CITIZENS OF HOPE AND GLORY

CITIZENS OF HOPE AND GLORY

The Story of Progressive Rock

STEPHEN LAMBE

AMBERLEY

For Gill,
the Prog Widow

First published 2011

Amberley Publishing
The Hill, Stroud
Gloucestershire GL5 4EP

www.amberleybooks.com

British Library Cataloguing in Publication Data.
A catalogue record for this book is available from the British Library.

ISBN 978-1-84868-190-3

Typesetting and Origination by Amberley Publishing.
Printed in Great Britain.

CONTENTS

INTRODUCTION

To my constant irritation, I missed it. I was born in 1962, so by the time I had had my Prog epiphany in 1978 it was all over. Here's how it happened. I was listening to a radio piece about Rick Wakeman and heard the last few moments of 'Heart of the Sunrise' by Yes from their 1971 album *Fragile*. It blew my mind. Friends at school, who up until 1977 had been bringing in Pink Floyd and Genesis albums to fawn over, had cut their hair and were now sporting the first Clash album and *Never Mind the Bollocks* by the Sex Pistols. Meanwhile, I had some catching up to do, and some vinyl to buy. Nowadays, I buy CDs and, yes, I even download (legally), but the catch-up process continues.

The question of what Progressive Rock actually is vexes even the most hardcore fan of the genre. In some books on the subject, the definition can run to several pages. I admit, however, that I am unable to do better than this definition from *The New Rolling Stone Encyclopedia of Rock and Roll*, so I reproduce it here:

> [Progressive Rock] denotes a form of rock music in which electric instruments and rock band formats are integrated with European classical motifs and orchestrations, typically forming extended, intricate, multi-sectional suites.

A few times in the book I refer to 'gateway' albums or songs. Progressive Rock can be deliciously melodic and accessible, but it can also be inaccessible, intense and difficult to listen to. On these occasions a simple melody line, refrain or lyric can make all the difference. Suddenly you 'get' the music you are listening to and a whole new vista of possibilities opens up. This happened to me with the music of Echolyn and Gentle Giant some years ago, after my initial attempts to listen to their music had resulted in bafflement. To show that this music never ceases to surprise and delight, during the writing of this book the music of Van der Graaf Generator has become a pleasure when before I had always been put off by singer Peter Hammill's earnestness and the angularity of the music.

Progressive Rock is considered by many to be a broad church, but to provide some sort of narrative focus to this book I have concentrated, in the main, on those artists that are sometimes referred to as 'symphonic'. If your tastes lie in the avant-garde, the space rock of Hawkwind, the horribly titled Krautrock movement, jazz-rock fusion, jam bands and a host of other subgenres, I am afraid you will be disappointed. Other artists and subgenres sweep in and out of the book where their inclusion becomes appropriate. Pink Floyd and Mike Oldfield – vitally important figures in the 1970s – are given scant coverage here, for instance. I do not believe that the world needs yet another plod through the history of Pink Floyd, although where their history coincides with the remit of this book, they feature. I do give some coverage to electronic music and the Canterbury scene, plus the ever-expanding world of Progressive Metal, but these are mere toes in the water, junction points to help the reader explore further.

You will note that the book contains no direct quotations from other artists or other publications apart from the above definition from *The New Rolling Stone Encyclopedia of Rock and Roll.* There are several ways of creating a book like this. One is to spend months interviewing the great and the good and then to assemble the text using their testimony as the basis for the narrative. This is perfectly valid, and a few books on the genre have done this beautifully. I have chosen to make this book a personal history, however, in the hope that my experience and opinions will strike a chord with other fans of the genre. This book contains fact *and* opinion. If I have made any factual errors I am sure that Progressive Rock fans will correct me, but I have done my best to make sure that the book is as accurate as possible. More importantly, where I have expressed an opinion, I hope I have adequately justified it. If I have not done so, feel free to tell me. Other opinions *are* available, of course. In the end this is a history of Progressive Rock filtered through my own tastes and experiences and I hope it is all the better for that.

Most importantly, in this book I make no attempt to be comprehensive. I may devote a whole page to one particular album or era of an artist's history, but then dismiss the next year's work or album in a few lines. I have done this to avoid repetition, and for narrative cohesion. However, if you require a comprehensive history of any particular artist, then the chances are that one is available. I list many in the Further Reading section of this book. I also apologise in advance if your favourite artist has not been given the space you feel their work deserves. I have listened to dozens of albums that I had never heard before in preparation for writing this book, particularly from Germany, Italy and the Scandinavian countries, and where I believe these make an important contribution to this history, they are featured. Progressive Rock developed in Britain initially and I am English, so it is artists from the UK that feature most prominently, particularly in the chapters on the 1970s. However, this is not to denigrate the huge contribution made by groups from other countries. I know that nations as diverse as Chile, Mexico, Australia, Finland, Estonia and Ukraine have produced some exceptional Progressive Rock bands, and I salute them all.

A wider bibliography can be found at the back of the book, but I am particularly indebted to authors Charles Snider and Jerry Lucky. Their respective books, *The Strawberry Bricks Guide to Progressive Rock* and *The Progressive Rock Files*, have been invaluable in helping piece together the timeline of this book, and I thank them for their research.

A NOTE ON THE STRUCTURE OF THIS BOOK

This book is a straightforward chronological history of the genre, written for the general reader rather than the expert. Some important features of this book are the 'pivotal albums' – sixty or so works that I feel are worth talking about in detail. This is not a 'Best Progressive Rock Albums of All Time' list. The albums featured are included either because they are essential or important albums in the history of the genre, or because they represent the work of one particular band. In the case of Radiohead and Dream Theater, the albums featured represent whole subgenres of Progressive Rock. In a few cases I am indifferent to the chosen albums myself, but feature them because they are important. By all means use this list as a starting point for further exploration, but do not buy them all and assume that you will be listening to 'the best Progressive Rock of all time'. I am not qualified to make that judgement.

95 per cent of the illustrations in this book have never appeared in print before. I am extremely grateful to all the photographers that have so generously allowed me to use their work – their names appear in the acknowledgements. I am particularly indebted to Neil Palfreyman, Chris Walkden and David Robinson for the time and effort they have taken in sifting through and preparing photographs for this book. Gentlemen, I salute you!

Most of all, I would like to thank all the Progressive Rock musicians of the last forty years that have given me and so many others so much pleasure. Occasionally, this music has brought the artists responsible untold wealth. Most often, however, the music was made at a time when the wider public were either indifferent or openly hostile to Progressive Rock. Thankfully, that is now changing. Progressive Rock seems now to have taken its place as a respected genre among many. Even today, however, talented musicians continue to toil away in bedrooms, small studios or on tiny stages in front of miniscule audiences, all for the love of Progressive Rock. These musicians are, to me, the Citizens of Hope and Glory, and this book is dedicated to them.

Stephen Lambe
Tewkesbury
August 2011

1

EVOLUTION

Rock music was barely in its teens when the story of Progressive Rock began. Looking back on the era now, it seems hard to believe that Bill Haley's 'Rock Around the Clock' and Elvis's appearance on *The Ed Sullivan Show* had taken place little more than a decade before 'Hey Joe' or *Sgt. Pepper's Lonely Hearts Club Band.*

During that time, rock music, itself a hybrid of jazz, country and blues, had been through all kinds of changes in an effort to keep its core audience, largely teenage kids, happy, stimulated and buying records. In the early days the focus was largely the American scene, with British stars like Billy Fury and Cliff Richard copying their American idols, but by the early 1960s the ground had begun to shift. The Merseybeat explosion, which spawned The Beatles alongside a flurry of less famous bands, led to the British Invasion, which moved the emphasis to our side of the Atlantic for a short while. The ground was thus laid for the future of British pop music. It would no longer be made by Americans, for Americans.

To survive, all musicians have to stay one step ahead, both of the opposition and the public. The best bands from the early 1960s adapted and survived. The others faded away. The Beatles, already famed for the quality of their songwriting, became more adventurous, and from *Rubber Soul* (1965) to *Sgt. Pepper's Lonely Hearts Club Band* (1967) their ambition grew. This was partly fuelled by consciousness-expanding drugs, of course, but also by their own growing maturity and confidence as musicians, as well as the talent of producer George Martin and the rest of the team at Abbey Road Studios.

The music business in the 1960s was smaller than it is today, largely an offshoot of the entertainment business, and the idea that the late 1960s was some sort of creative haven is largely a myth. As with now, profit was the main driver. However, while desperation has led to the championing of short-term gain in this modern age, some of the labels in the 1960s were prepared to take a long-term view, particularly with the new 'album' bands. Over a short period of time at the end of the 1960s and the beginning of the 1970s, the industry, never one to miss a bandwagon, signed up countless Progressive bands in the hope of finding another Led Zeppelin or Black Sabbath. Labels such as the slightly confused Deram (an offshoot of Decca), which boasted pop and rock groups including Procol Harum and the Moody Blues, slugged it out with Harvest (the Progressive wing of EMI), which had Deep Purple and Pink Floyd, and Vertigo (Phillips), which had Colosseum and Uriah Heep. Looking at the roster of artists in the then-new Vertigo's books, it's amazing to see how many of these bands are still listened to today, even if worldwide fame eluded them – bands like Jade Warrior or Magna Carta. Others have long since faded into obscurity, like Gravy Train or Tudor Lodge.

The mid to late 1960s, however, was also the era of the domineering manager, who usually claimed to know what the audiences and labels wanted. The best known of these was Brian Epstein, of course – he made The Beatles wear suits, opt for distinctive mop-top haircuts and bow at the end of each song. Most bands had an Epstein. Musicians in an up-and-coming combo could expect to be manipulated, styled, ripped off and, worst of all, told to sing somebody else's songs. While Epstein was one of the more benign managers, Don Arden was famed for his tough, manipulative, short-term approach to artist management. He managed Gene Vincent, and then, notoriously, the Small Faces, keeping them on low wages and pushing them into hastily recorded singles. The band soon moved from Decca and Don Arden to Immediate and Andrew Loog Oldham, who brought a more sophisticated approach to band management; crucially, the artists on his Immediate label were given decent budgets with which to record. Meanwhile, the fledgling Yes had a supportive manager in Roy Flynn, but he wasn't quite hard-nosed enough to get them where they wanted to be, so the band recruited someone else with a louder voice and better contacts – the all-powerful Brian Lane.

PSYCHEDELIA AND THE NEW UNDERGROUND SCENE

In 1966 an underground movement began to coalesce around a few key organisations in London, not least the short-lived but vibrant UFO Club. The house band at the UFO was a group of ambitious Cambridge graduates called 'The Pink Floyd'. Led by the charismatic, talented Syd Barrett and the brittle, ambitious Roger Waters, the band combined quirky, 'of its time' songwriting with ambitious, somewhat avant-garde instrumental passages. This is typified on record by 'Interstellar Overdrive' from the group's debut album *Piper at the Gates of Dawn*, which was released in 1967, at the end of the Summer of Love. That these pieces were too ambitious for the band's instrumental ability was incidental – without ambition, virtuosity has no purpose. Pink Floyd, as well as other psychedelic bands like The Move, The Crazy World of Arthur Brown, Traffic and The Pretty Things, began to gain mainstream interest, and by the end of 1967 psychedelia was becoming a real force in the British charts.

At the same time, the 1960s blues boom was beginning to change and develop. Having left The Yardbirds in 1966, Eric Clapton formed Cream with fellow virtuosos Ginger Baker and Jack Bruce, on drums and bass respectively. Over three albums, this supergroup, which played a mixture of original songs and rocked-up blues standards, set a precedent for improvisation having a place not just in jazz, its natural home, but also in rock music. Also flying the flag for virtuosity, albeit in a slightly more ramshackle way, was a striking young American of mixed race called Jimi Hendrix, whose single 'Hey Joe' and whose incendiary, unpredictable concert performances made him a worldwide star. Much of this virtuosity, of course, was to be experienced in the concert hall rather than on the record player, and the stage was already developing as the main outlet for these musicians – both psych artists and bluesmen – to improvise and to challenge what rock music had become.

Meanwhile, Midlands band The Moody Blues had moved on from their early rhythm-and-blues and Merseybeat roots, especially after the recruitment of singer-guitarist Justin Hayward, who replaced frontman Denny Laine. Hayward's softer voice and Mike Pinder's adoption of the Mellotron (a keyboard instrument using tape loops to mimic orchestral sounds) pushed the band in both more melodic and more orchestral directions. Having failed to honour a rather ambitious commission to create a rock version of Dvořák's *New World Symphony*, the band instead created *Days of Future Past*, a loose concept album (or song cycle) linked by brief orchestral pieces. To some Progressive Rock fans, the grandiose themes and use of the Mellotron make this the first proper Progressive Rock album. In my opinion, it is a pop-rock album with classical trimmings and instrumentation. It is an original and beautifully crafted album, but in our story it is merely a signpost. The Moody Blues remain on the fringes of our story. Their music retained grandiosity and a tendency towards instrumental experimentation, including an early and important use of the flute in rock, but rarely moved beyond the standard song format.

Even more than the Moodies, it was Procol Harum – whose chief claim to fame so far had been the classically influenced hit single 'A Whiter Shade of Pale' – who combined a strong classical music influence with rock. In the case of Procol Harum, the orchestra often existed alongside the band, almost as an extra member – something not seen again until the music of Renaissance in the mid-1970s.

The record that genuinely sparked the revolution was *Sgt. Pepper's Lonely Hearts Club Band* by The Beatles. As with previous Beatles albums it was a brilliantly crafted pop-rock album, but it was the arrangements and the studio wizardry that impressed. Audiences were wowed by the trip the album took them in a single sitting. This was not just a few singles held together by lesser tracks; it was full of tricks and studio wizardry, of exotic and unusual influences as varied as Indian music and the English music hall. The album was recorded over a positively luxurious four months at the beginning of 1967 and was released,

Procol Harum Live. The band have played with orchestras all over the world, and this album was recorded in 1971 with the Edmonton Symphony Orchestra. (*Salvo Music*)

significantly, during the Summer of Love. Unlike most bands, who often needed to keep playing gigs while recording, the decision by the band to stop touring gave them the time to make the best, most experimental and most cohesive album possible, and with no more than four-track recording technology. The eight-track machines already available in the USA did not appear in the UK until after the album was released.

The album featured several other innovations. The sleeve was lovingly created by artist Peter Blake with his wife Jann Haworth, and the band elected to print the song lyrics on the back of the cover – the first time this had been done on a pop album. Many guest musicians were invited to contribute, and the instrumentation was inventive and varied. It was the closing song, 'A Day in the Life', that was most influenced by classical music. In short, the album pointed a way forward. It showed what could be done.

KEITH EMERSON – THE BRIDGE

It is fitting that the first Progressive Rock superstar should be a keyboard player. Keith Emerson topped music industry polls in 1969 for his prodigious talent and extravagant showmanship with The Nice, a significant pit stop on the road to symphonic Progressive Rock. Emerson, like most of his keyboard-playing contemporaries, had been classically trained as a child, which had left him with brilliant technique. He did not, however, take this further, opting instead to follow his burgeoning interest in jazz, which helped create an interesting synthesis of styles in his playing. His rise through the ranks was fairly swift – via two hard-touring bands, The T-Bones and The VIPs, and an offer to put together a touring band to back rising soul singer P. P. Arnold. Arnold resulted in The Nice. Arnold had a hit with a version of 'The First Cut Is the Deepest' and planned to tour the clubs in support of her new-found fame.

The Nice were originally a four-piece, comprising Emerson, drummer Brian Davidson and two contrasting vocalists, Geordie bassist Lee Jackson and guitarist Davy O'List. From the beginning, the band were allowed thirty minutes at each gig to play their own set before the arrival of Arnold. On the strength of this, they started to play solo gigs. Initially the set consisted of music very much influenced by the psychedelic bands of the time – hardly surprising, considering their 1967 package tour with Pink Floyd, Jimi Hendrix and The Move. Indeed, Hendrix was an early fan of the band – an association that has done Emerson no harm throughout his career.

The band's first two albums, both featuring guitarist O'List, flopped but did well enough to keep audiences, the management and the label interested. In particular, the cover art of the band's version of Leonard Bernstein's 'America', which featured Martin Luther King, was controversial enough for the single to be banned in the USA. The band fanned the flames by burning a crude effigy of the American flag at a concert at the Royal Albert Hall, although whether this was genuinely political or, as some have suggested, clever marketing has never quite been established. From this point onwards, The Nice were hot property. Their eponymous third album and its live follow-up *Five Bridges* – with lyrics by Jackson about his home town – were huge successes. The band, now a three-piece, were by this time sharing the stage with string ensembles and orchestras. They were moving into the big league.

Given that the repertoire of The Nice included adaptations of Sibelius's *Karelia Suite* and Bach's *Brandenburg Concerto No. 4*, it has been suggested that the band were the first Progressive Rock group. I think not. Progressive Rock takes classical structures, tonality and ambition and applies these to rock music. The Nice were doing something a little different in taking existing classical pieces and placing them in rock, jazz and blues settings. While the use of an orchestra on the classical-meets-rock live album *Five Bridges* was extremely fashionable at the end of the 1960s, the 'rock' and the 'classical' sides of the music remained largely separate. The Nice were playing adapted classical music in a similar way to Walter Carlos (*Switched-On Bach*) and Jacques Loussier (*Play Bach*) by adapting composed classical pieces to their own styles. This music also provided a vital signpost on the way to Progressive Rock.

The Nice did see Emerson develop two important facets of his performance that were to become notorious as his career developed. His excitingly rough treatment of the Hammond organ – which involved throwing it around the stage and sticking knives into it – began in the 1960s. Also, 1969 saw Emerson's first use of the modular Moog synthesizer onstage. He was possibly the first man in the UK to do this. Large and cumbersome, it was an erratic instrument, and like the Mellotron it went out of tune on a regular basis. Within a few years it had been superseded by the classic compact design of the Minimoog, although Emerson plays the modular Moog to this day.

THE BEGINNINGS OF GENTLE GIANT

Simon Dupree and the Big Sound, from Portsmouth, were fairly typical of the mildly successful white soul bands that emerged during the mid-1960s British beat boom. A six-piece that included the prodigiously talented Shulman brothers, Phil, Derek and Ray, they have several claims to fame, one of which is their only hit single, 'Kites', released in 1967. They featured a young Elton John from Watford on keyboards for a while, and recorded at Abbey Road at the same time and in the same studio as The Beatles while *Sgt. Pepper* was being created (Simon Dupree recorded during the day, The Beatles at night). They were the subject of a risqué *Man Alive* documentary on ITV about the early 'groupies' phenomenon.

The band suffered the same interference from label and management as many of the less fortunate groups of the time. They toured widely and released a series of increasingly desperate singles as their fortunes faltered. The band split in 1969, the hopes of the three Shulman brothers seemingly thwarted by a lack of ambition in the rest of the band. Under the guiding eye of manager Gerry Bron, the brothers began working on more ambitious and rocky material of their own.

The recruitment of the classically trained Kerry Minnear was an essential step in shaping the new band's sound. The phrase 'classically trained' covers a multitude of sins, from someone that has passed Grade 1 piano to musicians like Rick Wakeman and Kerry Minnear. Whereas Wakeman failed to finish his course at the Royal College of Music when the lure of session and live work in the rock world became strong, Minnear was different. He completed a course in composition, having also developed piano and percussion skills, and his strengths as a composer were crucial in honing the precociously talented but untutored Shulman brothers. Londoner Garry Green, by contrast, had developed his guitar-playing skills on the semi-professional blues circuit, yet absorbed music like a sponge and adapted to this new environment brilliantly.

The band spent the early part of 1970 developing material and playing the odd gig and BBC session. Much of this early material was jettisoned as the band found a coherent sound that suited them, although most of it has appeared in one form or other recently, since a revival in interest in the band has seen much old audio and video resurface. 'City Hermit' is a good example of this material. It has a pseudo-classical organ line – albeit a slightly obvious one – that hints at Progressive Rock, yet the song itself is reminiscent of the soulful psych that Traffic were developing. The band had not yet discovered their signature sound.

YES – THE MOST INVENTIVE COVERS BAND IN THE WORLD

Jon Anderson and Chris Squire met for the first time at La Chasse, a drinking club not far from the famous Marquee club, which was much frequented by musicians. The meeting was brokered by Jack Barrie, the club owner, who had been attempting to find a suitable vehicle for the talented northern singer Anderson for some months. Squire was a rising bass player somewhat adrift following the recent break-up of his long-term project The Syn, and had recently been playing in a band called Mabel Greer's Toyshop. Barrie felt the two would have something in common musically. Finding that they did indeed have similar musical interests, particularly a love of vocal groups like The 5th Dimension, they soon set about forming a band. Their vision was that this was to be a rock band with an emphasis less on hit singles than on ambitious, sophisticated arrangements, great harmonies and high-quality players. Squire brought in his colleague from The Syn, guitarist Peter Banks. Advertisements and contacts brought in ambitious young jazz drummer Bill Bruford and organist Tony Kaye.

The band were noticeably *good*, and made a huge impression as a live act almost from the beginning. That all the players, except perhaps Bruford, were seasoned live performers obviously helped, as did the dedication of early manager Roy Flynn, who got them some regular gigs (including, famously, a support slot at Cream's farewell gig at the Royal Albert Hall) and a prestigious deal with Atlantic – the same label as Led Zeppelin, and then best known for its rhythm-and-blues acts.

The band began by playing radical rearrangements of other people's songs, gradually combined with their own material – a policy reflected in their first album *Yes*, released in 1969. This included covers of 'I See You' by The Byrds and the Lennon/McCartney song 'Every Little Thing'. Musically, it includes plenty of hints at the band to follow. Listen to the arrangement of 'Harold Land', for instance. While the song itself is a fairly typical example of 1960s anti-war whimsy, the arrangement is hugely ambitious, particularly Kaye's clever piano playing. Closing track 'Survival' is marvellous, perhaps the first genuine Progressive Rock track.

With the album out and selling modestly, the band continued to play the live circuit, and continued to impress. Their developing songwriting is reflected in their second album, released at the start of 1970. *Time and a Word* contains excellent pieces such as 'Then', 'The Prophet' and 'Astral Traveller', but the problem the album has is the rather ham-fisted use of the orchestra, which steals space from both Peter Banks's guitar and Tony Kaye's organ. Despite some fine playing, Banks became a casualty of that album, and the band reached its first crossroads. Where to turn next?

KING CRIMSON WINS THE PROGRESSIVE ROCK ARMS RACE

King Crimson charted their own course from very early in the band's turbulent, stop-start life. This was due in no small part to eventual band leader Robert

Fripp's distrust of the music-making industry. In fact, Fripp had already signed to Decca for one album with brothers Peter and Michael Giles in 1968. A strange piece of work, it was called *The Cheerful Insanity of Giles, Giles and Fripp*. Largely ignored at the time, it is now much picked over in its re-released form by Progressive Rock fans. That Decca allowed the band to release its own material shows remarkable faith for a time when bands were more often forced to play songs written by specialist songwriters, as was suffered by the Shulman brothers. Like the Shulman brothers, the brothers Giles had some past experience of the music industry, having played in a professional touring band called Trendsetters Ltd, which had toured extensively and backed a variety of big names, but made no headway of their own. Fripp's experience was far more local, but his virtuosity was without doubt. The trio, complete with whacky, Bonzo Dog Band-styling, moved to London from Dorset to make a go of it.

Even before the album was released, the trio had recruited talented multi-instrumentalist Ian MacDonald and worked briefly with former Fairport Convention singer Judy Dyble before a more rock-orientated path led to the departure of bassist and vocalist Peter Giles. The charismatic and talented Greg Lake – a friend of Fripp's from Dorset and already in a band called The Gods with various future members of hard rockers Uriah Heep – took up bass and vocal duties. However, the final piece in the puzzle was the involvement of Peter Sinfield. Sinfield is a crucial figure in the development of Progressive Rock, but his initial role in the newly named King Crimson was not only as lyricist, but as sound and lighting engineer as well. In particular, he became one of a breed of talented people who specifically designed light shows to enhance particular passages of music, even particular notes or chords.

In the early part of 1969 the band rehearsed and made a couple of attempts to record their debut album without a label, hoping to licence the finished item, a shrewd and unusual (although not unheard of) event. Decca, belatedly realising that Giles, Giles and Fripp were morphing into something very exciting, unsuccessfully attempted to assert their claim on the band, which may well go some way to explaining Fripp's lifelong distrust of record labels. Work on the album finally began during the summer, while the band performed gigs in the provinces and made appearances at the Speakeasy and the Marquee. The band adapted some of their live repertoire and jettisoned other pieces, with the studio acting almost as an extra instrument. The band, and MacDonald in particular, were adept at using the instruments lying around in the studio to good effect, especially an elderly Baldwin Electric Harpsichord. In July, the band took a break from recording to play with the Rolling Stones at Hyde Park in front of 650,000 people, a gig that turned out to be pivotal in getting the band's name known, despite their short thirty-minute set.

In the Court of the Crimson King was released at the end of October 1969. And all hell broke loose.

2

1969–1975: THE WAY UP

1969

By late 1969, lines were being drawn and allegiances to musical philosophies were being developed. Counterculture groups like Pink Floyd were deciding what sort of bands they should be. In the case of the Floyd, this sense of uncertainty manifested itself in the confused *Ummagumma* album. Other bands were taking hard rock into interesting corners. Led Zeppelin were reinventing the blues, while Deep Purple and Uriah Heep introduced hard rock to the crunching Hammond organ. Black Sabbath down-tuned their guitars and invented the sound and ethos of Heavy Metal. Meanwhile, the prototype Progressive Rock bands were locked in squalid country cottages and cramped, smoky rehearsal rooms up and down the country, developing a sound to call their own.

BUSINESS CHANGES

The early 1970s saw almost no crossover audience for the sales of seven-inch singles and twelve-inch albums in the UK. With *Sgt. Pepper*, the Beatles at last proved that the album could be a viable form in its own right, and so from then onwards artists were gradually allowed to develop their music in an album format. To a certain extent, the album charts in the UK reflected the tastes of the single-buying public, but by the early 1970s the really big sellers – the best example being Pink Floyd's *Dark Side of the Moon*, one of the highest grossing of all time – were viable entities in their own right, with no requirement to spawn hit singles. We remember the single successes of the Osmonds, for instance, but we remember the album successes of Led Zeppelin. Those artists that could count on success in both areas – Elton John, David Bowie and Stevie Wonder being significant examples – are rightly held in huge esteem.

The days of rock and roll as a humble offshoot of the entertainment business were on their way out, and in the early 1970s the label bosses began to exert

In the Court of the Crimson King, King Crimson's groundbreaking debut album. (*DGM*)

their power. The figure that towers above everyone else in those heady early days was Ahmet Ertegun, a Turkish immigrant in the USA. Ertegun was initially a rhythm-and-blues enthusiast and set up his own label, Atlantic, to produce and promote those artists, which included Otis Redding, Ben E. King and Solomon Burke. When Atlantic became part of Time Warner in the late 1960s, Ertegun remained at the helm, and saw an opportunity to move into rock music, signing Led Zeppelin, Yes, Crosby, Stills & Nash and Emerson, Lake & Palmer. A shrewd businessman of course, but a music fan first and foremost, Ertegun realised that creativity and commercial success need not be mutually exclusive. The early 1970s is often seen as a halcyon time of artistic freedom and music without consequences. This is not the case. Every band signed to a major label was expected to turn a profit. Artists *were* given the latitude to develop without the need to produce instant results – but it was on the understanding that the millions would follow. Ertegun combined the passion of an enthusiast with stupendous business sense and a real flair for contract negotiation. That he was also much loved was amply demonstrated by the outpouring of tributes after his death in 2006. Led Zeppelin in particular were persuaded to reform for one last time at a concert at London's O2 Arena that also included contributions from Keith Emerson and members of Yes.

Progressive Rock could not have developed as it did without the relative freedoms allowed by visionaries such as Ertegun, and by the end of 1969 all the pieces were in place for the most creative five years in the history of rock music.

King Crimson
In the Court of the Crimson King
Released November 1969

Months of gigging and a genuine buzz about the band meant that the album would have been a hit regardless of what it sounded like. But it was astonishing. No album had ever sounded like this, and, excepting its copycat sequel, *In the Wake of Poseidon*, no album ever would again. In many respects the album represents an intriguing dead end in the development of Progressive Rock. Had this version of the band continued, the genre may well have taken a very different path than that laid by the early works of Yes and Genesis.

Owing as much to jazz as rock, the extraordinary '21st Century Schizoid Man' kicks the album off. It is dominated by a heavy opening riff, Greg Lake's aggressive, distorted lead vocal and a big band middle section. The dissonant solos by Robert Fripp on guitar and Ian McDonald on sax are remarkably bold. 'I Talk to the Wind' is as sweet as the opening track is harsh, a triumph of woodwind and electronic piano, and practically a McDonald solo track bar Lake's tremulous lead vocal and a lush guitar solo from Fripp. 'Epitaph', however, takes the album in a different direction. Grandiose, pompous and dramatic, it is dominated by the haunting swirl of Mellotron strings. Again, Lake shines in one of his favourite tunes, which is why it has been included in many an Emerson, Lake & Palmer live set. It is for this track and for the title track that the album is so fêted among Progressive Rock fans.

Side two has only two pieces. 'Moonchild' begins gently, Lake's treated voice almost whispering over a gentle guitar and Mellotron backing. Michael Giles's sensitive cymbal work is also remarkable in its detail. The second part of the piece is the first of many King Crimson recorded improvisations – McDonald on vibes, Fripp on electric guitar and Giles on drums. Often ignored, this section rewards intense listening. As an example of spontaneity it is remarkable, but it is easy to understand why those that are in a hurry to get to the famous title track skip it, and like many improvisations it feels very much 'of its moment'. The album closes with the grandiose title track, which is again dominated by the Mellotron strings. Attention to detail is to the fore here, and the little pipe organ passage towards the end of the track is delicious.

The album made a huge impact on its release – not just commercially, where it rose to number five in the UK charts, but with other musicians. The sudden success of the group – in particular a US tour that was probably one step too far – took its toll, and the band fell apart in 1970. Ian McDonald, in particular, dominates the album; Fripp was to become central to later releases.

McDonald's departure was also a loss to Progressive Rock as a whole. He becomes a peripheral figure in our story from here on, and he found success in other areas of music, most notably as a member of hard rock band Foreigner. Peter Sinfield's lyrics must take their share of the credit, too, as should the amazing cover art of Barry Godber, which has a decadent and disturbing atmosphere that increases the album's considerable impact. That Godber died shortly afterwards, and therefore contributed no other work to the genre, only increases its reputation as work set apart from the mainstream of Progressive Rock. While this album is by no means typical of the genre that it helped originate, it remains one of its most pivotal, influential and vital examples.

THE TEMPLATE IS WRITTEN

In the Court of the Crimson King was a shock for many of the band's contemporaries. The gauntlet thrown down, it took a while for anyone to pick it up. Not that the world of experimental music was in any way quiet, but the symphonic form of Progressive Rock remained largely in its cauldron, brewing and not yet ready to be administered. Late 1969 also saw the release of Frank Zappa's genre-busting solo album *Hot Rats*, which set the template for his unique career and mashed together highbrow and lowbrow. He remains a huge influence, both to Progressive Rock guitarists and to composers. In 1970 Pink Floyd were still finding their feet as a band post-Syd Barrett, and released their first number one album *Atom Heart Mother*. Its title track is an early example of a side-long piece of music, and was written with composer and arranger Ron Geesin. Meanwhile, Keith Relf and Jim McCarthy of The Yardbirds experimented with classical influences in the first incarnation of Renaissance, who will come into our story a little later.

Elsewhere in England, the softer, jazzier movement that had grown out of Canterbury in Kent was finding its feet as Soft Machine. Originating in psychedelia, Soft Machine had by now become a fully-fledged jazz fusion project, and had almost completely ceased to be a rock band. Over the next few months they would change personnel completely. At the more song-based end of the market, Caravan released their second album, with the nudge-nudge, wink-wink title *If I Could Do It All Again I'd Do It All Over You*, for Decca. This was another template-setter, combining wistful, very English songwriting with semi-structured instrumental passages. Significantly, Caravan were one of the earliest bands to feature multi-part suites, as the pieces 'With an Ear to the Ground' and the magnificent jam that is 'For Richard' demonstrate.

Hastily reassembled following their notorious implosion at the end of 1969, King Crimson followed up their debut album with *In the Wake of Poseidon* in the middle of 1970. Despite the new dominance of Robert Fripp as band leader and most of the previous line-up present only as session men, the album follows the formula of its more illustrious predecessor fairly closely, with the Mellotron prominent as well as Fripp's varied guitar playing and Greg Lake's vocals. If it misses anything, it is Ian McDonald's attention to detail, but given the overall success of the band at the time, it is hardly surprising that the album was a major commercial success.

Paul Whitehead displays the artwork for *Trespass* and *Nursery Cryme* at Nearfest in 2007. (Steve Reed)

Young graduates Van der Graaf Generator, who had formed at the University of Manchester in 1967, signed to Tony Stratton Smith's new Charisma label and released their only album to chart in the UK, *The Least We Can Do Is Wave to Each Other*. With David Jackson's sax and Hugh Banton's organ taking the lead (alongside Peter Hammill's unique vocals), the band were already developing a sense of dynamics, drama and tension that was to underpin their greatest work.

Genesis
Trespass
Released October 1970

Genesis were formed from the ashes of two bands – The Anon and Garden Wall – at Charterhouse School in the mid-1960s. Having released *From Genesis to Revelation* for Jonathan King in March 1969 to minimal impact and sales, Genesis signed to Chrysalis and 'retired to the country' to write and to rehearse a live set. The result was *Trespass*. While most Genesis fans consider it to be the first 'true' Genesis album, it tends to be overlooked in favour of the two records that followed and which featured Phil Collins and Steve Hackett: *Nursery Cryme* and *Foxtrot*. To me *Trespass* is a seminal album, and the origin of the strand of Progressive Rock that remains most popular to this day.

Listening to it now, you can almost smell the newness and the intensity of the rehearsals. Yet there is also a naïvety about it that is very appealing. There is much about the way the music sounds that will be familiar to bands struggling to develop their own character today, for example John Mayhew's rather amateurish drumming. But in the main, this is the album that sets the template for Neo-Progressive Rock. A timeline that began in the 1970s, continued into the 1980s via Marillion and IQ, into the 1990s with Grey Lady Down and Jadis and finally brings us to Agents of Mercy and Credo in the new millennium, begins here with *Trespass*.

It is all there in opener 'Looking For Someone', which combines a grandiose choral quality with much busier passages, including an early use of multiple keyboards with organ and piano, sometimes in unison – not to mention the ubiquitous Mellotron. Peter Gabriel's flute is also vital. This may be the most influential and yet unsung track in the history of the genre, since its structure is so familiar now. Elsewhere, the album takes on a more pastoral, melancholic tone with the doubling of electric and twelve-string guitars (a Genesis trademark though out the 1970s). Gabriel sounds like Dave Cousins of The Strawbs on 'White Mountain'.

'Visions of Angels' is dominated by its charming piano intro and organ riff, while 'Stagnation' revolves around sweeps of piano, Mellotron and twelve-string guitar, before ebbing and flowing towards a wonderful, repetitive climax. 'Dusk' is a 1960s-style folk interlude before the bold, brash, crowd-pleasing 'The Knife' boisterously carries the album home.

Trespass is not the finest Progressive Rock album of all time, and the band's early masterpiece was to come three albums later. Yet, structurally, it is vital. Aside from the distinctive and instantly recognisable performance of vocalist Peter Gabriel, Tony Banks on keyboards also deserves praise for his inspirational choice of sounds, especially given the relatively small options open to him. His piano work, in particular, is exceptional. After the album's release, guitarist Ant Phillips departed for a more solitary musical existence. It is his textural work rather than his lead playing that impresses on *Trespass*, and with bassist Mike Rutherford he originated the band's signature multi-layered guitar sound. Drummer John Mayhew, however, was simply not up to the task. Phillips and Mayhew's replacements were to develop and refine the sound of the band, but it is *Trespass* that defines it.

THE END OF 1970

In a crucial and frenetic three-month period at the end of 1970, Genesis released *Trespass*, Pink Floyd released *Atom Heart Mother*, Van der Graaf Generator released *H to He, Who Am the Only One* and King Crimson released *Lizard*. Van der Graaf's album featured Crimson's Robert Fripp as a guest, and it is the first to feature the 'classic' four-piece line-up – with Nic Potter's bass replaced by Hugh Banton's organ pedals. Once again, the dynamics are shattering. King Crimson's *Lizard* featured a new line-up of the band, with Gordon Haskell (an interesting choice) singing and playing bass, and Mel Collins providing woodwind. A transitional album, and another to feature a side-long suite, it feels like an attempt to recapture the magic of the first album. However, it also takes the music into different places, including some astonishing piano from jazz/contemporary specialist Keith Tippet. Very much a studio project, the band would return to the road with a different line-up the following year.

Sonja Kristina and Curved Air onstage in 2010. (*Neil Palfreyman*)

Two other bands released their debuts during this period. Fronted, unusually, by a woman – the exotically named Sonja Kristina – Curved Air released *Airconditioning*, which combined neo-classical sensibilities similar to The Nice, courtesy of violinist Darryl Way and keyboard player Francis Monkman. The band also gave off a strong whiff of the US West Coast, with Jefferson Airplane often referenced. Gentle Giant also emerged reborn with their eponymous first album. No longer blue-eyed soul merchants, they were now hard-nosed proto-Proggers, albeit retaining many of their 1960s trappings. Soul and blues influences were intact, but in the main this is a coherent, rather jazzy, riff-dominated album, as typified by opener 'Giant', in which organ and Mellotron are prominent. The entire song built around a solid bass riff. 'Alucard' (with a searing Moog riff) and 'Isn't It Quiet and Cold?' demonstrated some of the quirkiness that was to become a trademark on later albums.

But the album with the biggest profile during this amazing three-month period was the eponymous debut of Emerson, Lake & Palmer. Having extracted themselves from their other commitments with some difficulty, the three of them put the album together pretty quickly, accumulating solo material into a decent forty minutes made up of recycled classical themes by Emerson on 'The Three Fates', Palmer's percussion *tour de force* 'Tank' and two lovely Lake songs, 'Lucky Man' and 'Take a Pebble', featuring some delicate piano from Emerson. Emerson's simple but effective modular Moog solo on 'Lucky Man' has also been hugely influential over the years. The band's appearance at the Isle of Wight Festival in August 1970, where the majority of their hastily arranged set featured an arrangement of Mussorgsky's *Pictures at an Exhibition*, acts as a gateway to four years of frantic activity from the first wave of Progressive Rock pioneers. Thanks to rock DJ John Peel's biting and dismissive comment that the performance was a 'waste of talent and electricity', the performance also marks the first of the genre's spats with the rock press.

1971

1971 was the most important and creative year in Progressive Rock. In fact, you might very well choose to stop at the end of this section – it never got any better than this.

Perhaps it would be useful to pause for a moment, and to put all this into context. While Progressive Rock was starting to develop as a cohesive genre, it is only possible to see this with hindsight. Most of the Prog bands were seen at the time to be playing broadly similar music for a broadly similar audience. Today, many of these same bands would certainly not be considered suitable for touring together. There was a constant stream of live gigs on the club and university circuits in those days. The Marquee in London was the Mecca for up-and-coming bands, but there was also a vibrant club scene all over the country (including some large pubs). Not that many bands necessarily had the opportunity to tour as such. A group might be in a studio one day, dismantle their gear to play a gig hundreds of miles away, and then return to the studio to record again. Only bands like Pink Floyd or King Crimson, who had some success behind them, enjoyed the luxury of larger venues and a tour manager. Otherwise, it was a club in Burnley and the gear in the back of a Ford Transit.

In the early spring of 1971, Charisma boss Tony Stratton-Smith took something of a risk by booking a package of three bands on his roster to tour together. Van der Graaf Generator, folk rockers Lindisfarne and Genesis were booked into major halls throughout the country. An itinerary from April of that year shows the nature of the tour – good 1,000-plus venues like the Fairfield Halls in Croydon and the Manchester Free Trade Hall. The plan was to charge a bargain price of six shillings for tickets. If the venues sold out, the tour would break even, and this they did. Van der Graaf Generator, the only band of the three to have had an actual hit album at that point, headlined with Lindisfarne (who were looking the best bet for future fame) second, and Genesis (with new guitarist Steve Hackett) opening. The tour became the most famous of its type until the notorious Stiff tour in 1977, during the punk era.

Of the albums that we will look at in detail, six were released in 1971. Other albums – to which I will give only passing attention – included supposed classics *Fragile* by Yes, *Nursery Cryme* by Genesis, *Meddle* by Pink Floyd, *Second Album* by Curved Air, *The Polite Force* by Dave Stewart's Egg and *Islands* by King Crimson. Emerson, Lake & Palmer, Focus, Van der Graaf Generator and Caravan all made their masterpieces, while Yes and Gentle Giant had the audacity to leave us waiting another year for theirs. Genesis made us wait for two. 1971 was that good.

By 1971, most of the originators of Progressive Rock had had time to find their musical feet. Weaker band members had moved on; mistakes had been made and corrected; albums had been made; equipment had been acquired. Most crucially, for the first time, Progressive Rock ceased to be just an English phenomenon. The Europeans were having a go, too.

Yes
The Yes Album
Released March 1971

Things had not been going well for Yes. With two largely ignored albums under their belts and an increasingly impatient record company on their heels, the band decided to fire their manager, Roy Flynn – which led to a temporary end to the wages they had been enjoying. They rented a house in the Devon countryside and began working on new material. New guitarist Steve Howe was a crucial part of the pattern. A self-taught virtuoso, Howe had been around the London scene for years, in cult psych outfit Tomorrow and later Bodast, and had even rehearsed with The Nice for a day before joining Yes.

Two important things need to be said about *The Yes Album*. Firstly, with Eddie Offord in place at Advision Studios as engineer, this is the first album to sound truly 'modern'. Almost all albums up to that point – including all Beatles albums produced by George Martin and many of the discs recorded at around the same time as *The Yes Album* – sound primitive to modern ears, no matter how good the material or arrangements. The production on *The Yes Album*, however, sounds clean and crystal-clear. Some commentators have even suggested that the band went too far here, tipping over into sterility. Later live performances of the same songs are often cited as far more impressive.

Whatever the sound quality, there is no denying the huge leap in the quality of material and imagination on this album compared with *Time and a Word*. All adherence to simple song structure had disappeared; here was the multi-part, multi-layered symphonic Progressive Rock album in all its multicoloured, melodic glory. Take, for instance, the glorious choral 'Dillusion', which is preceded by Steve Howe's gorgeous country acoustic section. The 'Würm' section of the same piece was surely written with live jamming in mind. Elsewhere, the hard-driving and yet complex 'Yours Is No Disgrace' and 'Perpetual Change' show that rock songs could be extended without boring the listener. 'Your Move' again shows delicacy without sentimentality.

Overall, this was Yes finally fulfilling their potential. The vocal harmonies are delicious, and Chris Squire and Bill Bruford, far from the normal rhythm section, raise their games to match the material, while Jon Anderson delivers a vocal performance full of confidence. Only organist Tony Kaye seems subdued. His playing, mainly organ but with some piano and Moog, is solid enough but lacks the swagger he showed on *Time and a Word*. He was to move on shortly after the album's release.

At times of adversity, there is a tendency for us all to play safe. With *The Yes Album*, the band did the exact opposite, crafting a classic and a deserved commercial success.

Caravan
In the Land of Grey and Pink
Released May 1971

Caravan recorded their third album at around the same time as Yes, but with a rather different agenda. *In the Land of Grey and Pink*, while not representative of their later output after the departure of bassist and vocalist Richard Sinclair, remains a high-water mark both in the Canterbury movement and Progressive Rock as a whole. Side one of the album contains four tracks based around a standard song format. 'Golf Girl' has a very 1960s lyric, but its lightness of touch and gentle good humour has ensured that it remains a fan favourite. 'Winter Wine' is more complex, although it has a simple, folky base. Dave Sinclair makes his Hammond sing as the track gives way to an elongated instrumental section. Improvised soloing, rather than the structured approach of Yes or Genesis, was always a feature of this strand of Progressive Rock, although Sinclair cleverly never strays too far from the main song melody. Pye Hastings's wry and rather slight 'Love to Love You (And Tonight Pigs Will Fly)' gives way to the psychedelic musings of Richard Sinclair in the title track.

However, it is the side-long 'Nine Feet Underground' that is most impressive. A masterpiece of organ pyrotechnics and groove bolstered by piano in its later sections, it has become not just the archetypal Caravan piece but the symbol of a whole movement.

Emerson, Lake & Palmer
Tarkus
Released June 1971

After the bombast of the band's first album, Emerson, Lake & Palmer wisely chose to write a record of original material for its follow-up, and in June they released *Tarkus*. The side-long title track is a stupendous piece of work, hugely intense and complex, with Emerson's organ punctuated by thrilling Moog fanfares and Palmer's busy and complex drumming, a kind of progressive shuffle, carrying the piece, along with vocal interjections by Greg Lake about the futility of war. As well as the amazing complexity of the piece, it is the drama of it that works best, the intensity beautifully judged against the vocal sections to produce passages of real majesty. Like *In the Court of the Crimson King*, it also benefits from remarkable artwork,

Tarkus, ELP's remarkable second album. (*Sony*)

this time by painter William Neal, which depicts Tarkus as part-armadillo, part-tank – a surreally literal interpretation of Lake's abstract lyrics about war and organised religion. However, combined with the music, the artwork certainly creates a heady atmosphere.

The rest of the album is a relative disappointment by comparison, and rarely even registers as Progressive Rock. 'Jeremy Bender' is a throwaway and offensive track when looked at with our twenty-first-century sensibilities, while 'Bitches Crystal' is much more interesting, returning to the complexity of 'Tarkus' via piano, washes of synth, and an impassioned vocal from Lake. 'The Only Way' pastiches church music while Lake again questions religion, before switching to a Jacques Loussier-style jazz piano section that segues straight into 'Infinite Space', a jazzy, piano-led instrumental. 'A Time and a Place' is again dominated by the organ, and then the 1950s rock-and-roll pastiche 'Are You Ready Eddy?' closes the album – a smug in-joke that might have been better left on the cutting-room floor.

While the 'Tarkus' suite shows what the band could really achieve, the rest of the album gets so bogged down in showing us how many styles the band can play in that it loses its way. But the title track remains one of the finest pieces of music in the Progressive Rock canon.

Gentle Giant
Acquiring the Taste
Released August 1971

Gentle Giant also took things up a notch with their second album. The statement on the sleeve notes for the record famously read:

> It is our goal to expand the frontiers of contemporary popular music at the risk of being very unpopular. We have recorded each composition with the one thought – that it should be unique, adventurous and fascinating. It has taken

> every shred of our combined musical and technical knowledge to achieve this. From the outset we have abandoned all preconceived thoughts of blatant commercialism. Instead we hope to give you something far more substantial and fulfilling. All you need to do is sit back, and acquire the taste.

This statement is often taken, particularly by journalists hostile to the genre, to be a pretentious statement of intent, and not just for Gentle Giant or the album, but for Progressive Rock itself. Of course, what the band were actually doing was throwing their potential audience an elaborate double bluff. 'We are making uncommercial but substantial music,' they seem to be saying, 'so why not buy it and see for yourself?'

Almost all the blues-based riffery of the first album had gone, to be replaced, as promised, by eight finely crafted pieces of music. Every member of the band was a multi-instrumentalist, so with no sound out of reach, the versatility of the band comes to the fore, particularly in the opening track, 'Pantagruel's Nativity', which opens with an eerie theme played on the Moog, while keyboardist Kerry Minnear, one of three vocalists in this initial incarnation of the band, sings in his gentle falsetto. When the whole band comes in, the listener is not allowed to settle, and the sheer variety of instruments on display – trumpet, vibes and sax being three of the more unusual instruments deployed – surprises throughout. The tone is maintained on 'Edge of Twilight' with Minnear again singing eerily over cello, restrained organ, acoustic guitar and a disturbing backwards drum pattern, before the first (and only, I think) kettle-drum solo in Progressive Rock . The overall effect of these opening tracks is unsettling, yet the versatility on display is amazing. 'The House, the Street, the Room' , while following a more conventional rock format for part of its duration, again throws in everything but the kitchen sink, particularly during the lightning-fast medieval-style 'round' midway through the song. The title track feels like a Walter Carlos-style Moog pastiche, while still sounding like a lot like Gentle Giant.

Side two opens with the menacing, riff-driven 'Wreck', followed by the delicious 'The Moon Is Down', which makes terrific use of unusual harmony vocals and features the bass guitar as lead instrument. This is the closest the album gets to the traditional Progressive Rock of Yes or Genesis. The quirky, jazzy 'Black Cat', perhaps the only conventional song on the album, leads into album closer 'Plain Truth', a showcase for the electric violin of Ray Shulman and the only track to feature an extended solo section.

Acquiring the Taste is important, not just because it is a fine album, but because it is one of the first records in the Progressive Rock era to forgo jamming and rehearsal room composition in favour of a gradually compiled series of pieces (and little or no thought as to how they might be performed live). As might be predicted, the album was not a huge success. To this day it has a reputation, I think undeserved, for inaccessibility. It rewards repeated listens handsomely.

Van der Graaf Generator
Pawn Hearts
Released October 1971

Although popularised by Yes, the three-track album – with one piece covering an entire side and two other long-form pieces on the other – was originated by Van der Graaf Generator with this, their early masterwork. Like Gentle Giant's *Acquiring the Taste*, this is an album that has few pretensions towards populism. On 'Lemmings', Peter Hammill's vocals dominate, and the first five minutes of the track are a full-on sonic assault. Everything from the organ to the sax to the vocalist *despairs*, although the main riff holds the piece together. It all seems to peter out into chaos, and then the stately piano of 'Man-Erg' pulls it back together. Its more conventional and melodic song structure gives way to organ apocalypse before a more reflective final section (with a rare use of the Mellotron by the band and guitar by guest Robert Fripp) builds to a hymnal climax. US versions of the album at this point include the George Martin tune 'Theme One', an instrumental entirely out of keeping with the tone of the rest of the album.

'A Plague of Lighthouse Keepers' examines, in abstract form, the feeling of alienation and madness of a lighthouse keeper. An initial vocal section gives way to a quiet, eerie instrumental section with saxes seemingly imitating foghorns. The main character assesses his own feelings of isolation and alienation via a brooding passage dominated by electronic piano, which then explodes into a frenetic passage featuring saxes, piano and Moog. As the piece continues, Hammill's vocals take on a quiet, reflective tone – as if he were Kerry Minnear's evil twin – and there is a rare moment of melody and stillness before a final multi-keyboard charge, stirring piano chords and the guitar solo (again from Fripp) that closes the piece.

Pawn Hearts is not an easy listen. Intense and often cacophonous, its fleeting moments of melody and refection sometimes feel like welcome oases of calm among the din. There is little doubt, however, that this version of the band – particularly with David Jackson's sax prominent as a lead instrument in place of lead guitar – produced a truly innovative take on the genre. Crucially, Hammill is one of Progressive Rock's most perceptive lyricists. Ignore this album at your peril.

Focus
Moving Waves
Released October 1971

If Van der Graaf Generator took this exciting new genre and hung it out to dry, Dutch band Focus kept their music closer to the classics, in this case medieval and baroque music. Formed, essentially, as a collaboration between Brainbox guitarist Jan Akkerman and keyboardist and flautist Thijs van Leer, the band's first line-up recorded a slightly uncertain debut before a revised rhythm section was established, which included Akkerman's Brainbox bandmate Pierre van der

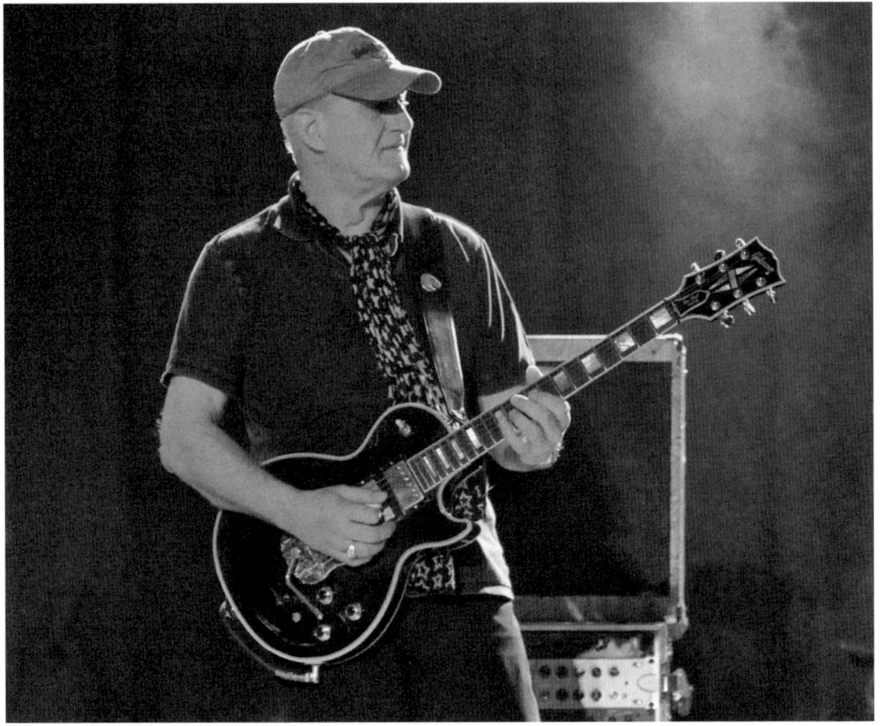

Jan Akkerman at Montgomery Theatre, Wath, in 2009. (*Chris Walkden*)

Linden on drums. The band then convened to record a second album in London with producer Mike Vernon.

The opener is the unique 'Hocus Pocus', one of those tracks that has seeped into the public consciousness over the years, thanks to its searing hard rock riff and very unusual yodelling by Thijs van Leer. Amazingly, the track doesn't overbalance the album too much, and the next track, 'Le Clochard', a delightful duet for classical guitar and Mellotron, calms things down gracefully. 'Janis', a flute-dominated instrumental, sails a little close to 'lift music' for comfort, and the florid piano-and-vocal title track has a throwaway quality to it. 'Focus II', which closes side one, is a sublime, deliciously restrained showcase for Akkerman's guitar, underpinned by piano and Mellotron.

But it is the side-long piece 'Eruption' that makes the album the classic that it is. Based on the Orpheus and Eurydice story, it is in turns stately and playful, and wears its baroque influences on its sleeve. After this call-and-response section, the delicious guitar instrumental 'Tommy' (with guitar amp feedback left intact) continues the suite, and leads into a thrilling, jazzy unison passage that heralds a section of jamming. This is the only section where the album strays from tight, economical arrangements. The delightful closing melody makes its first appearance, and then all of a sudden we are in a monastery with Gregorian vocals. 'Eruption' concludes with a drum solo and a reprise of the themes we have already heard.

Nothing in Progressive Rock sounds like 'Eruption' – or indeed Focus. On this track they perfectly balance composition with jamming. The band were to be less lucky on the following year's *Focus 3*, where some excellent short material was unbalanced by some of the most tedious jamming committed to record – in particular the tortuous 'Anonymous 2'.

Moving Waves was released to great acclaim in Holland, but not elsewhere. However, some hard touring and a triumphant appearance on the BBC television rock show *The Old Grey Whistle Test* lifted the band to star status in a matter of months – helped by the success of 'Hocus Pocus' and 'Sylvia' as singles. The band continued to chart into the mid-1970s, but the international success they enjoyed in 1971 and 1972 was never to be repeated until van Leer reconvened a tribute version of the group without Akkerman in the early 2000s.

MORE INNOVATION FROM YES AND GENESIS

Yes released a fourth album at the end of the year, *Fragile* – perhaps an early suggestion that the personalities in the band would always clash. With organist Tony Kaye now departed, the band invited youthful and lanky keyboard player Rick Wakeman to join them. He was clearly wasted in an early semi-electric incarnation of The Strawbs. Aside from a prodigious technique – a good match for the talented Steve Howe – Wakeman was far more than just an organist. He was happy to absorb the technical requirements for playing any keyboard instrument the music required. His work on *Fragile* was exceptional, mixing organ with Mellotron, electronic piano and Moog, often within the same piece of music. He also showed an admirable restraint on this particular album, serving the track rather than his personal vanity. The album itself refined the long-form composition of *The Yes Album* and also included such tracks as US hit single 'Roundabout', 'South Side of the Sky' and fan favourite 'Heart of the Sunrise'. Each member of the band also contributed a shorter solo piece, and the variability of these pieces is what leaves the album short of classic status.

Genesis also released their next album with new members Steve Hackett and Phil Collins. *Nursery Cryme* made as little impact as *Trespass* had done before it, and despite the affection that fans hold for it, to me it seems poorly recorded, the material nowhere near as strong as its predecessor's. It was, however, well performed, with both of the new musicians acquitting themselves well. Steve Hackett pioneered his 'hammering on' guitar technique, where the strings are played by hammering the fingers on the fret board to produce a note, rather than holding a string down and plucking with fingers or plectrum. Phil Collins, as well as drumming fluidly, was allowed a brief lead vocal on the charming 'For Absent Friends'.

Pink Floyd made another patchy album, *Meddle*, in Progressive Rock style before their music began to move in a more song-orientated, stadium rock direction. The side-long 'Echoes' was the pivotal track, largely instrumental and deliciously brooding. The throbbing 'One of These Days' was a highlight alongside some barely memorable song-orientated material.

Curved Air's *Second Album* was a big improvement on their first, and included some excellent material. Particularly strong were the lengthy album closer 'Piece of Mind' and the short but glorious 'Everdance'. On this album Francis Monkman's synthesizer work was particularly impressive in conjunction with Darryl Way's lead violin.

Emerson, Lake & Palmer and King Crimson also put out further albums, with ELP releasing a live rendition of *Pictures of an Exhibition* at a budget price, and King Crimson, now totally dominated by Robert Fripp, releasing *Islands*. The latter's line-up was the last version of the band with any sort of connection to the 1969 version that had imploded only two years before, even if it was only to be found in the material they played. The pivotal track on the album was 'Ladies of the Road', a cynical exposure of the world of the groupie, and one of the last songs that lyricist Peter Sinfield would help write for the band. To me it feels competent but directionless, and while the band were thought of as a good live outfit – as documented on the poorly recorded *Earthbound* album – tensions between Fripp and the other musicians soon led to King Crimson's dissolution once more, while on tour in the USA.

Progressive Rock was still largely a British phenomenon in 1971, and it was the year that many bands found their feet. Several made their finest music; for others, the best was yet to come.

1972

The beginning of 1972 saw some bands beginning to find success, while others continued to struggle. Gentle Giant, Genesis and Van der Graaf Generator made little progress in the UK, but found that there was a market for their music in mainland Europe. Holland and Belgium were sympathetic, but it was Italy that really embraced them. Whereas Yes bypassed these sorts of territories initially, moving fairly quickly from the UK club circuit to larger concert halls, both in the UK and in the United States, other bands found that the dramatic nature of the music they were making was best suited to the Italian temperament. It was an odd synergy, considering the traditional British reserve. Van der Graaf Generator, despite some chart success in Italy, folded amicably for the second time in 1972 for financial reasons, and Peter Hammill pursued an enigmatic and artistically credible solo career for the next few years. King Crimson, the band name remaining with Robert Fripp after the split, spent the latter part of the year on hiatus.

Close to the Edge, Yes's finest album, recorded in 1972. (*Rhino*)

YES SET THE BAR EVEN HIGHER

With the USA the biggest market for rock music in the world, some bands would spend months playing the American sports arenas, particularly on the northern West Coast and in the Midwest. Jethro Tull were one of the earliest bands to play this circuit, and Yes played their first gigs supporting them in the summer of 1971. By 1972 the latter were back headlining, but late in the spring they began work on their follow-up to *Fragile*.

Yes
Close to the Edge
Released September 1972

Recorded at Advision studios in London under the supervision of regular engineer Eddie Offord, who had also engineered *Tarkus* by ELP a few months before, *Close to the Edge* is arguably the finest statement that the Progressive Rock movement made. It blends adventure with melody to produce some of the most inventive yet accessible music ever recorded. Created over a then-lengthy three months, and largely pieced together in the studio, the album consisted of just three pieces of music.

The title track may not have been the first side-long piece of music committed to vinyl, but it may well be the most concise. Not a moment of its eighteen minutes and forty-three seconds is wasted. There is no flab, and only one solo, courtesy of Wakeman's urgent organ playing towards the end of the piece. All the choices made by the band seem perfect, to this day. The cacophonous opening resolving into the main theme of the piece; the opening and closing vocal sections that use the same song structure but with such different arrangements; and the 'I Get Up I Get Down' section, which builds tension before the remarkable release of the ending. The other two pieces are by no means passengers on the album, presenting very different moods and structures. The gentle twelve-string guitar intro to 'And You and I' builds into an inspiring, stately middle section, and has been played at almost every Yes concert since, whatever the line-up. The album closes with the relentless 'Siberian Khatru', complete with its famously unexpected harpsichord solo.

What Yes showed they were masters of were intricate and varied arrangements, with Chris Squire's bass in particular weaving astonishing patterns around the music, while the instrumental stars – guitarist Steve Howe and keyboard player Rick Wakeman – add flavour without ever getting carried away in excess. Wakeman, in particular, uses the Moog synthesizer not as an instrument for soloing as he was to do in his solo career, but as a support instrument for texture. The band were also masters at the building and releasing of tension – a masterful and satisfying trick in music if it can be carried off. Produced in a lavishly simple and atmospheric gatefold sleeve, this was the first album to feature the famous Roger Dean Yes logo.

The album was a huge hit all over the world, reaching the top five in both Britain and the USA. Given the level of invention on display, the success of the album is almost impossible to envisage these days. Here was a record that, while not short of melody, was a real challenge to listen to. And it made Yes one of the biggest bands in the world.

Jethro Tull
Thick as a Brick
Released July 1972

Jethro Tull, whom Yes had supported in the USA in 1971, had gradually converted themselves from a blues band into something rather more interesting. Their 1971 hit album *Aqualung* had been misinterpreted as a concept album by the press as a result of some of the tracks having similar themes (specifically, they attacked organised religion). The similarity in appearance of Ian Anderson and Aqualung (the title character pictured on the cover) gave the press even more material to get their teeth into. All of it was an irritation to Anderson and for their next album he set about doing something about it.

The music of *Thick of a Brick* is an astonishing step forward from its predecessor in terms of arrangement and complexity. It would have been easy, presumably, to churn out another hard rock album after the success of *Aqualung*, but Ian Anderson was having none of it. The band presented the album as one continuous piece of music split over two sides of vinyl – one of the first times this was attempted. Whether the first side of the album should be seen as a whole or just a series of short pieces spliced together is open to debate, although it does hang together very well.

JETHRO TULL

The St. Cleve Chronicle & Linwell Advertiser

Friday January 7th 1972 — No.1003 — Price 3p Weekly

THICK AS A BRICK

JUDGES DISQUALIFY "LITTLE MILTON" IN LAST MINUTE RUMPUS

THE SOCIETY FOR LITERARY ADVANCEMENT AND GESTATION, (SLAG), announced their decision late last night to disqualify eight year old prizewinner Gerald (Little Milton) Bostock following the hundreds of protests and threats received after the reading of his epic poem "Thick as a Brick" on B.B.C. Television last Monday night.

A hastily reconvened panel of Judges accepted the decision by four leading child psychiatrists that the boy's mind was seriously unbalanced and that his work was a product of an "extremely unwholesome attitude towards life, his God and Country". Bostock was recommended for psychiatric treatment following examination "without delay". The first prize will now be presented to runner up Mary Whiteyard (aged 12) for her essay on Christian ethics entitled, "He died to save the little Children".

ART DEMO FORCES CLOSURE

U.F.O. SIGHTING SENSATION

LITTLE MILTON IN SCHOOL – GIRL PREGNANCY ROW

DIRECTOR ACCUSED

Mongrel dog soils actor's foot

HEAD INJURY

Jethro Tull's astonishingly detailed newspaper format cover to *Thick as a Brick*. (*Chrysalis*)

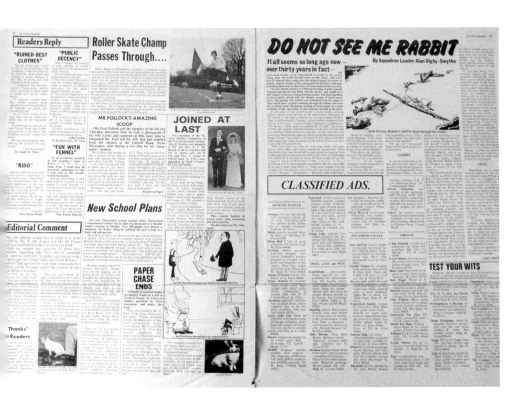

Readers Reply

"RUINED BEST CLOTHES"

"PUBLIC DECENCY"

"FUN WITH FENNEL"

"RIDO"

Roller Skate Champ Passes Through....

MR. POLLOCK'S AMAZING SCOOP

JOINED AT LAST

New School Plans

PAPER CHASE ENDS

Editorial Comment

DO NOT SEE ME RABBIT

It all seems so long ago now — over thirty years in fact—

By Squadron Leader Alan Digby-Smythe

CLASSIFIED ADS.

TEST YOUR WITS

The album starts deceptively with a simple acoustic guitar and flute refrain before launching into pure Progressive Rock complexity, with impressive performances by both Martin Barre on guitar and John Evan on organ. Evan, in particular, is a star throughout, his bluesy organ and piano work holding the album together with great style. Although side two contains that most hated of things, a drum solo on a studio album (yuck), it still builds to a terrific climax. The continuous nature of *Thick as a Brick* means that it is not easy to get into, but perseverance brings great reward. Like much of Progressive Rock, the music of the album falls into place after several listens.

A little bit like Yes in the same year, Tull hit the peak of their creativity with *Thick as a Brick*, and spent the next few years attempting to live up to it.

Gentle Giant
Octopus
Released December 1972

After the complexity of *Acquiring the Taste*, Gentle Giant recorded two albums in 1972. They began with the more accessible and cohesive concept album *Three Friends* and then, later in the year, with new drummer John Weathers on board, they returned to the much-used Advision Studios to record their most celebrated album to date, *Octopus*.

While no Gentle Giant album sounds like any other, *Octopus* feels to me like it is the most cohesive, even though it is musically very diverse. The quirky opener, 'The Advent of Panurge', gives way to a more overtly medieval influence on the

Gary Green of Gentle Giant at Nearfest. (*Kevin Scherer*)

charming 'Raconteur Troubadour', which is followed by the harder rock of 'A Cry for Everyone'. Side one finishes with the hugely influential 'Knots' mixing complex multi-part vocal harmonies with Weather's xylophone pyrotechnics. Side two kicks off with the deliciously complex instrumental 'The Boys in the Band' before Phil Shulman's last lead vocal on a Gentle Giant album, accompanied by violin and cello, on the charming tribute to the band's roadies, 'A Dog's Life'. The gorgeous ballad 'Think of Me with Kindness' – perhaps Kerry Minnear's finest lead vocal – finally leads into the complex album closer 'River'.

Despite its popularity, it is tempting to see *Octopus* as a lesser album in the Gentle Giant canon simply because of its relative accessibility. However, to me it is their most consistent and charming work. For a band that could sometimes be clinical and complex for the sake of it, this is an album full of emotion, and for me that makes it their best.

THE ITALIANS ARE COMING

By 1972 the music was beginning to seep into other territories. Not only did Italy become an important territory for sales, it started to produce its own florid and dramatic take on the genre. *Pawn Hearts* by Van der Graaf Generator was the inspiration for many of these bands; amazingly, it was a number one album in Italy for twelve weeks in 1972. Genesis and Gentle Giant in particular found that while their fortunes remained muted in the UK, with club gigs and support slots their main staple, they could play decent-sized halls to large and appreciative audiences in Italy.

The New Trolls had already released their seminal album in 1971, *Concerto grosso per i*, which featured some challenging orchestral arrangements, not unlike similar efforts by Deep Purple and Yes. But in the same way as the orchestral efforts by those two bands, the album fails to blend the orchestra with the bluesy rock of the band itself. However, three bands in particular made a real impact on the international scene.

Banco del Mutuo Soccorso, from Rome, built their complex, keyboard-orientated sound around the playing of two brothers, Vittorio and Giani Nocenzi. As with many early Progressive Rock bands, organ was important to their early sound, but the band weaved piano and some innovative synth textures around it. There were other innovative features on display, too – saxophone and other woodwind instruments added Van der Graaf-style textures, while the classically inspired vocals of tenor Francesco di Giacomo added a genuinely operatic quality to the music. The band released two albums in 1972, their self-titled debut and the concept album in Italian, *Darwin!*, of which more in a moment.

Premiata Forneria Marconi, from Milan, had a similar lineage to bands like Yes and Gentle Giant. Since the group was made up of seasoned musicians

Banco at Nearfest. (*Kevin Scherer*)

Franz Di Cioccio of PFM at Nearfest. (*Kevin Scherer*)

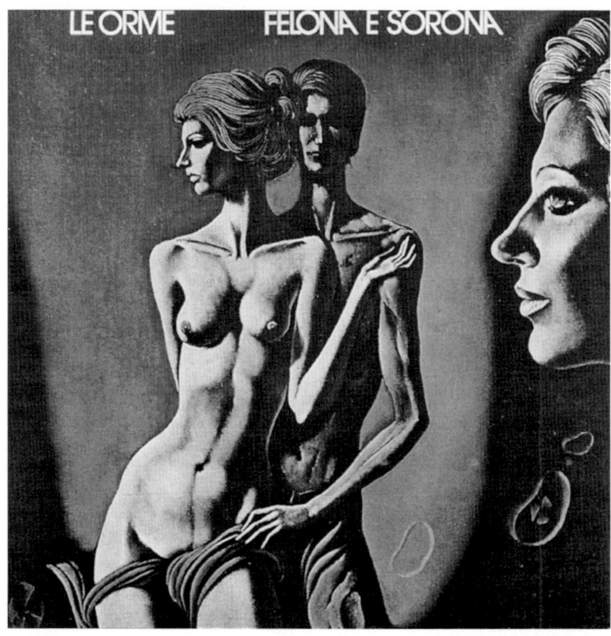

The cover of the Le Orme classic *Felona e Sorona*. (*Polygram*)

used to playing a variety of styles, by the time they formed their Progressive incarnation in 1970 they were perfectly capable of playing complex material. After the band had signed to the Italian wing of RCA, their first recordings brought them major success in their homeland. Like Banco, the band released two Italian language albums in 1972, *Storia di un minuto* and *Per un amico*, before being signed to ELP's Manticore label. Peter Sinfield was assigned to write English language lyrics.

Le Orme, from Venice, had had a longer career as a psychedelic combo in the late 1960s before morphing gradually into a Progressive Rock band in the early 1970s, when the band had its greatest success as a keyboard-led three-piece, with virtuoso Tony Pagliuca on keys. They were a little like ELP in that the lack of a guitarist for their key albums gave them a very special sound.

Banco del Mutuo Soccorso
Darwin!
Released 1972

Premiata Forneria Marconi
Photos of Ghosts
Released 1973

Le Orme
Felona e Sorona
Released 1973

These three albums, all released within an eighteen-month period, are typical of the Progressive Rock emanating from Italy at the time, while all sounding completely different to each other. It is hard to separate them in terms of quality either.

Darwin! is a remarkable piece of work, often hard-edged, yet with a level of complexity that is quite astonishing for the year that it was created. The band also show that they have to ability to build real atmosphere and tension, as is shown on the opener 'L'Evoluzione', a mixture of Genesis lyricism, ELP synth fanfares and Gentle Giant angularity. 'La conquista della posizione eretta' on the other hand is an expressive ELP-style instrumental with some remarkable synth textures, while later in the album '750,000 anni fa... L'amore?' brings genuine warmth and emotion. Hugely powerful and at other times showing a tenderness that the English bands would struggle to attempt, this album remains arguably their finest work.

It is not hard to understand how PFM came to the attention of Emerson, Lake & Palmer. Whereas Banco had power and neo-classical lyricism, PFM had huge amounts of class. Not unlike Gentle Giant, they were able to mix moments of acoustic delicacy and full-band electric power in a heartbeat. This is all evident on 'River of Life', which goes from a delicious flute and classical introduction into a full-band workout. If PFM had a fault, it was that ideas come and go all too suddenly without really establishing themselves, and 'River of Life' has almost everything the band had to offer: delicious melody, instrumental dexterity and lovely vocal harmonies. 'Celebration', with its exuberant synth line and choral vocals, on the other hand, feels like a deliberate hit-single attempt. The title track again has a delicacy and beauty that most bands would envy, while 'Old Rain' introduces violin as a lead instrument, with hits of delicate, intricate jazz. 'Il Banchetto' is the only piece sung in Italian, while 'Mr. 9 'til 5' is the only song that has aged badly, sounding like an ELP novelty outtake. The album closes on the wonderful 'Promenade the Puzzle'. Of all the Italian bands, I recommend PFM as the group to try first, since they have many elements that British fans in particular will find attractive. A little like Gentle Giant without the inaccessible edge, the band mix plenty of Genesis and even a touch of Canterbury into a formula that is melodic, beautiful and accessible.

On the other hand, we have Le Orme. *Felona e Sorona* is their most celebrated album and it is not hard to understand why. Like Banco's work, it has lyrics in Italian, but this should not put any potential listeners off. This is a Progressive Rock power trio (in ELP style) of the highest order. The album is dominated by the powerful organ and synth playing of Toni Pugliuca and the bass and vocals (again, Greg Lake style) of Aldo Tagliapietra. Opening piece 'Sospesi nell'incredibile' is the only lengthy track on the album, and allows the band to stretch out. Elsewhere, the story – about two feuding planets – is allowed to develop over short passages mixing intense keyboard rock with lovely Italian-style acoustic guitar-driven vocal pieces. At thirty-three minutes, it is quite a short album, but the overall result is charming and very powerful.

ELSEWHERE IN EUROPE

It was not only Italy that began to emerge as a force internationally in 1972 and 1973. The insultingly titled 'Krautrock movement' began to emerge. This was a different, although obviously related, genre.

Not all German bands chose this path, as evidenced by the hard rock/Progressive hybrid of Eloy, who released their second album *Inside* in 1973. French band Ange also had a unique take on Progressive Rock and began to emerge internationally, particularly via a very well received appearance at the 1973 Reading Festival in the UK promoting their excellent second album *Le Cimetière des arlequins*. Often thought of as a German band, although actually from Britain, Nektar also began to win a following internationally with their groove-based music and in 1973 released their best-known album *Remember the Future*, a major hit in Germany and also a success in the USA.

However, the most striking and original album released outside the UK in 1973 came from another French band, the extraordinary Magma.

Magma at Nearfest 2007. (*Kevin Scherer*)

Magma
Mekanïk Destruktïw Kommandöh
Released 1973

Magma were formed in 1969 by drummer Christian Vander, who has an unusual, ecological world view. He invented a story based around the exodus of a colony of humans to a new planet, Kobaia. Most of the band's subsequent albums revolve around conflicts on Kobaia, and often stretch out into jazz-fusion territory. However, *Mekanïk Destruktïw Kommandöh* is important in that it follows a more minimalist, symphonic path.

Unlike most British Progressive Rock bands and particularly unlike the Italians (whose inspiration tended towards the pastoral and romantic), Magma's music was rather more atonal and Teutonic in character, with composer Carl Orff clearly a major influence. This is particularly evident in the choral, almost hysterical vocals that carry the music forward, particularly on the relentless album opener 'Hortz Fur Dëhn Stekëhn West'. Despite the reputation of the band, the music is not always attritional. Although percussion and brass are prominent, so are traditional Progressive Rock instruments such as electronic guitar, organ and piano, and it is also possible to hear shades of jazz wizard John Coltrane, the classical swirls of Emerson Lake & Palmer, and even vocal group The 5th Dimension.

All the lyrics are also sung in 'Kobaian', a sort of invented part-language with suggestions of both German and French, giving the music an unearthly quality that is unlike anything else produced in the Progressive Rock era. Magma produced only a few albums blending the symphonic and the otherworldly in this way; their subsequent music moved in a jazzier, more fusion-based direction. 'Zeul', as this strand of music came to be known, has become its own subgenre, with various Magma-related bands playing in a similar style. If *Mekanïk Destruktïw Kommandöh* appeals, then delve further.

PINK FLOYD AND MIKE OLDFIELD CLEAN UP

1973 was an exceptionally busy year. The British album chart, and indeed the public consciousness as a whole, was dominated by two albums. These were Pink Floyd's *Dark Side of the Moon* and Mike Oldfield's *Tubular Bells*. There is always debate as to whether these two albums 'count' as Progressive Rock. Both certainly carry the spirit of invention typical of a lot of music at the time. *Dark Side of the Moon* is a selection of very fine songs linked by some devilishly clever instrumental sections. Its cleverness lies as much in its conception as its execution. Despite the album's adult subject matter, it is an album for the big stage, full of crowd-pleasing guitar solos. It works beautifully as a complete work, but also as a collection of powerful but relatively simple songs. Effectively, *Dark Side of the Moon* became the first stadium rock album, and the public lapped it up.

Tubular Bells, on the other hand, was the product of a unique imagination. Mike Oldfield wanted to make music in a solitary way, and his first three albums, which include the often overlooked *Hergest Ridge* and the more accessible *Ommadawn*, show extraordinary vision. Of course, they are not rock albums at all, but they *are* Progressive, weaving and developing themes in an unusual and sophisticated way. *Tubular Bells* shows what can happen when one rather obsessive man is allowed into a recording studio on his own for an extended period of time. While its impact has been somewhat muted by fame and familiarity, it deserved its astonishing success.

KING CRIMSON REFORM (AGAIN)

King Crimson re-emerged in an entirely new incarnation. Having recruited Bill Bruford and John Wetton as a high-quality rhythm section, Robert Fripp also picked young violinist David Cross and extravagant percussionist Jamie Muir for a new version of the band that mixed complex, angular instrumentals with improvisation and some melodic vocal sections sung by Wetton. The band released the first of an excellent trio of albums, *Larks' Tongues in Aspic*, in March 1973. Jethro Tull also released *A Passion Play*, their poorly received follow-up to *Thick as a Brick*. The press antipathy to this album seems mystifying now. It seems to me to be almost on a par with its better-known predecessor and in some areas it is more expansive and inventive. Caravan also released a notable album, *For Girls Who Grow Plump in the Night*, with a different line-up, introducing John G. Perry on bass and the hugely talented Geoffrey Richardson, the only lead viola player I can think of. The album contains some of their most inspiring pieces since *In the Land of Grey and Pink*, with the opening 'Memory Lain, Hugh/ Headloss' and the dated lyrics but sweet melody of 'The Dog, the Dog, He's at It Again' particularly prominent.

After the relative accessibility of *Octopus* in 1972, Gentle Giant hit problems with a more ambitious work, *In a Glass House*. For me, the more accessible material on this record is not quite up to the usual standard. However, 'An Intimates Lullaby' – aside from the vocal played entirely on tuned percussion – remains hugely underrated and one of the most ambitious and haunting pieces in the Progressive Rock canon. It is also about as close to contemporary classical music as Prog gets. The baffled record company failed to release the album in the USA, but it sold well as an import for many years.

However, 1973's most important achievement belongs to a British band finally ready to challenge Yes and ELP. Genesis.

Genesis
Selling England by the Pound
Released October 1973

This was the third album to feature the 'classic' Genesis line-up of Gabriel, Collins, Banks, Rutherford and Hackett, and after the patchy (though much-loved) efforts *Nursery Cryme* and *Foxtrot*, they needed to deliver something special. They did.

Three important factors brought about the huge improvement. First of all, the material the band came up with was more mature and better structured than anything they had written previously. Secondly, co-producer John Burns achieved a much warmer and sympathetic sound for the band at Island Studios. Finally, and crucially, this was the first album to feature the use of the synthesizer as a lead instrument. Its contributions to the sound of 'The Cinema Show' and 'The Battle of Epping Forest' in particular are warm and fluid, with Tony Banks taking to the instrument as if he had always played it.

The lyrics of this album read like a love story to England. They are playful, very funny at times, and have an engaging wistfulness that went on to inspire a host of imitators. Album opener 'Dancing with the Moonlit Knight' begins with Gabriel's solo vocal, and introduces this new, warm, unified Genesis. 'I Know What I Like (In Your Wardrobe)' is the hit single, a weird tale of domesticity with the band's first sing-along chorus. However, 'Firth of Fifth' is the first of two classics on the album. Not only is it deliciously structured, it contains two of the most fêted moments in Progressive Rock – Banks's elegant and fiendishly difficult piano introduction and Hackett's signature guitar solo, a part of his solo live set to this day. After the Collins-sung ballad 'More Fool Me', side two opens with the least successful track on the album, the complex 'Battle of Epping Forest', which is followed by the soothing, neo-classical instrumental 'After the Ordeal'. 'The Cinema Show' is the album's other classic, its Beatles-esque introduction building to a climax dominated by Banks's remarkably fluid synth solo. 'Aisle of Plenty' neatly repeats some of the themes from the beginning of the album.

Selling England by the Pound is one of the great achievements of the 1970s Progressive Rock era. It is not perfect, but when it fails it does so with such style that it is difficult not to love it. It remains my favourite Genesis album, by quite a long way.

CRISIS, WHAT CRISIS?

The autumn and early winter of 1973 represent another important period in the evolution of Progressive Rock. At a time of strife in the Middle East, the ongoing Watergate scandal in the USA, and a worldwide oil crisis, the key artists in the Progressive Rock book were becoming very rich indeed. Their output at the end of 1973 displayed huge ambition, but creativity was starting to suffer.

Emerson, Lake & Palmer
Brain Salad Surgery
Released December 1973

In the main, while the music on *Brain Salad Surgery* never quite hits the euphoric heights of *Tarkus*, it does benefit from greater consistency, and has several moments that are genuinely startling. As usual, ELP throw in a few cover versions (if we can call them that) with a grandiose version of that very English hymn 'Jerusalem' – the closest Progressive Rock ever came to an alliance with the Women's Institute – and followed that up with a piece by composer Albert Ginastera, 'Toccata', probably the best showcase for Carl Palmer's percussion skills on record. 'Still... You Turn Me On' is a Greg Lake ballad, one of many on ELP albums and one of the finest. 'Benny the Bouncer' is the obligatory joke track, and has not held up well. However, the showpiece of the album is the astonishing 'Karn Evil 9', which spills over from side one of the vinyl LP and takes up all of side two. The track jumps straight into the first vocal section, and so fails to repeat the impact of 'Tarkus', but it is still heady stuff, with powerful lyrics from Peter Sinfield, and the band's famous 'Welcome Back My Friends to the Show that Never Ends' motif, as borrowed by Alan 'Fluff' Freeman for his radio rock show. To be honest, that is the high point of the thirty-minute piece, which continues with a jazzy piano section and has plenty of classical flourishes that show off Emerson and Palmer's versatility. The climactic vocal section recalls 'The Great Gates of Kiev' from *Pictures at an Exhibition*.

Five albums in, *Brain Salad Surgery* cemented the band's reputation as world-beaters. The UK album charts in the third week of December showed the impossible,

The unusual pull-out cover for ELP's ambitious *Brain Salad Surgery*. (*Sony*)

with Yes at number one and Emerson, Lake & Palmer at number two. Progressive Rock was at the height of its commercial powers at the end of 1973. Things could only get better, surely?

Yes
Tales from Topographic Oceans
Released December 1973

Momentum is an amazing thing. Even though neither *Close to the Edge* nor the sumptuous triple live album *Yessongs* had gone to number one in the UK album charts, the band was doing such amazing business as a live act that their reputation was at fever pitch. For a few short months in 1973 they were vying with the likes of Led Zeppelin, ELP and Deep Purple to be the biggest band in the world. Pre-orders for the band's next album went through the roof, guaranteeing them a number one slot for at least a week.

Tales from Topographic Oceans, Yes's most controversial album, released at the end of 1973. (*Rhino*)

However, all was not well in the Yes camp. Initially, the band could not decide whether to record in the countryside or the town. Finally a decision was made to record at Morgan Studios in London, but for some reason it was judged a good idea to move bales of hay and other clichéd symbols of the countryside into the studio to generate a rural spirit. This incident is often held up as a perfect example of the decadence and pretentiousness of Progressive Rock. In reality, it is no worse than many of the slightly bonkers schemes embarked upon by many rock stars in the mid-1970s, including Led Zeppelin, Elton John and of course ELP. It is simply what happens when rock stars have too much money and not enough perspective.

Jon Anderson and Steve Howe had devised a four-track double album based on the Shastric scriptures, and there lies its trouble. One of the main arguments against Progressive Rock – that it overstays its welcome – is exemplified by this flawed album. By deciding that the record would have this format in advance, the band became stuck with it, and had to come up with eighty minutes of material. Whereas the nineteen-minute 'Close to the Edge' had been a model of precision and concision, the band simply did not have enough ideas to do this four times with *Tales*, and sadly it shows.

The album starts well enough with 'The Revealing Science of God (Dance of the Dawn)', probably the strongest of the four pieces. However, it takes an age to reach the most thrilling moment, Rick Wakeman's Minimoog solo, so perhaps even this piece might have been shorter. 'The Remembering (High the Memory)' is less successful, however, and plods along for three quarters of its length. This is a common feature of *Tales*. Dull material is persisted with, and more interesting moments seem far too short. The third piece, 'The Ancient (Giants under the Sun)', is supposedly most ambitious and difficult to listen to, pre-empting as it does the jazzier material to come on 1974's *Relayer*. I must admit I rather like it. It showcases Steve Howe's electric guitar throughout, although new drummer Alan White also demonstrates an interest in exotic percussion and the final acoustic guitar section, 'Leaves of Green', is one of Yes's prettiest songs. 'Ritual (Nous sommes du soleil)' closes the album, this time showcasing Chris Squire's bass. As with 'The Revealing Science of God' there are some excellent ideas, but they take too long to establish themselves.

The album was released to largely hostile reviews and is often held up as a symbol of a genre going too far. That the band played the whole thing on tour a month before its release was perhaps asking a bit too much of its audience. To many Yes fans, including me, it is too long and short of ideas, but still has some wonderful moments. To others, perhaps a minority, it is the best thing the band has ever done. To many of Progressive Rock's detractors, however, it has come to represent how ridiculous Progressive Rock could be. This reputation is undeserved, but understandable.

1974

1973 had been a heady year, and 1974 was something of an anticlimax as a result. For the bands that had broken into the lucrative American market, life remained good. Emerson, Lake & Palmer toured incessantly, headlining the famous California Jam festival in April 1974 above Deep Purple and Black Sabbath. Their performance included Keith Emerson's infamous revolving piano, with Emerson and piano suspended in mid-air and revolving while he played. So much for health and safety! Yes toured *Tales from Topographic Oceans* to a mixed reaction, then lost keyboard player Rick Wakeman, who was dissatisfied with the band's direction. They recruited Swiss virtuoso Patrick Moraz to replace him. He had made a well-received Progressive Rock album with two former members of The Nice, Brian Davison and Lee Jackson. The resulting album, *Relayer*, is an amazing piece of work, although not an easy listen, with music that borders on jazz-rock fusion at times. Yet in the delicious 'To Be Over', the band produced one of their most lyrical pieces of music. A little chastened, and embittered by American label Columbia's reaction to *In a Glass House*, Gentle Giant returned with a powerful and accessible record that had a strong concept. *The Power and the Glory* was particularly relevant given the continuing Watergate scandal in the USA. The album contains a couple of classics, the gloriously languid 'Aspirations' and the manic 'Cogs in Cogs'. The band's creative run continued into 1975 with the equally impressive *Free Hand*. This again trod a more accessible, hard-rocking path while containing two further classics, 'On Reflection' and the exquisite 'His Last Voyage'.

ALL CHANGE IN THE GENESIS CAMP

For Genesis, 1974 was to be a pivotal year. Tensions were starting to run high, despite increasing success in the UK and, for the first time, the USA. Both Phil Collins and Peter Gabriel came close to leaving the band. Yet despite this, they decided that the next album was to be a full-blown double album with a story written by Peter Gabriel. Given that *Tales from Topographic Oceans* had already been released to a mixed reaction, the band were probably wise to choose a grittier subject, albeit one from the fertile, surreal mind of the troubled singer. The double album *The Lamb Lies Down on Broadway* is yet another work that splits Progressive Rock fans. To some it is their masterwork, to others it has some great material and the odd track, particularly on the second record, which feels as if the band were becoming tired. I tend to agree with the latter camp. By the time the band had set off on a very theatrical tour in support of the album, Gabriel had already decided to leave.

King Crimson had a two-album year, although the first, *Starless and Bible Black*, mainly consisted of live improvisations with studio overdubs. Not that it is any the worse for that, but it pales in comparison with what was to come next.

King Crimson
Red
Released October 1974

Nothing in Progressive Rock sounds quite as savage as the title track of King Crimson's final 1970s album. It is an astonishing piece of work, with wild, almost uncharacteristic drumming by Bill Bruford and a thundering bass line from John Wetton. When it is not delivering its main riff, it is full of impending doom. As an album opener, it is one of the most shattering and heavy in Progressive Rock.

This was a band in meltdown. Robert Fripp, in the grip of some sort of spiritual awakening, had disappeared within himself, so Bruford and Wetton took control of many aspects of the record, the line-up having slimmed to a three-piece. 'Fallen Angel' is a relatively restrained vocal track, with guest oboe and cornet, but it builds to another powerful climax. 'One More Red Nightmare' returns to the heavy riffing, combined with an almost funky vocal from Wetton that sounds like a precursor of his band of the late 1970s with Bruford, UK. This track also has a returning Ian McDonald, and his sax recalls the 1969 line-up.

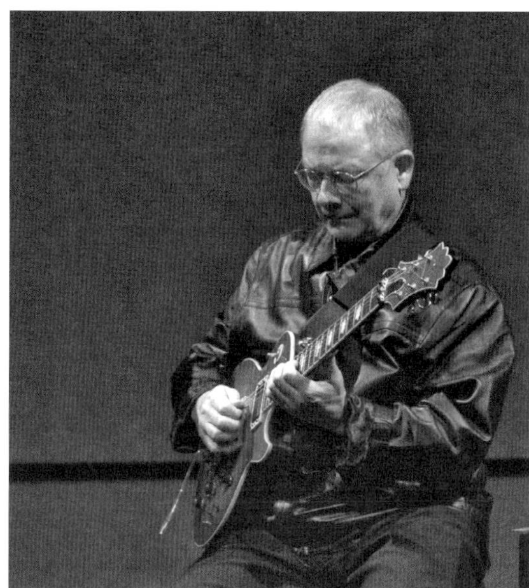

Robert Fripp in concert in 2010. (*Hightea*)

'Providence', a live improvisation from the middle of 1974, features David Cross on violin, and for me this is the best improvisation on a Crimson album since 'Moonchild'. As the piece builds up tempo with Bruford's drum pattern driving it forward, Wetton and Fripp vie for attention. Wetton is loud as well as dexterous, and it is not difficult to understand why tensions had begun to build. The album ends with the brooding 'Starless', its lyrical opening once again enhanced by the sax of Ian McDonald. The song's amazing final section is built around a huge bass riff and a repetitive, wailing guitar figure that eventually breaks into something more urgent. A haunting Mellotron fittingly underpins the last few moments of King Crimson in the 1970s.

The internationalisation of Progressive Rock continued apace in 1974 with further excellent albums from PFM, Ange and Cologne band Triumvirat. Despite the loss of drummer Pierre van der Linden, Focus recorded the well-received *Hamburger Concerto*, although to me the shorter pieces are better than the rather plodding side-long title track.

SPACE ROCK AND ELECTRONICA

An entire book could be written about the rise of electronica, of course, and while Rick Wakeman and Keith Emerson are important figures in the development of synthesizers in the 1970s, it was in the area known initially as 'space rock' that those synthesizers began to dominate. Two albums in particular stand out as great examples of where Progressive Rock and electronics collide.

Tangerine Dream
Phaedra
Released 1974

Phaedra is a hugely influential album and many of the textures created on it can be heard time and time again by artists using synthesizer loops and sequencers. This was the album that first developed that sound. But it is important to remember, especially when listening to the side-long title track, that they were not just using synths to create their sound palate. Mellotron, piano and other instruments like bass guitar play their parts as well. *Phaedra* itself is a deliciously serene seventeen-minute journey. Sounds build and fade, only changing gradually so that the listener is never startled, the instruments washing through the mix gradually. The three tracks on side two are starker, less groundbreaking, one-idea pieces using treated Mellotron (on 'Mysterious Semblance at the Strand of Nightmares') and flute (on 'Moments of a Visionary').

So influential was the title track, however, that it became the stylistic lynchpin of Tangerine Dream albums for years to come, including the band's biggest UK hit, 'Force Majeure' in 1979. By this time the band had also introduced guitars and drums to give their music more commercial appeal. In 2010 Andy Tillison of The Tangent – who had himself put out an electronic album, *Fog* – introduced to his band's live set an improvised tribute to Tangerine Dream called 'After Phaedra'.

Vangelis
Heaven and Hell
Released 1975

Greek keyboard player Vangelis had previously been in Aphrodite's Child, best known for their hugely pompous double album, *666*, based on the Book of Revelation, and had been linked with Yes after Rick Wakeman's departure. However, he had been developing a solo career that was to culminate in film soundtrack work, but which in the mid-1970s placed him in the centre of Progressive Rock. He was also developing a very individualistic approach to synthesizers, and by the mid-1970s his music had become instantly recognisable.

Heaven and Hell is a hugely varied work, with moments of dramatic neo-classicism. The English Chamber Choir is used in the early part of the work to dramatic effect, especially on the opening section 'Bacchanale', on which drums and electronic piano are also prominent. This is followed by the three-movement 'Symphony to the Powers B', the glorious third movement of which was used as the theme tune for the TV series *Cosmos* in the mid-1970s. The first side concludes with the ethereal vocal piece 'So Long Ago, So Clear' sung by Jon Anderson of Yes – a pairing that would be formalised a few years later. Side two is perhaps less memorable, but still contains some glorious moments, in particular Greek singer Vana Veroutis's lovely vocal on 'Twelve O'Clock'. Vangelis is often dismissed as a purveyor of film soundtracks;

it is easy to forget what an innovator he was on his 1970s albums. Like Tangerine Dream, he used instruments such as piano and Mellotron to create his textures, and also had a talent for big melodies several years before Jean Michel Jarre cornered the market with *Oxygène*.

A SECOND WAVE OF BRITS

1974 and 1975 are really marked by the rise to prominence of a second wave of British bands, each presenting a further variation on the genre. Several groups took the dynamics and instrumental expansiveness of Progressive Rock and applied them to song-orientated material with considerable artistic and commercial success. The two most notable of these were Barclay James Harvest and Supertramp. *Crime of the Century* was Supertramp's breakthrough album in the UK, and combined skilful songwriting – like the insanely catch single 'Dreamer' – with more Prog pieces like opener 'School' and the title track. They went on to have huge commercial success by embracing the more commercial side of their music in the late 1970s.

John Lees of Barclay James Harvest at the Cambridge Rock Festival in 2009. (*Stephen Lambe*)

Barclay James Harvest
Everyone Is Everybody Else
Released 1974

Having formed in the late 1960s in Yorkshire, Barclay James Harvest might never have survived had they formed twenty years later. Initially on the Harvest label, they had been around for four albums before a switch to Polydor gave them greater commercial potential. While *Everybody Is Everybody Else* did not chart on release, it did the groundwork for the relative commercial success that the band was to have in the latter half of the decade, particularly in mainland Europe.

In a sense, this album is here to represent all the bands that took inspiration from Progressive Rock in terms of their instrumentation and instrumental prowess, while sticking to a fairly rigid song structure. Barclay James Harvest were similar to the Moody Blues (with whom they were sometimes unfavourably compared) in that a sense of grandeur was applied to dramatic and well-constructed pop-rock songs. I can find very little Progressive Rock in *Everyone Is Everybody Else,* which seems in songs like 'Mill Boys' to owe as much to the intense, narrative-based songwriting of Neil Young as it does to anything by Yes or Genesis. But the album is beautifully constructed and the Mellotron work, in particular, is delicious.

RENAISSANCE, GRYPHON AND CAMEL

Other bands were also coming to maturity in the mid-1970s. Three very different bands that had been around for a while, developing their sound, were Renaissance, Gryphon and Camel. There is a knowing expansiveness to these bands not evident in the grittier, more pioneering work of the artists that had emerged a few years before, and while no new ground was broken sonically, the different take that each of these bands had on the genre provides interesting variations on the classic sound of those early bands. Having begun as a vehicle for Keith Relf and Jim McCarthy of The Yardbirds to explore more experimental music, Renaissance rapidly became an entirely different outfit, based around the romantic, classically trained piano playing of John Tout and the remarkable voice of Annie Haslam. Renaissance were unique among the 1970s bands in that they wore their classical influence, mainly nineteenth-century romantic composers, on their sleeves. It was more than merely structural – as might have been the case with Genesis and Yes, for instance.

Strong on melody and drama, the band's music usually replaced the traditional lead guitar with orchestral textures. Unusually for the 1970s, the band was at its best when accompanied by a full orchestra, although this was of course an expensive proposition. Renaissance had practically no success in the UK in the mid-1970s, and so concentrated on the lucrative US East Coast market. 1974's excellent *Turn of the Cards* for Miles Copeland's BMG label, which included band staples 'Running Hard' and 'Mother Russia', established a winning formula, but the best was to follow.

The reformed Renaissance, live at the Ottawa Bluesfest, Canada, in 2010. (*Roy Layer*)

Renaissance
Scheherazade and Other Stories
Released August 1975

Scheherazade and Other Stories shows the band at their most ambitiously neo-classical, yet also displaying their finest melodies. The opening few minutes of the eerie 'Trip to the Fair' are dominated by John Tout's glorious piano introduction, but the song itself is carried along by Annie Haslam's gorgeous lead vocal and a tantalising and memorable melody. The mercurial 'Vultures Fly High' is followed by the evocative pop-folk of 'Ocean Gypsy'. Side one of the album is wonderful, but it is side two, the multi-part 'Song of Scheherazade', based on *One Thousand and One Nights*, that shows how unique Renaissance were. Here the use of orchestra is magnificent, perhaps the most cohesive on a Progressive Rock album. The piece mixes vocal sections with some delicious instrumental passages, and the contrast between Annie Haslam's yearning, crystal-clear voice, the orchestra and the band itself works beautifully.

Gryphon were also a band that could only have developed in the way that they did in the 1970s. Originally an acoustic early music ensemble formed by multi-instrumentalist Richard Harvey and woodwind specialist Brian Gulland, the band incorporated more traditional rock instruments. At the height the Gryphon's powers, which included a tour supporting Yes in 1974, the band combined early instruments like Krumhorns and bassoons with rock instruments in a completely unique style. As the 1970s wore on, however, conventional instruments began to replace the more exotic ones, and the group's distinctiveness disappeared. The band's best album is probably *Red Queen to Gryphon Three*. While it is certainly a Progressive Rock album, the group had not quite completed their turn to more conventional instruments. As a result, what made Gryphon unique – especially the use of Krumhorns and bassoons – remained intact.

Camel, who came from Surrey (with the exception of veteran keyboard player Peter Bardens), had released two albums by 1975, both of which found the band developing their style from bluesy rock into something with a more symphonic character. Often (although wrongly in my view) linked to the Canterbury movement due to the jazzy nature of some of their music, the key to the 'classic' Camel sound is Andrew Latimer's bluesy, melodic guitar playing and the hugely distinctive and fluid keyboard playing of Peter Bardens. Bardens chose lighter sounds – using the Solina string ensemble rather than the Mellotron for his string sounds, for instance – and played more Fender Rhodes electronic piano than any other keyboard player in Progressive Rock. *Mirage*, which included the classic 'Lady Fantasy', had been a considerable advance on Camel's eponymous debut, and had charted in the USA.

Camel
Music Inspired by The Snow Goose
Released April 1975

Music Inspired by The Snow Goose was something of a tangent after the hard-edged *Mirage* and to this day I wonder how they came up with the idea. True enough, using an orchestra remained fashionable as strings were all over pop, rock and soul in the mid-1970s. However, with it came a change in the band. Some Prog fans do not like this album because for them it is too similar to easy listening, so smooth and autonomous is its production. The melodies are sweet, the playing tasteful, and of course there are few vocals, but then these were never Camel's strong point in the first place.

Camel's breakthrough album, the delicious *Music Inspired by The Snow Goose*. (*Decca*)

The album is a musical illustration of Paul Gallico's novel *The Snow Goose*, and it opens with a sonic impression of the Great Marsh before the orchestra comes in with the first of a set of wonderful melodies, leading into the familiar Camel live favourites 'Rhayader' and 'Rhayader Goes to Town', the latter probably the hardest-rocking moment on the album. The album is awash with delicious moments of guitar, and 'Sanctuary' is one of them. This is followed by 'Fritha', played on the synthesizer until the glorious main guitar theme. The quirky woodwind of 'Friendship' is next. A clip of this track being played by a woodwind ensemble on *The Old Grey Whistle Test* is often cited as an example of Progressive Rock pomposity, yet to be honest it's harmless, and the piece itself is less than two minutes long. Side one closes with the mournful 'Rhayader Alone'.

Side two contains longer pieces, with the up-tempo, synth-dominated 'Preparation' leading into the ambient, haunting 'Dunkirk', which builds towards the sadness of 'Epitaph'. The stately piano of 'Fritha Alone' leads to the final, triumphant strings of 'La Princesse Perdue' before 'The Great Marsh' closes the album as it had begun.

Why do I love this album so much? After all, it breaks no new ground. I enjoy it simply because it sums up so many of the themes of the novel so well and so simply, with such emotional use of texture and melody. It is beautifully composed by Latimer and Bardens with great economy and, unusually for a Progressive Rock album, the whole is far greater than the sum of its parts. The album was the breakthrough record for Camel in the UK although some, including me, marginally prefer the live version recorded later in 1975 with the London Symphony Orchestra, and released on *A Live Record* in 1978. The live version loses a little of the subtlety, but gains in the way the piece flows. The orchestra sounds wonderful.

Hatfield and the North
The Rotters' Club
Released 1975

Back in Canterbury, Caravan bassist Richard Sinclair had left the band to form the short-lived but influential Hatfield and the North with former Egg keyboard player Dave Stewart, guitarist Phil Miller and drummer Pip Pyle. Having released a well-received eponymous debut, they followed this with *The Rotters' Club* in 1975. The album mixes some complex, jazz-influenced instrumentals with Sinclair's very English and somewhat stream-of-consciousness-derived songs. The result is quirky, recalling both the Monty Python-inspired humour of jazz-rock band Brand X, and the technical, contemporary/jazz hybrid sound that Stewart and Miller were to utilise in the famously difficult band National Health. Stewart was later to take this approach to the band Bruford at the end of the decade. Often the music of *The Rotters' Club* is charming and lyrical, making excellent use of Caravan flautist Jimmy Hastings, and at other times it is rather more baffling. Ultimately, however, its charms win out over its complexities. The title of author Jonathan Coe's best-selling novel is a tribute to this unique album.

1974 and 1975 were the years that Progressive Rock became fashionable. For a short period, perhaps only a few months, some of the trappings of Progressive Rock – particularly extreme dynamic shifts, changes in time signature and some of the keyboard technology – began to creep into the world of mainstream rock. Listen, for instance to Elton John's *Captain Fantastic and the Brown Dirt Cowboy* and some of the textures he created on a variety of keyboards. The Strawbs, not naturally a Progressive Rock band despite having had Rick Wakeman as a past member, recorded their most Prog album in *Hero and Heroine*. The band for that album included keyboard player John Hawken, previously of Renaissance, and his Mellotron playing on that album is a particular highlight.

In December 1975, British rock band Queen released their fourth album, *A Night at the Opera*. While far from Progressive Rock, it was the band's most grandiose and ambitious album yet, full of great songwriting and Prog influences. It was to be their most extreme statement – they tempered their ambition with the follow up *A Day at the Races* a year later. It is a neat symbol of the furthest reach of the Progressive Rock movement. In 1975, if you played what you liked, wrote what you liked and recorded what you liked (and had the money), you could get away with it. Less than a year later, attitudes had begun to change.

The remarkable six-minute single 'Bohemian Rhapsody' is one of the most famous and revered pieces of popular music ever written. Occupying the number one spot in the UK singles chart over the 1975 Christmas period, it provides a neat but coincidental bridge between Prog in its prime and the move to more aggressive songwriting. The song itself feels like a grotesque (although probably unintentional) parody of Progressive Rock, switching between torch song ('Mama, I just killed a man') to bonkers choir ('Galileo, Galileo'), to hard rock ('Just gotta get out') back to torch song again ('Any way the wind blows… *CLANG*'). It was the last time the public would buy such a record is such colossal numbers.

3

MACHINE MESSIAH: TECHNOLOGY AND PROGRESSIVE ROCK

ADVANCES IN MONITORING AND PA SYSTEMS

As we have seen, the late 1960s and early 1970s saw huge strides in analogue recording equipment, allowing musicians, for the first time, to get their musical visions out of their heads and onto vinyl. The problem of how to take this material into a live setting, however, remained.

Live concerts are very unpredictable. Most venues are not purpose-built for loud, amplified sound, so creating a viable live setting for music, especially something with the complexity and dynamic range of Progressive Rock, was always going to be a challenge. However, it was a challenge eagerly taken on by the technologically ambitious. Even in the twenty-first century, a band is likely to be presented with a very different scenario for a gig in a local pub or bar, compared with a large hall or arena.

The small venue is likely to have a small public address system only. Take the 'classic' Progressive Rock five-piece of vocals, guitar, bass, keyboards and drums – it is likely that the drummer will be heard acoustically, while the bassist and guitarist will play through their amps direct to the audience. Only the singer and keyboard player, both of whom would not normally have any form of intermediary amplification, would play through the PA. This will give the sound engineer a tricky problem. He will have to balance the sounds of the instruments he can do little about – drums (whose only volume control is the power of the playing), bass and guitar (who can turn their amps up or down) – with the instruments playing through the PA. The band may, or may not, have some sort of primitive monitoring system allowing them to hear what is being played. This is an imprecise art at the best of times, but, hey, it's only a pub gig.

In a large venue, with today's multi-channel control desks and high-power PA systems, every instrument is catered for. A guitarist's amp will be linked to the PA using a specialist microphone acquired specifically for the purpose. A bassist will usually have a feed from his amp plugged directly into the PA. The keyboard player can either create a submix of his own playing then offer that to the PA

The sound desk at Nearfest. (*Kevin Scherer*)

in two channels, or feed each individual keyboard directly into the PA. Most importantly, the drummer is quite likely to have every drum individually miked, with a couple of overhead microphones thrown in to pick up the ambient noise of his cymbals and the rest of the kit. Moreover, a sophisticated monitoring system, traditionally delivered via a 'wedge' on the floor, but more often these days supplied with in-ear earphones, allows each performer a sophisticated mix of whatever he wants to hear of the band, in order to allow as strong a personal performance as possible.

In the mid-1960s, all concerts were like pub concerts. When The Beatles were drowned out by screaming fans at Shea Stadium, it's unlikely that the audience would have heard much of any clarity anyway, such was the lack of power in the PA system. TV coverage of live performances from the late 1960s reveals very little miking, even on instruments that were being recorded for the TV soundtrack. However, more ambitious and more complex music required a new approach to live sound that mirrored the advances taking place in the studio, with mixing desks increasing from four to eight, sixteen, twenty-four and finally thirty-two input channels.

Giant on the Box, an excellent DVD chronicling several Gentle Giant performances from the mid-1970s, demonstrates the band's heroic attempts to make the best of some relatively primitive sound equipment. As well as standard rock instrumentation, the band use acoustic guitars, vibes, cello, violin, recorders, multiple vocalists and a variety of other instruments, most using relatively basic microphones to capture the complex live arrangements. How their engineer achieved it all without howling feedback remains a miracle and is real testament to his skill. Sir, I salute you!

Acoustic guitars were rarely used in a rock setting, as the sound rarely cut through with the primitive pickups available, despite the innovative work of folkier artists like John Martyn, who would route his acoustic guitar, via a primitive pickup, through a fuzz box and echo unit (see below). Flute players had more success making themselves heard, which partially explains their relative frequency in a Progressive Rock setting. Today, of course, anything is possible, and a guitarist no longer needs an acoustic guitar to make a sound like one, with an acoustic 'simulator' pedal fitting right into an effects board at a cost-effective price.

THE MELLOTRON

There is a great Pathé newsreel feature from the early 1960s that shows nattily besuited TV magician David Nixon demonstrating the Mark 1 Mellotron. The clip is in full colour, and aims to show the versatility of the instrument in creating orchestral sounds. It looks and feels more like an advert for a Bontempi organ, with a boffin-like figure teaching Nixon how to use the beast. Yet it was the world of rock music that would embrace the Mellotron in all its glory.

If you needed string sounds in the 1970s – and if you were in a Progressive Rock band you probably did – what choices did you have? You could try to produce that sort of sound on the Hammond organ, of course. At a pinch, that would be bearable, but for a more authentic sound there really were two choices. Firstly there was the Mellotron. This remarkable instrument featured tape loops of real orchestral instruments, and was activated by depressing the relevant key on a piano-style keyboard. It soon became clear that authentic though the samples were, the overall effect had an unmistakable haunting quality all of its own. The

This and next page: The three ages of studio recording at Rockfield. Right, 1960s equipment on display. Overleaf, top, engineer Tim Lewis and the forty-eight-channel Neve console in the Coach House Studio at Rockfield. Overleaf, bottom, Rob Reed of Magenta's completely digital set-up. (*Stephen Lambe*)

famous Mellotron reed sound at the beginning of 'Strawberry Fields Forever' by The Beatles is a renowned early use of the instrument. Progressive Rock provides the most impressive CV for the Mellotron, however. The sweeping grandeur of the introduction to 'Watcher of the Skies' by Genesis is a classic example of the orchestral power of the instrument. For a more disturbing, aggressive use, try 'Larks' Tongues in Aspic' and 'Red' by King Crimson.

The Mellotron had its faults. For all its studio usefulness, once out on the road it proved problematic. It regularly broke down and even more regularly went out of tune, requiring constant maintenance, and often manual assistance during the gig. However, from 1974 bands had a more reliable alternative, because the ARP company introduced its 'Solina' String Ensemble. One particular acolyte was Peter Bardens of Camel, and it can be heard to particularly good effect at the beginning of the band's excellent instrumental 'Lunar Sea'. The downside of the Solina was simple – the noise it made. Thin and reedy, its synthesised sounds lacked the authenticity and bite of the Mellotron's, yet it was a far more practical alternative, and became synonymous with jazz funk and disco in the late 1970s, before being superseded by the polyphonic synths of the early 1980s.

The Mellotron, even more than the Modular and Minimoog synthesizers, has become the key instrumental symbol of the Progressive Rock movement. The unearthly sound that the instrument makes – as well as the striking white exterior of the Mark 4 – has reached such iconic status that modern synthesizers have specific Mellotron samples as opposed to generic orchestral samples. Whether this is a good thing or not is debatable, since the purpose is no longer to mimic the sound of an orchestra, but to mimic the sound of the Mellotron itself. Yet it is such a distinctive instrument that perhaps it deserves its own place in the instrumental palette. I leave it to the reader to decide.

TINKLING THE IVORIES

Progressive Rock relies on keyboards for its colour and atmosphere. Keyboards also provide opportunity for soloing. Most importantly, they channel the genre's link with the symphonic, which in turn provides a link to the past and helps give the genre the credibility it craves. Forty years on, Progressive Rock is surer of itself as a style, so it is no longer essential to have a keyboard player at all. A very fine contemporary band called Diatessaron from Canada weave all their textures from the pool of sounds available to the electric guitar. With guitar synths and effects now able to mimic the same instruments as keyboards, a guitarist can, potentially, do it all. More usually, however, it is left to a keyboard player to provide those textures.

In the early 1970s, if you wanted a 'noise' or effect you had to find a keyboard that could provide it. Acquiring such a keyboard might depend entirely on your ability to pay for it and then to transport it. If you were playing the clubs, you

Rick Wakeman's 1972 keyboard rig, as shown on the cover of *The Six Wives of Henry VIII*. (*A&M Records*)

might get a piano, but more often you would carry your own electronic piano or organ. In the studio there were more options, limited mainly to acoustic piano, electronic piano and organ. The development of the Mellotron was a vital addition to the keyboard player's sound palate, providing strings and woodwind whenever he wanted it.

THE HAMMOND ORGAN

The keyboard instrument that defines the early part of the Progressive Rock era is the organ. In the early 1960s, small, portable models like the Vox had been important, but their thin, very specific sound did not suit musicians who required a more varied and powerful sound palate. The solution to this was to use the Hammond organ. First manufactured in the early 1930s, the Hammond was first produced to give churches a low-cost alternative to the pipe organ, and as such was never intended to be particularly portable. However, with its large arsenal of sounds, its double keyboard, and its foot pedals giving much more varied playability, it soon became the first choice for rock keyboard players. Indeed, if you only had one keyboard, it had to be the Hammond. The rich, whirring sound of the Hammond played through its companion, the Leslie speaker cabinet, can now be produced pretty accurately with samples, of course, but certain musicians still take them on tour. Although on the classic Focus albums he played piano, Mellotron and other keyboard instruments, Thijs van Leer tours to this day with nothing more than a Hammond B3 and a flute. The Hammond is a very reliable

Anthony Phillips, Genesis's original guitarist, plays the Hammond organ in a slightly unusual way at Penarth, January 2005. (*Chris Walkden*)

piece of equipment but the cost of transportation, not to mention carrying the thing upstairs (I've done it), caused smaller bands financial issues. Bill Bruford, in his typically ironic way, cites transporting the Hammond as one of the main reasons that his band Bruford broke up.

OTHER CLASSIC KEYBOARDS

Piano, organ, string simulation and synthesizers were essential parts of the Progressive Rock keyboard player's arsenal. However, other instruments also played a more peripheral part in the set up. The Fender Rhodes electronic piano was originally invented in the 1950s as a portable alternative to the acoustic piano; however, its soft, ethereal sound made it an interesting alternative to its more strident cousin. The harpsichord has often been used by musicians wanting a baroque feel to a piece of music, and the Baldwin Electric Harpsichord provided a live alternative, while the Hohner Clavinet, made famous by Stevie Wonder for its hard, percussive qualities, provided the same service for Rick Wakeman and Kerry Minnear in particular.

The piano itself has also seen some changes. Until the end of the 1970s, if you needed an authentic piano sound you had no choice but to carry one on tour and hope that the microphone systems of the PA made it sound as good as possible. The Yamaha electronic piano was a conventional instrument with pickups below the strings, slightly increased portability, and sound that could be channelled directly into the PA without microphones. However, the rise in digital synthesizers and weighted, touch-sensitive keys removed the need for acoustic pianos completely.

SYNTHESIS

It is no coincidence that the rise of Progressive Rock in the 1970s ran in parallel with the development of what is still known as 'the synthesizer'. The operation of the analogue synthesizer is easy to understand, since all it does is produce sounds by generating electrical signals of different frequencies. Simple!

While the synthesizer itself dates back to the nineteenth century, the first commercially available synth was built by Robert Moog in the mid-1960s. Initially a toy of the super-rich, they were only available to artists such as The Beatles and the Rolling Stones, although the most famous early use of the modular Moog was Walter (later Wendy) Carlo's album *Switched-On Bach*. Given the modular Moog's size, expense and lack of portability, the novelty soon wore off, and models were often made available second-hand, which is how Keith Emerson, then of The Nice, came across one. Several bands used the instrument on stage, but nobody has made such extensive live use of it as Keith Emerson, and it remains a part of his touring set-up.

Thankfully, the Moog soon slimmed down to a much more portable version, and the first Minimoog, with its iconic raised dial board and wood styling, appeared in 1970 and became a part of any monied keyboard player's arsenal. Rick Wakeman became the most famous exponent of the Minimoog, the instrument's thick, powerful analogue sounds perfectly suiting his florid playing style. With his long-term sponsorship by digital manufacturer Korg from the 1980s onwards, Wakeman stopped using the Moog for a considerable period of time, choosing other lead sounds, but it is interesting to note that the Minimoog has been back in his keyboard rig since the mid-1990s. In 2002 Moog Music produced a remodelled digital version of the Minimoog, the Moog Voyager, and the company is also marketing an analogue reproduction of the original model to meet growing demand for this iconic instrument.

Other synths existed. The VC3 (the Putney) has reached almost the same iconic status as the Moog due to its usage on Pink Floyd's *Dark Side of the Moon*, while Tony Banks of Genesis used ARP synthesizers to great effect on *Selling England by the Pound*. As the 1970s wore on, the industry strove for the next key instrument in the genre, which was obviously the polyphonic keyboard (up to then, only one key could be played at a time). At the end of the 1970s these finally appeared via companies like Sequential Circuits, who manufactured the Prophet 5 and Prophet 10 machines, made famous on early 1980s Genesis and Phil Collins recordings

Andy Tillison of The Tangent on stage in the USA in 2005, playing a modern set-up including a PC and a Moog Voyager – the latter a digital recreation of the Minimoog. (*Stephen Lambe*)

particularly. The time of analogue polyphony was a short one; the rise in digital synths at the beginning of the 1980s swept them aside. The Yamaha DX7, which has its own iconic status, was the first digital synthesizer to penetrate the market and, at around £1,500, it was within the price range of most serious musicians. Around the same time, the first samplers appeared – the Fairlight and the Synclavier – which were used by such artists as Kate Bush and Tears for Fears. Since the early 1980s, digital synthesizers have been developing and improving constantly. The 1980s and early 1990s were synonymous with a rather cheesy palate of sounds, but since then sampling technology has improved to such an extent that the sound of vintage keyboards can be reproduced with stunning accuracy, as can the piano itself. MIDI is icing on the cake, allowing a musician to keep all his sounds on a laptop if he wishes, and to use his keyboards to control and trigger those sounds. Should he wish it, a Progressive Rock keyboard player can spend hours programming his sounds on a laptop so that every song, or every moment within a song, will have its own programme triggered by buttons on the keyboard, foot pedals or the computer. While this may not be quite as much fun as carrying around trucks full of equipment, it actually gives today's musicians many more options.

A typical guitar effects board. (*Chris Walkden*)

GUITARS AND EFFECTS

For guitarists, authenticity is everything. Of all the instruments in this chapter, it is the electric guitar that saw least development during the early Progressive Rock era. Whereas a modern keyboard player will generally want to get newer and more advanced kit as they become more affluent, a Fender Stratocaster player with an improving income is more likely to sell that £200 Squire 'Strat' for a 1959 Fender classic. In the twenty-first century, of course, there are dozens of manufacturers making deliciously crafted guitars, both electric and acoustic, for the discerning guitarist with a couple of thousand pounds in their pocket. In 1970 this was not the case. Generally, you owned a guitar by Mr Fender, Mr Gibson or Mr Rickenbacker, or you owned a copy of one.

Progressive Rock musicians had as good an understanding of tone and the power of different instruments and pickup settings as anyone, however. Few musicians from the era used only one make or model of guitar, yet most favoured the Gibson Les Paul above other makes, largely for its thickness of tone and the sustain that the guitar's solid wood body produced. Both allowed the guitarist to be heard among other instruments, especially when playing lead lines and solos. Robert Fripp, Garry Green of Gentle Giant and, most famously, Steve Hackett of Genesis are largely associated with the Les Paul. Hackett's famous gold-top model from 1957 looked good and sounded great, allowing him the extreme sustain and hammering-on playing techniques for which he became well known.

Although best known for playing an unusual Gibson model, the hollow-body ES175, Steve Howe of Yes has used a huge variety of guitars for both studio and

Steve Hackett plays the Les Paul, famous for having a thick sound with plenty of sustain. (*Stephen Lambe*)

live work over the years. His choice of the Fender Telecaster on the Yes album *Relayer* was controversial, since its trebly tone was normally associated with country music and the rootsier forms of rock and roll. Fellow bandmate Chris Squire was one of many musicians to use the striking Rickenbacker bass. Like its six- and twelve-string counterparts, the Rickenbacker was a naturally trebly instrument. Squire often played it as if he were a lead guitarist. More regularly, bassists favoured the Fender Jazz or Fender Precision models.

The early 1970s also saw a huge explosion in the use of guitar effects and pedals. Once cumbersome studio toys, the first effects, pedals or modules – inserted between the guitar and the amp and controlled with the feet – were used in the 1960s by Jimmy Page and Jimi Hendrix. While the two most popular effects were the distortion pedal (or fuzz box) and the wah-wah (or cry baby) pedal, many others were invented. As a guitarist of rudimentary talent in the early 1980s, I had endless fun with the only pedal I could afford, a simple Flanger, which produced a sonic phase shift. It wasn't long before guitarists were gathering multiple effects onto a single piece of wood, and the 'effects board' was born. The EBow was another useful effect invented at just the right time, in 1969. This was a battery-powered electronic device used to vibrate the strings of an electric guitar, giving sustain without an initial 'plucking' tone. The producer of an atmospheric, eerie effect, the EBow is often credited, somewhat pompously

Left: Bryan Josh of Mostly Autumn playing the popular Fender Stratocaster. (*Chris Walkden*)

Right: Phil Mercy of Thieves' Kitchen using an EBow. (*Chris Walkden*)

I have always thought, as an instrument in its own right. It is not; that master technician Jan Akkerman of Focus was able to produce a similar effect merely by expert manipulation of his Les Paul's volume knob. The EBow is good fun, though, a useful addition to the guitarist's range of sounds.

DRUMS AND PERCUSSION

Once a primitive art, drumming took on a new sophistication from the late 1960s onwards. On the early rock-and-roll records, the drummer provided a steady backbeat, normally in 4/4 time. This was one of the principle elements that separated rock from jazz. In the latter, the role of the drummer was more varied and polyrhythmic, providing swing and texture as necessary. In classical music the percussionist provided rhythm, yes, but also drama and – via the mallet percussion instruments – even melody.

The Beatles, with their leisurely hours of studio time, moved the rock drummer forward, creating effects and using 'close-miking' of the drums to bring a new sophistication and intimacy to the role of the drummer. As the new virtuosity of the late 1960s (typified by Ginger Baker of Cream) gave way to the Progressive Rock era, bands realised that the drummer now had the potential to be as creative as any other member of the band. The first pioneer of this new-found creativity was Bill Bruford of Yes and later King Crimson. Fiercely intelligent and pragmatic, Bruford was a jazz man at heart, and it was his sense of the experimental, derived from jazz, that pushed his music forward in a rock setting. His legendary precision, typified by the crisp 'thunk' of his snare sound,

Bill Bruford in late-career action. (*Fernando Acaves, www.billbruford.com*)

has rarely been copied, and his ambition and willingness to improvise set him apart from many of his rock contemporaries.

Not only was the 'miking up' of the full kit possible in the studio, but advances in microphone and mixing technology made a sophisticated arrangement of microphones on the kit achievable in a concert setting as well. It is worth pausing for a second to consider what possibilities are available to a sound engineer with even a modest mixing set-up in the modern age. Say the engineer has twenty-four input channels available to him. He might dedicate eight of these to a typical drum kit. This will make it possible to place individual microphones on the snare, the bass drum, the three tom-toms and the hi-hat, with two available overhead to pick up the ambient noise from the cymbals. Once he has mixed these to his satisfaction he can then group them together, allowing him to manipulate the sound of the kit as a whole if he so wishes. Better still, he can add effects – perhaps a little reverb on the snare for atmosphere. Compare this to the early rock-and-roll era. A single microphone picking up your kit would have been the height of sophistication. Compare the two scenarios and you begin to see the possibilities available.

Bruford was to become an innovator once again in the 1980s, when the first electronic drum kits became available. He became the poster boy for the Simmons company, giving it much-needed credibility in an era when Simmons's hexagonal pads often adorned *Top of the Pops* courtesy of the New Romantics. By the time Bruford had rejoined Yes in the late 1980s and early 1990s, his electronic kit had reached the height of sophistication, allowing him to sound like a 'regular' drummer, an exotic percussionist or a purveyor of melody within seconds. It also left him vulnerable – a computer malfunction on the Union tour in 1991 left him inaudible and embarrassed in front of 10,000 people. Before long, he had scaled back his experiments and reverted to the traditional acoustic kit.

In truth, the sound of the Simmons kits has dated very badly, and has become largely synonymous with the 1980s. This is typified by the famous closing theme music to the British TV soap opera *EastEnders*, which was recorded in 1985. Even Bruford's worthy efforts have not aged well, and in the twenty-first century the electronic kits have largely been confined to the practice room, where they provide sophisticated imitations of real drum kits in places where space or volume are an issue.

Progressive Rock's second innovator was Carl Palmer, who brought real showmanship to ELP, thanks to a prodigious and versatile technique, astonishing speed and a tendency to take his shirt off a lot – factors that remain a part of his performance to this day. Whereas Bruford was the master of precision, for Palmer drumming is rather more macho. There is a classic clip of Palmer on TV in around 1974, demonstrating his famous engraved stainless-steel kit, which was also one of the earliest kits to trigger electronics, albeit in a fairly unsophisticated way. Palmer is shown hitting pads attached to his acoustic kit, which start basic sequences and rather twee synthesizer sounds. By the mid to late 1980s, Bruford was using his electronic kit to play melodies and mimic tuned percussion. But if Bruford was the catalyst in the development of electronic drums, Palmer was the pioneer. He was also a trained percussionist, and in films of Keith Emerson performing his piano concerto on tour with ELP in 1977, Palmer can be seen as one of the percussionists in the orchestra.

In the modern era, a Progressive Rock musician with a few pounds in his pocket can create any sound he wants at the press of a button. Creativity is limited only by lack of ambition. In the 1970s, musicians had to find or if necessary *invent* the sounds they wanted. In the new millennium there are practically no limitations.

4

1976–1980: THE WAY DOWN

1976–1978

1976 was an odd year. With the benefit of hindsight, it feels like the calm before the storm. Most of the Progressive Rock and hard rock bands that had come to prominence at the start of the decade (some of them by now very rich and famous indeed) were either on tour in America or simply on hiatus. The full impact of punk was still a year away and disco was not yet at its height. What was left was a creative vacuum dominated by established stars. A quick look at the UK singles charts for that year shows how moribund pop music was at the time, with the public buying lesser tracks from safe, middle-of-the-road, established names. In 2011 the BBC showed every 1976 episode of the iconic pop charts show *Top of the Pops* in sequence and these shows are nigh-on disastrous, with appallingly smug presenters introducing lacklustre performances. The UK album charts in 1976 reveal little improvement, dominated as they were by compilations from the likes of Abba, The Beach Boys, Glen Campbell and guitarist Bert Weedon.

Led Zeppelin had two number one albums in 1976, neither considered their finest. The second, the soundtrack to their bloated concert film *The Song Remains the Same*, was to be superseded in later years by the emergence of better live material. Studio album *Presence*, meanwhile, was lacklustre, although it did contain the classic 'Achilles Last Stand', a ten-minute *tour de force*. Although it is 'Stairway to Heaven' from 1971 that is usually stands accused of being the band's attempt at Progressive Rock, 'Achilles' is the closest the band ever came to the genre in reality. It is a precursor of the pomp rock already making a mark in the USA and which would become popular in the UK towards the end of the 1970s.

Among the greatest-hits packages and old-school rock acts, the high-energy blues band Dr. Feelgood scored a number one album in the UK with *Stupidity*. The writing was on the wall.

Genesis finally solved the problem of the loss of Peter Gabriel by taking a chance with drummer Phil Collins. Despite the different personalities of each singer (Collins was the chirpy everyman, Gabriel the earnest intellectual), the similar timbre of their voices had meant that they always blended well both on record and in live performance. As a result, when singing lead vocals Collins could sound like Gabriel while giving the band a more accessible face. At a stroke, all the band's hard edges were ironed out. It was a brilliantly fortunate commercial decision taken for non-commercial reasons. The album they had been working on, *A Trick of the Tail*, was finally released at the beginning of 1976. Still very much in the Progressive Rock idiom, the emphasis shifted slightly towards the songwriting side of the group's talents. While male fans were kept happy with the complexity and Mellotron surges of 'Dance on a Volcano' and 'Los Endos', the band found a new sensitivity in gentler pieces like 'Ripples' and 'Entangled', and started to win a more general rock audience. For the first time, women started listening to the band. Later in the year the band undertook their biggest tour yet, recruiting the ubiquitous Bill Bruford to fill in on drums. The band's double drum kit set-up – which allowed Collins to carry on playing drums when not singing – became a template for many bands after that. This was assuming bands could afford to cart around two drum kits while on tour, of course. Two kits lent visual novelty and a pleasing symmetry to stages in larger concert halls and the front cover of this book shows contemporary US band Izz on stage with a similar set-up on a smaller budget.

For the resurgent Van der Graaf Generator, this was a period of intense activity and creativity, even if success in their native country remained as elusive as ever. Having streamlined their sound somewhat from the relative excesses of the *Pawn Hearts* era, they recorded *Godbluff* in 1975 and then two albums in 1976, one at the start of the year, *Still Life*, and the other towards the end in *New World Record*. The beginnings of change in the music industry are evident even in these albums. While *Still Life* sees the band in familiar, organ-led territory, the latter album is the first to feature extensive use of electric guitar, albeit somewhat eccentrically played by Peter Hammill, to mixed effect.

Van der Graaf Generator
Godbluff
Released October 1975

The first album recorded by the reformed Van der Graaf Generator is, to me, the band at their best. The excesses of *Pawn Hearts*, magnificent though they were, seem to have been replaced by more concision in the writing and the playing on this first album of their third 'sequence' as a band. *Godbluff* is one of several Progressive Rock albums to feature four tracks, two on each side of the vinyl LP. Here, the relatively accessible and melodic 'The Undercover Man' is the opener, based around a satisfying melodic line sung and played on flute and piano. For me, this was a 'gateway' track, a way to penetrate and understand some difficult music. 'Scorched Earth', however, is as intense, powerful and hard-rocking as the band ever got. 'Arrow' moves in jazzier territory initially, before Hammill's vocals increase the intensity levels, and album

Van der Graaf Generator onstage as a three-piece. (*Roy Layer*)

closer 'The Sleepwalkers' again begins relatively gently before rocking hard in its conclusion, with David Jackson's sax particularly impressive. *Godbluff* represents Van der Graaf Generator at their intense yet concise best.

YES GO SOLO

1976 was not a particularly exciting year for Yes. A period of inactivity, as a band at least, at the end of 1975 was not concluded until the beginning of an American tour the following summer, with Patrick Moraz still in place on keyboards. However, this period is notable for the release of solo albums from all five members of the band. They were not all released at the same time, and vary in quality. Drummer Alan White's *Ramshackled*, while decent enough, would have garnered little attention had he not been the drummer of one of the biggest bands in the world, while guitarist Steve Howe's *Beginnings* was spoilt by his somewhat unpalatable lead vocals. Howe would release a large number of solo albums later in his career, and a better starting point is *The Steve Howe Album* from 1979.

The other three albums are more worthy of note. While Howe was first out of the blocks, Chris Squire soon followed with *Fish out of Water*. Of the five albums, this was the one most like Yes, but with an interesting twist. It would have been easy to overbalance the album by favouring the bass guitar, and while that is indeed a lead instrument, it is not overbearing and is combined with the subtle use of an orchestra and some wonderful organ playing by Patrick Moraz. *Fish out of Water*, then, has an atmosphere of its own that has never been repeated by Squire or anyone else. The album is not perfect – 'Safe', in particular, overstays its welcome by at least five minutes – but Squire showed he was essential to Yes, not just as a musician but as a writer.

Released in the spring of 1976, Patrick Moraz's *The Story of i* remains one of my favourites from the era, a frenetic and hugely inventive forty-minute ride through the fervent imagination of the Swiss keyboard player, taking in jazz fusion, funk, electronica, pop and South American rhythms on the way. Like Alan White, had Patrick not been a member of Yes at the time, it's likely that this remarkable and slightly bonkers album might not have received anything like the attention that it did. I will not linger too long on it since it is so unique that it is difficult to fit into my narrative, but I heartily recommend it.

Jon Anderson
Olias of Sunhillow
Released July 1976

Cover art was a vital factor in the success of the Progressive Rock movement, and while Roger Dean was not involved in Anderson's first solo album, the fantasy artwork by David Fairbrother-Roe could not have happened without him. Anderson laboured for many weeks in the studio on this extraordinary album, and its unique atmosphere is created both by his vision and his instrumental limitations.

Olias of Sunhillow, Jon Anderson's typically otherworldly solo album. (*Elektra*)

Anderson concentrates on the instruments that he either has some competence on – including percussion, acoustic guitar, keyboards and harp, as well as his extraordinary multi-layered vocals – to tell a wonderfully imaginative fantasy story. These limitations give the album a unique, otherworldly feel. Synthesizers are very prominent throughout, typically on the lovely 'Qoquaq En Transic', leading to speculation than Vangelis might have been involved in the album. However, to me it is Patrick Moraz who sounds the greater influence; indeed, it is rumoured that he assisted Anderson in assembling the keyboards used on album, without contributing directly to the playing or writing. It is the imagination with which Anderson uses the instrumental palate available to him that is so extraordinary here, whether it is with massed percussion, synths or choral voices. Significantly, the lack of conventional rock instruments helps too, particularly the absence of lead guitar and kit drums. Anderson had nobody to hide behind in making this album and that discipline was his masterstroke. Structurally, too, this is a clever piece of work. Just when an instrumental section might be about to overstay its welcome, the mood changes to a slightly more conventional song format, like the two lovely vocal pieces that close each side of the album, 'Flight of the Moorglade' and 'To the Runner'.

If your experience of Anderson has been slightly poisoned by some of his spiritual outpourings and the relative mediocrity of his later solo albums, then do not be put off by this unique piece of work. The story is imaginative without having the more extreme spirituality of later albums, and the gatefold sleeve is so stunning that it demands you seek out a vinyl copy just to own it – even if you also buy the CD or a download.

MORE ACTIVITY IN 1976

Gentle Giant, meanwhile, released the last of their truly Progressive Rock albums, the very patchy *Interview*. Clearly worn down by years of (at best) partial success, the band had developed a cynical attitude to the record industry and the music of this album simply sounds tired, while the mock interviews that fall between the tracks fall flat. Jethro Tull released the least Prog album of their Prog sequence with the equally tired *Too Old to Rock 'n' Roll: Too Young to Die!*. In the UK, it was the second wave of bands that were more active and creative, with Camel in particular really hitting their stride with the excellent *Moonmadness*. While this album followed a more conventional song structure after the relative excesses of *Music Inspired by The Snow Goose*, its key tracks straddled the line between the symphonic and Canterbury-influenced jazz, best typified by 'Song within a Song', its sweet, flute-led main part leading into a delicious synth-dominated final section, while the wonderful instrumental 'Lunar Sea' saw the band moving even further into fusion territory.

Robert John Godfrey, the enigmatic leader of The Enid. (*Chris Walkden*)

The Enid
In the Region of the Summer Stars
Released February 1976

One band that were to find their own niche as the punk movement took hold were The Enid. Given that their symphonic nature made them an almost typical Progressive Rock band, they were able to sidestep the main criticisms of the genre by playing slightly ironic classical pastiches and peppering their live sets with popular classics like 'Dambusters March' and 'The Skye Boat Song', while band leader (and only constant member) Robert John Godfrey played on his convincing and humorous 'old-school teacher' stage manner.

The band's first album, *In the Region of the Summer Stars*, sums the band up beautifully, combining convincing and powerful classical pastiches with more conventional Progressive Rock pieces. Kit drums and guitar are prominent. The band made excellent and convincing use of synthesizers in a time well before sampling, and without resorting to the stylised orchestral sounds of the Mellotron. Often these two factors combine, as on 'Death, the Reaper', which begins as a classical piece with a faint medieval feel but later adds guitar and drums as the track builds towards a climax. Elsewhere, the romanticism of 'The Lovers' – dominated by grand piano and orchestral synths, Vangelis style – gives way to the madcap hard rock of the 'The Devil'.

This particular album was based around the Tarot, and would have been recorded as *Voyage of the Acolyte* had Steve Hackett not already released an album of the same title. An accident of circumstance, in this case a tragic one, led to the instrumental nature of these tracks and much of the band's later output. Singer Peter Roberts killed himself, forcing Godfrey to reconstruct the tracks in instrumental form. The band released the album in expanded form in 1984 after its deletion from the EMI catalogue.

ENTER THE AMERICANS

We have already seen how groups from mainland Europe had begun to enter the scene as early as 1972, but aside from the bands from Italy that signed to ELP's label Manticore, their influence remained in their own countries until the CD boom of the 1990s made many of these recordings available to a wider audience. It is important that we acknowledge the contribution made by bands like Eloy, Hoelderlin and Novalis from Germany in contributing to the bank of knowledge that is Progressive Rock. Both Banco and PFM released excellent Progressive Rock albums in 1976. For PFM it was all change. Peter Sinfield no longer contributed English lyrics, and the band also brought in a distinctive new singer, Bernardo Lanzetti, for the much-praised *Chocolate Kings* album, while Banco recorded another intense concept album, *As in a Last Supper*, perhaps their finest since *Darwin!*.

This might be a good point to mention the growing emergence of American bands in the Progressive Rock scheme. Beginning with a largely British and European genre in both conception and content, it took the integration of bands like Yes, ELP and Jethro Tull into the touring circuit of the USA before the influences began to rub off onto American musicians. Given the closeness of the blues to American roots music, Americans were one step closer to the origins of blues and jazz than Europeans, for whom rock and roll was received almost as an intensely cool but somewhat alien experience. Whereas musicians like Chris Squire, Rick Wakeman and Keith Emerson came to rock music via their grounding in the classics or church music or both, Americans had experienced the blues and jazz at first hand. Whereas Led Zeppelin fed the blues back to an American audience in a much more exciting and youthful way – as The Beatles had a decade earlier – what were our Atlantic neighbours to make of this new European music, which ignored the blues almost completely?

The response was to integrate Progressive Rock into what they were already playing – to a greater or lesser degree. Whereas in the case of many British bands the ejection of the blues from their music was almost a matter of pride, to the Americans Prog simply became part of a greater whole. For some bands like Happy the Man, Starcastle and Yezda Urfa, an interest in European Progressive Rock became almost total; for other bands like Styx and Kansas the hybrid between rock and roll and Progressive Rock became a winning and commercially very successful one.

Yezda Urfa
Sacred Baboon
Recorded 1976

To show what could be done in 1976 and how far the American scene had come by this time, we turn to this remarkable lost classic. Later in the book, as we head into the 1990s, we will talk about another US band, Echolyn, and there is a strong lineage between Yezda Urfa's music, which only saw the light of day in the late 1980s, and one of the best contemporary US bands. Having released their debut demo album *Boris* in 1975, the band signed to a small label, intending to release songs from that album plus some new material they had been working on. After that label folded, the album was never released and the band broke up in 1981. Musically, the band are one of few to combine the influences of Yes and Gentle Giant. Singer Rick Rodenbaugh certainly has a voice in the Jon Anderson mould, but he also has an ethereal quality reminiscent of Kerry Minnear when required. Musically this is frenetic, complex stuff, full of varied and eclectic instrumentation, with the band's unison playing particularly effective. The band's vocal harmonies, more Gentle Giant than Yes, are also extraordinary. The melodies are strong, although the complexity of the music gives them very little breathing space. Given how tight Yezda Urfa sound on record, they must have been quite a band live. Most importantly, this album is one of the first examples of an American band completely ignoring its own heritage to play music drawn from a new genre. This is second-hand music, but it is of exceptional quality

Given that the sincerest form of flattery is imitation, it is no surprise that one or two of these bands should sound rather like their British peers, and this an accusation often aimed specifically at Starcastle, who, like a number of bands that pursued rock music as a career, came from the Illinois area. It is not hard to see why. Vocalist Terry Luttrell sounds quite like Jon Anderson, Herb Shildt's synth-heavy keys are reminiscent of Rick Wakeman and the two guitarists chime rather than grind. Nonetheless, greater analysis reveals something quite different and rather appealing. The band's first two albums, *Starcastle* (1976) and *Fountains of Light* (1977), are awash with great melodies and fantasy imagery, while *Citadel* moved in a poppier direction and a final effort, *Real to Reel*, which attempted to take the band in a grittier, more commercial direction, tried to sound like Styx without pleasing anyone (apart from me, for whom it remains a guilty pleasure). The band re-emerged in the late 2000s to play the Rosfest festival in Pennsylvania and even released a new album.

Another band to reform in more recent years are Happy the Man (named after an obscure Genesis track), who signed to Arista in the mid-1970s and released their eponymous debut in 1977. Hailing from Virginia but later moving to Washington, D.C., the band played what would now seem very uncommercial music – completely instrumental and with feet in both the symphonic and fusion

Kerry Livgren of Kansas onstage at Nearfest with Proto-Kaw. (*Kevin Scherer*)

camps. Parallels with Camel and Focus are pretty accurate, as well as suggestions of Gentle Giant and Gryphon, but as a unit the band were a major influence on some of the American bands to emerge later in the 1990s and 2000s.

Styx – yet another band from Illinois – absorbed the Progressive Rock influence early on, but shamelessly combined this with hard rock and light pop influences, so that while their early albums were actually quite adventurous, they became best known for schmaltzy ballads like 'Lady' and 'Babe', which were massive hit singles. In the final analysis, they were much more of a pomp rock band with the odd Prog moment, as shown on albums like *Cornerstone* during their most successful period. It is difficult to blame them for following a more commercial path.

However, the band that most typified the fusion between hard rock and Progressive Rock were Kansas, who hailed from Topeka, not unsurprisingly in Kansas. The band's music was an almost seamless mixture of hard rock, Southern rock and Progressive Rock. In Robby Steinhardt they had a versatile violinist who could play classical pieces almost as well as he could boogie, and as a vocalist he was a useful foil for the extraordinary Steve Walsh, who had the sort of voice that could only come out of America, even though the origin of his style of singing is Paul Rogers of British band Free, with vocalisations and phrasing more synonymous with blues and hard rock than Progressive Rock. Yet within the hybrid that was Kansas, Walsh's voice worked supremely well. Walsh also provided keyboards alongside multi-instrumentalist Kerry Livgren, with extra guitar from Richard Williams. The band also benefitted from a drummer with more influence on the band than most in the gifted Phil Ehart.

Kansas
Point of Know Return
Released 1977

The band were never particularly well served by their studio sound, and their finest statement from their early years is probably *One for the Show*, the live double album recorded in 1978. Their material was normally excellent, so I have picked their top five US album *Point of Know Return* as a typical example. It also includes the huge American hit 'Dust in the Wind'. The title track and 'Paradox', which follows, are both fine examples of their mixture of Prog adventure and good tunes, while 'The Spider' moves into full-on ELP territory. 'Portrait (He Knew)' moves the band onto safer hard rock ground while 'Closet Chronicles' has a grandiose, pomp-rocking feel and 'Lightning's Hand', sung by Steinhardt, combines Southern rock with pomp rock flourishes. After 'Dust in the Wind' , 'Sparks of the Tempest' continues the hard rock theme before two mini-epics close the album, 'Nobody's Home' and 'Hopelessly Human'.

It is amazing that an album this varied should hang together so well, but it does. There are plenty of unifying factors, Walsh's voice being one and Steinhardt's ubiquitous violin being another, yet the point seems to be that there's no snobbery here. The band is not trying to say that it is a Prog band being forced to play Southern rock. Kansas play like they mean all of it and this reflects the experience of American audiences in the mid-1970s. There was no particular sense that Progressive Rock was 'art', or at least no more than any other genre of music people were listening to. It was just rock music.

PUNK

There is little doubt that by the start of 1977 the pop music industry was in a bit of a state. This has nothing to do with Progressive Rock specifically. The development of the genre in the early 1970s had been as exciting as anything else that had happened in that period. The bands were new, fresh and creative. Yet by 1976 the rock world was divided into haves and have-nots. Yes, Pink Floyd, Genesis and ELP, to varying degrees, had made it big and were either on hiatus or touring incessantly in the USA, playing large halls and stadiums. Meanwhile, Van der Graaf Generator and Gentle Giant, along with the better-known Italian bands, were finding that the money was not finding its way down to them. This malaise did not just apply to the Progressive Rock bands. Led Zeppelin, Deep Purple, The Who and Elton John all had creative difficulties around this time, and in the USA it was no better, with cocaine fuelling the decadence of those whose music had shone so brightly seven or eight years before. Both pop and rock had lost touch with their audience.

Yet on the surface all was well. The music press still gave these artists all their attention, and its leading lights still featured in yearly music press polls. Most of these bands were excellent financial bets – why stop backing a winning horse? – but for artists who had been less successful the pressure was on.

Punk, on the other hand, was no more than a news story until well into 1977. Although the first album by the Ramones, released in early 1976, was a major influence on the British punks – some of whom, like the Sex Pistols, were already gigging – it was not a massive commercial success in the UK. Punk and the New Wave did not become major commercial propositions until late 1977 or early 1978. Gradually, however, this new music began to seep into the consciousness of the record-buying public. Teenagers who had previously brought Yes albums to school began to bring albums by The Stranglers or The Damned, and no wonder. This was new and exciting. Compare, for example, buying a new album by The Clash, which would talk to you personally about social issues, to a poorer than average album by Gentle Giant.

The record companies began to follow this fashion. Marginal artists that had been supported for years were either dropped or put under pressure to change into something else that might fit the current fashion better, and even the biggest artists had the words 'hit single' whispered in their ears. This particularly affected Gentle Giant, whose 1977 album *The Missing Piece* blended the band's traditional material on pieces like 'For Nobody' and 'Memories of Old Days' with shorter, snappier songs. In truth, on this first effort the band did the short stuff rather well, and both 'Two Weeks in Spain' and 'I'm Turning Around' are rather wonderful attempts at the shorter song format. The same cannot be said of the following year's *Giant for a Day*, however, and while *Civilian* in 1980 showed what might have been, by then it was too late; the band folded shortly after its release.

1977 represents a final creative hurrah of many of the big names of the Progressive Rock scene. While many bands released albums of considerable quality, few demonstrated any new ideas. However, a surprise was in store from one of the biggest bands in the world.

Pink Floyd
Animals
Released January 1977

Since *Meddle*, Pink Floyd had released three albums in the 1970s, including the ground-breaking and massive-selling *Dark Side of the Moon* and the more reflective *Wish You Were Here*, another massive commercial success. With a formula established, they might have played it safe. However, with Roger Waters taking more control over the band, they came up with a Progressive Rock album of astonishing power, invention and savagery. The subject matter, in typically Orwellian style, was politics and society in 1970s Britain. Here the animals mirrored Orwell's allegorical creatures in *Animal Farm*, with the sheep easily led, the dogs warlike and the pigs despotic and manipulative.

Roger Waters onstage in 2011. (*Neil Palfreyman*)

But it is the music that is most surprising, and while the lengthy 'Dogs' treads fairly familiar Floyd territory for its first half, it drips with invention after the halfway point, as does the biting and funky 'Pigs (Three Different Ones)'. The final main piece, 'Sheep', rocks as hard and as inventively as anything the band have done before or since.

Animals was a commercial success, of course, but it marks a minor dip in the band's fortunes, being relatively inaccessible for the group's mainstream audience. The subsequent tour, which saw Waters suffer a nervous breakdown of sorts, was to provide inspiration for the massively successful concept album *The Wall* in 1979. However, for me *Animals* represents the peak of the band's creativity.

A FINAL HURRAH

Also released early in 1977 was a surprising album by Genesis in *Wind & Wuthering*. After the tuneful romanticism of *A Trick of the Tail*, the band returned to full-on Progressive Rock in an album that marks guitarist Steve Hackett's swansong with the band. It is the album on which his contributions are most evident. Although in 'Afterglow' and 'Your Own Special Way' the band began to think in a radio-friendly way, they also pleasured their hardcore fans with extended pieces like 'One for the Vine' and the Hackett/Collins nostalgia fest 'Blood on the Rooftops', featuring a genuine integration of Hackett's classical guitar into a Genesis song for the first time. What a shame there was no more of this to come. Within a few weeks, Jethro Tull had released the delightful folk/Prog hybrid *Songs from the Wood*, which combined Prog quirkiness and interesting time signatures with lush, folky melodies to winning effect.

After three years away from recording, the fruit of Emerson, Lake & Palmer's efforts finally emerged with the ambitious double album *Works Volume 1*. While punk was not yet a commercial force, this was the perfect album for the burgeoning genre to attack. It contained four sides of vinyl, a side for each member's solo work and one containing two band pieces. The solo tracks are mixed at best. Although I am a fan of Keith Emerson's 'Piano Concerto No. 1', Greg Lake's earnest singer-songwriter contributions are not particularly memorable and nor are Carl Palmer's percussion-based workouts. Side four is great, however. 'Pirates', while grandiose, makes excellent use of its orchestra, and the final track, a typical reworking of Aaron Copeland's 'Fanfare for the Common Man', is lovely, even if it does outstay its welcome a little. It also became a huge hit single in the UK in its abbreviated form. The trio took the album (and an orchestra) on tour in the USA – an ill-conceived move that lost the band a fortune, and which required a later tour as a three-piece to recoup the loss. The changing times and the band's financial situation seemed to knock the stuffing out of the trio, and after one last lacklustre album, *Love Beach*, they called it a day.

Meanwhile, Yes had reconvened in Switzerland to work on their next album. Rehearsals with Patrick Moraz had not begun well, so Rick Wakeman was called back in as a session player. Delighted with the material, he agreed to rejoin the band, beginning a very lucrative couple of years for them. The album itself, *Going for the One*, was a return to relative brevity, containing as it does five tracks, although side two contains only the UK hit single 'Wonderous Stories' and the epic 'Awaken' – arguably the band's finest individual track. Overall, despite an unsympathetic production, the album is a triumph and shows that even if the band were no longer innovating, they could still produce music that could move, charm and rock.

These 1977 albums by Genesis, ELP and Yes were commercial successes, with *Going for the One* reaching number one in the album charts. *Animals* got to number two but stayed on the UK chart a few weeks longer.

For most of the bigger bands, the 'album and world tour' rollercoaster continued. Europe, the USA and the Far East, particularly Japan, provided huge markets. This was the era of the live album, with Jethro Tull's *Bursting Out* and the Genesis live double album *Seconds Out* particularly successful, alongside Camel's *A Live Record*. Even the medium-sized bands like Camel and Gentle Giant found audiences to be healthy enough. Camel headed off in a jazzier direction following the recruitment of ex-Caravan and Hatfield and the North bassist Richard Sinclair for the excellent *Rain Dances* and the patchier, poppier *Breathless* in 1978. Both albums contained some great material but had significant nods towards shorter, more song-orientated material in pieces like 'Highways of the Sun' and the title track from *Breathless*. Camel were always classy songwriters, but lacked a 'commercial' vocalist, so hit singles were usually an aspiration rather than a likelihood.

For Yes and Genesis, times were good and it was as if punk didn't exist. Having lost Steve Hackett, Genesis continued as a three-piece, and released *...And then there Were Three...*, which, while still fairly Prog in style, was mainly made up of shorter pieces, not to mention the charming hit single 'Follow You Follow Me'.

Yes, meanwhile, released the rather odd *Tormato* album. As with Genesis, the emphasis had shifted towards shorter songs, and 'Don't Kill the Whale' was even a minor hit. The *Tormato* tour, with the band playing 'in the round', was a massive success, beginning in late summer 1978 and continuing well into 1979. My first ever live music experience, aged sixteen, was Yes at Wembley Arena in October 1978. The band sold out for three nights, and even played a matinee on the Saturday – hardly very rock and roll, but the public demanded it.

The opportunities for new bands had dried up, however, and fewer people were discovering Progressive Rock for the first time. Nevertheless, there was still room for one more supergroup.

UK
UK
Released 1978

Since the dissolution of King Crimson in 1974, Bill Bruford had played as a sideman and a session player with bands like Gong and Genesis on the *A Trick of the Tail* tour. He had also rehearsed with Rick Wakeman and John Wetton in 1976, with a view to forming a supergroup that failed to come together. By 1977 he had completed a fine solo album, *Feels Good to Me*. Far from the usual drummers' fare, this supremely musical album made excellent use of the jazzier chord structures and virtuosity of guitarist Alan Holdsworth, also a member of Gong for a while, and American bassist Jeff Berlin alongside erstwhile Egg and Hatfield and the North keyboard player Dave Stewart. Vocalist Annette Peacock also performed as a guest.

Before long, a supergroup had been planned, with Bruford and Holdsworth teaming up with Wetton once more. Eddie Jobson, the former Curved Air and Roxy Music *enfant terrible*, played keyboards and violin. This version of the band was only to produce one album, but what an album it is.

The glorious tension that produced *UK* is obvious from the start, with the stabbing unison playing that begins 'In the Dead of Night', and Wetton's aggressive, rather distant vocal. The moment when this fine, melodic Wetton song gives way to an astonishing solo from Holdsworth (which Bruford still cites as one of the great moments in rock music) is typical of the album as a whole. The first three tracks form a sort of suite, while 'Thirty Years', which closes side one, builds from near stillness into a marvellous opportunity for Jobson (on synth) and Holdsworth to show off. Jobson's 'Alaska' opens side two with high drama, although the latter part of the piece is perhaps too ELP (more specifically, too *Tarkus*) for its own good. It segues into the terrific 'Time to Kill', which is followed by the brooding 'Nevermore', its gentle acoustic guitar introduction leading into searing jazz fusion. The album closes with the largely overlooked 'Mental Medication', a delicious hint of the glories to come from both Bruford and Holdsworth.

It is not hard to see why this line-up could last one album only. Wetton was writing melodic rock, while Jobson was a traditional 'symph' man, full of grand gestures, big chords and keyboard pyrotechnics. Bruford and Holdsworth, however, were there to express themselves in a rather purer way (they were jazzmen, after all). According to Bruford, Holdsworth supposedly infuriated Jobson by refusing to play his parts the way he had on record. It was a beautiful album and tour, but UK had no chance of surviving.

UK continued without Bruford or Holdsworth, and produced a wonderful, if far more melodic and symphonic, second album, *Danger Money*, plus a live album recorded in Japan. However, for the two jazzier players, even better was to come the following year.

Bruford
One of a Kind
Released 1979

Following their departure from UK, Bruford and Holdsworth returned to most of the musicians that had played on Bruford's solo album *Feels Good to Me*, specifically Dave Stewart (keyboards) and Jeff Berlin (bass). Bruford had decided that being a band leader was what he wanted to do, and this was the third of the albums he recorded in fairly quick succession at Trident Studios in London, the second of which had been the *UK* album.

The album is unique – melodic, complex and hugely English. Its unique approach to Progressive Rock evokes a variety of moods, typified by the humorous introduction to the delicious 'Fainting in Coils' and the shatteringly melodic album opener 'Hell's Bells'. The band is a delight throughout – at times languid, at others frantic. Bruford's drumming is typically sensitive and precise, while Jeff Berlin's bass playing is a virtuosic delight, hopping and skipping all over the album. Dave Stewart's varied textures and innovative use of the (then) brand new polyphonic synths are wonderful, but perhaps the star of the show is the amazing Allan Holdsworth, who turns in something of a guitar masterclass. The writing, mainly by Bruford, holds the album together and gives it such a consistent yet varied tone.

After a live album recorded in New York with new guitarist John Clarke (later to play in Cliff Richard's band), Bruford's band had one more album in them, *Gradually Going Tornado*, released in 1980. The vocals by Berlin are an acquired taste. I saw the band live as part of a double bill with Brand X and remember being impressed, not just by the band but also by Bruford's deliciously dry announcements. The

Alan Holdsworth, a member of Bill Bruford's brilliant supergroup. (*Kevin Scherer*)

band finally broke up, but Bruford was to use this band – which to my mind was a Progressive Rock band in the Canterbury tradition – as a springboard to a further career in jazz with his band Earthworks.

Steve Hackett
Spectral Mornings
Released June 1979

Steve Hackett owed a lot to the popularity Genesis had brought him, but his solo success at the end of the 1970s and the start of the 1980s came about from a combination of factors. He picked his material carefully, mixing some Prog pieces with some shorter, song-orientated tracks without seeming to compromise on quality. He also put in a lot of hard work, touring medium-sized venues incessantly with a group of excellent musicians including his brother John on flute. His second album, which he recorded in America, was even more varied than his first. *Please Don't Touch* included performances from Steve Walsh (of Kansas), Richie Havens and soul singer Randy Crawford.

However, by 1979 he had recruited a band, and this gave his next album *Spectral Mornings* a more cohesive structure. Not only were the textures provided by Hackett himself beautifully judged, but in keyboard player Nick Magnus he had a sidekick with an unusual sound palate created using traditional analogue instruments. Magnus had the ability to make keyboards sound like they had never sounded before. The album kicks off with 'Everyday', part song, part guitar workout, and a fan favourite to this day. The delicate 'The Virgin and the Gypsy' floats on John Hackett's flute and some delicious guitar synth textures. 'The Red Flower of Tachai Blooms Everywhere' is a showcase for the Japanese koto, which is deliciously

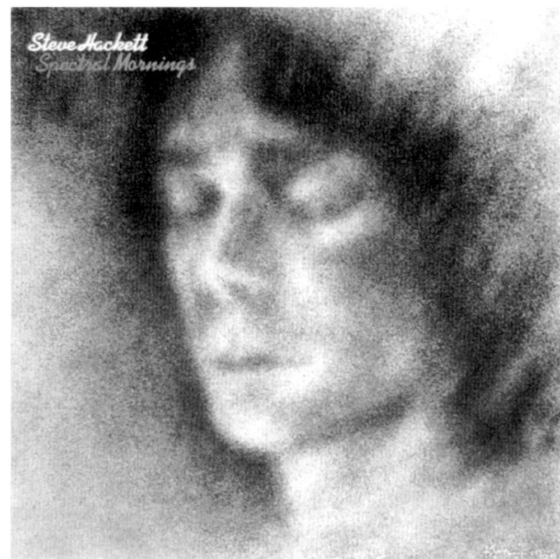

Spectral Mornings, Steve Hackett's brilliant third solo album from 1979. (*Virgin*)

combined with the Mellotron. This is followed by the powerful instrumental 'Clocks' and the low-key, faintly satirical 'Ballad of the Decomposing Man'. Side two contains only three tracks, the deliciously evocative 'Lost Time in Cordoba', which combines Spanish guitar with flute, 'Tigermoth', which combines a powerful instrumental with a wistful, ghostly First World War ballad, and the beautiful title track, a showcase for Hackett's wonderfully melodic guitar.

The same band were largely responsible for an excellent follow-up, *Defector,* in 1980. It reached the top ten in the UK album charts, although by the mid-1980s Hackett's fortunes as a solo artist had begun to falter.

THE SHORT HIBERNATION OF PROGRESSIVE ROCK

By the end of the 1970s almost all the artists that had made Progressive Rock the force that it had been, regardless of country, had either stopped making music completely, or were making music so different that their Progressive Rock roots were hardly apparent. Kansas, whose music had always combined AOR with Progressive Rock, held out the longest. Having made the decent *Monolith* in 1979, their next album *Audio-Visions* moved in a more pop-oriented direction, and by 1982 most of the Prog trappings had gone. PFM and Banco in Italy were already making song-orientated music, and even bands like Camel and Renaissance had had to modernise to keep making music.

For Renaissance in particular, changing with the times had been a challenge. After the success of their albums in the mid-1970s, they had produced one more Progressive Rock album, *Novella*, before finding relative success in the UK, almost by accident, when 'Northern Lights' became a hit in 1978. The supporting album, *A Song for All Seasons*, clearly took the band in a more commercial direction, but the follow-up, *Azure d'Or*, failed to cash in on the success. This was a continuing story throughout the late 1970s and early 1980s. Very fine Progressive Rock musicians were being asked to dumb down by their record companies. A few, like Genesis, succeeded, and a few, like The Enid, developed niches for themselves. However, most bands floundered.

However, the 1970s still had one major Progressive Rock album left, even if it was actually released in the summer of 1980.

Yes
Drama
Released 1980

Following some abortive sessions in Paris after the *Tormato* tour, Yes found themselves without a singer or a keyboard player. The band might have folded at that point, yet the remaining three-piece had a final gambit, and it was quite a shock. The Buggles – bassist/singer Trevor Horn and keyboard player Geoff Downes – were already famous for their bubblegum pop hit 'Video Killed the Radio Star'. Yet even looking at the famous video for that song, it was clear that Downes's heart lay in Prog, and the rig he sported (even if he did play it while wearing rubber gloves in the video) could have graced any 1970s Prog stage. The duo were big Yes fans and approached the band with the song 'We Can Fly from Here'. Suddenly they found themselves in the band.

It all seemed to fit. Downes had a modern approach, but a 1970s sensibility. Horn sang in a similar register to Jon Anderson. The resulting album was very much in the classic Yes style, but was perhaps a tad more aggressive, the New Wave influences apparent in the overall fire of the playing rather than in the songwriting, bar the reggae-inflected, Police-influenced 'Run Through the Light'. If the band were all-new, then other aspects of the album played it safe. The core threesome, Squire, Howe and White, recorded their backing tracks with stalwart sound engineer Eddie Offord. Roger Dean was invited back to produce a striking album cover.

Built around three epics, 'Machine Messiah', 'Into the Lens' and 'Tempus Fugit', the music itself is superb. The three existing members sound rejuvenated and on top form, with Howe in particular at the top of his game. It is also the best-recorded Yes album since *Relayer*. Downes turns in a sympathetic, unflashy performance and Horn's singing is excellent, close enough to Anderson to sound like Yes but with plenty of character of his own.

Two problems remained. Firstly, was this Yes? *Drama* causes confusion with diehard Yes fans since its quality was achieved without Jon Anderson, who embodies the spirit of Yes to many. So it cannot be Yes. To me, it's a Yes album through and through, and one of the best at that. The second problem lay in what would happen when the band went on tour, and this was to be the downfall of this line-up. In America, the dates had been marketed without mentioning the line-up changes, and although the band played well, there was some hostility. By the time the band got to Europe, however, the inexperienced Horn was struggling. I caught the band at Hammersmith Odeon on this tour, and while he sang the *Drama* material beautifully, he really struggled on the older material; 'And You and I' was particularly painful. The tour completed, the line-up fell apart. Nonetheless, *Drama* remains a fan favourite, to the extent that when the band found itself once again without Anderson in 2009, the new line-up returned to the album and played 'Machine Messiah' and 'Tempus Fugit' live.

CODA: THE STRANGE SOLO CAREER OF MR RICHARD WAKEMAN

If there is a single person that embodies the Progressive Rock musician, it is probably Rick Wakeman. This is not just for his prowess, flamboyance and pioneering work in developing new keyboard technology. In recent years, he has become everyone's Prog expert. Need a sound bite for a TV special? Call on Rick. Need an anecdote about 1970s excess? Call on Rick. In the UK especially, he has become an avuncular spokesman for the genre. He is the archetypal Grumpy Old Rock Star and in 1977 he was my god.

That year I was fifteen and developing an interest in music with more depth than just ABBA. Leafing through a catalogue for the A&M Records, I bypassed the albums by the Carpenters and Herb Alpert and my attention was caught by the striking cover of Rick's *The Myths and Legends of King Arthur and the Knights of the Round Table*. History *and* rock music! I bought that album and played it to death. This, surely, was real music. It was dynamic and dramatic and had such great melodies.

Rick's two big budget albums, *Journey to the Centre of the Earth* and *The Myths and Legends of King Arthur and the Knights of the Round Table*, released eleven months apart in 1974 and 1975 respectively, are unique albums in the Progressive Rock canon. *Journey* was recorded live at the Royal Festival Hall when Rick was still in Yes, and has a brash, almost child-like grandeur. It certainly has its moments, and as a showcase for Rick's keyboard playing, particular his lead Minimoog work, it has few parallels. Of course, it is also wildly naïve and both the lyrics and the text written for the narration are functional at best, but this only adds to the charm. *King Arthur* repeats the formula, but the relative safety of the studio elicits better performances from his two lead vocalists, Ashley Holt and Gary Pickford Hopkins, and Rick's left-of-centre choice of musicians from his local pub's pickup band works well. The themes and arrangements are also more convincing, and in 'King Arthur and the Black Knight' Rick wrote his most fiendish orchestra part and delivered the most exciting Minimoog solo (actually a duet) of his career. These two albums almost transcend the Progressive Rock movement. Enormously successful in the UK, they have more in common with brash theatrical albums like *Jeff Wayne's Musical Version of War of the Worlds* than the work of Yes and Genesis, yet I cherished them nonetheless.

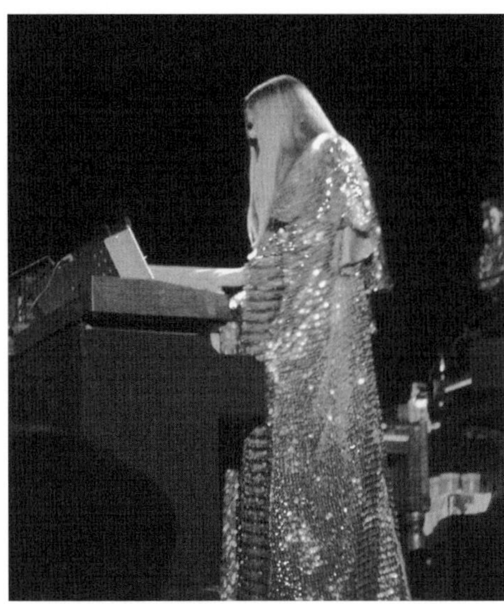

This page and oppposite: Rick Wakeman then and now. Left, onstage with Yes in 1974 (*Rich Greene*) and right, in Leamington Spa in 2010 (*Neil Palfreyman*).

The albums that bookend these two are actually more conventional Progressive Rock works. Rick's first solo album, *The Six Wives of Henry VIII* features six instrumental profiles of the wives in a rather more stripped-down way, whereas *No Earthly Connection* from 1976, actually my favourite of his first four, replaces orchestra and choir with a small horn section and is the first recorded work of the pretentiously titled English Rock Ensemble. His next two albums also have plenty to recommend them. *White Rock*, from 1977, was the soundtrack album to the 1976 Winter Olympics and features some gorgeous melodies, while *Rick Wakeman's Criminal Record* from the same year – recorded at the same time that Yes were recording *Going for the One* in Switzerland – also has some great playing and memorable arrangements.

There were follies, even in the early years. He made and lost a fortune. There were failed businesses, the *King Arthur on Ice* incident (for details of this I recommend his book of anecdotes, *Grumpy Old Rock Star and Other Wondrous Stories*), heart attacks and alcoholism. Perhaps the most interesting and least-remembered Wakeman folly was his financial backing for the Birotron. This was a Mellotron-type instrument that allowed eight-track tapes to be played on a continual (rather than an eight-second) loop, allowing for gradual modulations in sound or instrument samples. Production issues caused by unseen problems converting the prototype into a machine that could be mass-produced at a price that made sense for anyone other than the super-rich meant that few models were manufactured. By the time these issues were ironed out, digital polysynths were revolutionising the keyboard market. The Birotron can be heard on *Rick Wakeman's Criminal Record*, and was used on tour with Yes from 1977 to 1979. It is now one of the rarest musical instruments in the world.

After this, Rick's career began to slide into post-punk desperation. His last album for A&M was the patchy double album *Rhapsodies*, which combined ham-

fisted covers like a disco 'Rhapsody in Blue' and a piano version of 'Summertime' (jazz not being his strongest suit) with some variable originals, of which the best was the serene 'Sea Horses'. There followed a succession of labels and comebacks, of which the most successful was a version of Orwell's *Nineteen Eighty-Four* with lyrics by Tim Rice. It was released, like Anthony Phillip's electronic album *1984*, in 1981. Rick soldiered on, with soundtrack work and niche music plus the odd Christian album following quickly. For a while, his stock-in-trade was solo piano albums for New Age labels interspersed with the odd rock album that left his Progressive Rock heritage far behind. There was one more Progressive Rock album in him, though. In 2003 he recorded an album called *Out There* that owed as much to the growing Progressive Metal movement as it did to the 1970s. A stylish return to form rather than huge commercial success, it is his most recent album in the Progressive Rock style in a musical career that has became more settled as he entered his sixties.

As well as being the archetypal Progressive Rock musician, Rick remains one of the figures that suffered the most when the New Wave came along and cluttered the market place. For a while hugely popular, he was never really 'cool', and when the 1980s came along it was not just his music that fell out of favour. His sense of humour, which is resolutely traditionalist, and his politics, which are resolutely Conservative, fell out of favour as alternative humour and left-wing, anti-Thatcherite and anti-Reaganite material began to dominate the stages of Britain. Yet he has survived as a national treasure, with regular appearances on TV as a witty raconteur. While the two big orchestral albums have dated somewhat, they remain a staple of his solo live set. They do not represent the pinnacle of the Progressive Rock artistry, but they do contain plenty of musical wit. For those interested in 1970s keyboard wizardry, they remain a must-listen.

5

COMING TO YOU LIVE: PROGRESSIVE ROCK ON STAGE

Live performance has always been important to Progressive Rock artists, both as a source of income and as a form of self-expression. However, two sometimes complimentary but often contradictory principles seem to underpin these performances: 'give the audience a show' and 'let the music speak for itself'.

In the early days of the genre, these two principles often combined, for practical as well as aesthetic reasons. A Genesis performance in the early 1970s, for instance, would feature singer Peter Gabriel standing while the other four members sat down to play. The band were seated to aid performance and concentration, yet the lack of any sort of visual focus meant that Gabriel had to compensate, particularly as there were long periods of tuning between songs. He started to tell surreal stories to keep the attention of the audience, and then, famously, came the costumes. The Peter Gabriel of the twenty-first century has all the gravitas and stature of a world leader, but when we look back at archive clips we see man in a red dress and fox's head, or dressed as a flower. Wasn't it all a bit silly?

By way of complete contrast, the King Crimson of the early 1970s believed that the music should tell you all you needed to know about the band. Robert Fripp would sit down (of course, he preferred to play that way anyway) and any personal expression came from the joy of playing and not from a desire to pose or look serious. In Heavy Metal, for instance, the sexual swagger that has been in rock music since Elvis played *The Ed Sullivan Show* in the mid-1950s is often exaggerated. Microphone stands and guitars become phalluses. Drummers play huge kits, most of which they barely use. In Progressive Rock however, sex was played down completely. If the keyboard player had a big rig, and many did, it was because he needed all those instruments to create the colours he wanted. Or that was the theory, at least.

Every convention has its exceptions, and Keith Emerson was one. Beginning with his days in The Nice, Emerson developed a knife-throwing and Hammond-beating act that was straight out of cheap theatre. His way of sexualising his instrument (prior to the development of the ghastly keytar in

Keith Emerson at Nearfest in 2006 with his ever-present – and somewhat cumbersome – modular Moog in the background. (*Kevin Scherer*)

the late 1970s – a handheld synth and later a MIDI keyboard controller) was to attach pyrotechnics to the ribbon controller of his Moog. Emerson has in some areas become a victim of his own pioneering spirit. As an early exponent of the innovative yet cumbersome modular Moog in 1969–70, Emerson took to using one on stage, and as a result has transported one around with him from country to country, venue to venue, big and small, for forty years. He doesn't need it, *really* he doesn't, but there is still a thrill to seeing it played. Admittedly, his crew have no doubt got the packing and transportation of the beast down to a fine art these days, but this instrument is a museum piece.

The wonderful Mellotron, the polyphonic keyboard developed in the early 1960s, still crops up on stage from time to time. We had an M400 model on stage at the Summer's End festival in 2008, played by Thomas Johnson of Thieves' Kitchen. Thomas need not have brought one – he had the digital patches to do the same job – but it was a thrill all the same. As already mentioned, after fifteen years without one, Rick Wakeman wisely returned to using the Minimoog on stage. It is true that while accurate digital imitations of the instrument now exist, nothing quite compares to hearing *and* seeing this iconic instrument being played.

All music creates its own conventions, and if you attend a concert featuring a keyboard player who rose to prominence in the 1970s, chances are he will still have and use a big keyboard rig, even though he probably doesn't need one. MIDI technology makes more than a few keyboards unnecessary; Andy Tillison of The Tangent, for instance, takes this to an extreme and will go as far as programming a single key to play a specific sound for a brief period of time. As a result, he can play the most complex of sound palates with two MIDI keyboards.

Rick Wakeman or Geoff Downes, on the other hand, use a broader brush, both because they can afford to and because they believe it is expected of them.

Yes were also innovators in set design, with Roger and his brother Martyn Dean designing sets for the band's *Tales from Topographic Oceans* and *Relayer* tours. These designs referenced Roger's otherworldly album cover designs – large fibreglass pods were littered around the stage, for example. Drummer Alan White notoriously became stuck in one of these pods in 1974, an incident that provided inspiration for a hilarious scene in the movie *This Is Spinal Tap*. As with many aspects of the Progressive Rock era, Yes revisited such stage sets for their 2004 world tour. Sadly, the cut-price nature of the tour lead to the fibreglass stage props being replaced by giant inflatable shapes that were not quite so impressive.

Yes did have one more innovation up their sleeve, since copied by many artists. On their 1978–79 world tour, and again in 1990, they played large arenas 'in the round', placing a round, revolving stage in the centre of the hall, giving all parts of the hall a great view and allowing more tickets to be sold.

As Canadians, Rush moved into bigger venues at the end of the 1970s. They began to use a huge overhead screen to illustrate some of the set. The song 'Red Barchetta', for instance, showed an animated car being driven from the driver's point of view, video-game style. This was thrilling stuff, and was sparingly used by a band so as to enhance rather than overwhelm the music. Many other artists have used screens to provide atmosphere, two recent examples being Porcupine Tree and IQ, whose projections have become an integral part of their live shows to the extent that it is almost impossible to imagine a live concert with either band without their projections. The relative cheapness of laptops and media manipulation software means that such projections are within the budget of many more artists than was once the case; often it is the limitation of the venue that prevents such innovations, rather than the band's budget.

The 1980s Neo-Prog revival would often reference the theatricality of early Genesis. While once again there was a feeling of small boys dressing up, it was often used to decent and in some cases extreme effect. Fish's face paint, although he dropped it eventually, certainly helped get him noticed, and Euan Lowson's performance of 'The Ripper' at early Pallas concerts was chillingly effective. Peter Nicholls of IQ, also an artist, used extreme make-up in the 1980s that was both effective and disturbing. Later, the band's performances of their much-lauded 1997 double album *Subterranea* featured live performances by singer Peter Nicholls that must have been exhausting. The spectre of two world wars still hung over musicians and audiences that were born in the 1950s and 1960s, so when Geoff Mann of Twelfth Night performed 'Sequences' in full army uniform at the Reading Festival in 1982 and 1983, the impact was considerable. This sense of theatre is not as common as it used to be, although Robert Ramsay of current British band Tinyfish offers an engaging variation on the theme by using costumes in his spoken word sections at various points in the band's set.

Geddy Lee and Alex Lifeson of Rush onstage in 2010. (*Peter Hutchins*)

Whereas the theatricality of the 1980s was generally somewhat serious and had little ironic content, the interjections of Ramsay are rather more knowing, almost as if they are an in-joke in which both the band and the audience are complicit.

THE RISE OF THE FESTIVALS

The modern era has brought with it some tension between live performance and the perceived seriousness of the music. Some Progressive Rock fans are wary of pitting 'performance' against 'music'. This tends to vary depending on the venue, or even the country in which the concert is being played. There is an interesting contrast, for instance, between the Nearfest and Rosfest festivals that take place every year within a hundred miles of each other on the eastern side of the USA. Nearfest, with its eclectic 'art rock' programme, tends to have a slightly reverential atmosphere – a 'Prog church', as Kurt Rongey of US band The Underground Railroad once called it. Rosfest, on the other hand, is rather more of a party with a slightly more 'rock-and-roll' aesthetic. This has caused some problems at Nearfest, particularly for British bands. When Pallas played Nearfest in 2004, there was some criticism of singer Alan Reed's ebullient, rabble-rousing style, which was considered inappropriate by some. This would not have been an issue

The concourse at the Zoellner Arts Center, Bethlehem, PA, the home of Nearfest. (*Kevin Scherer*)

at Rosfest. This is not to criticise Nearfest at all – I have attended it three times and have always greatly enjoyed the experience.

Since the mid-1990s, a steady stream of festivals has helped sustain the Progressive Rock scene. I have a much-treasured VHS tape of Progfest from 1995 featuring White Willow from Norway, Ars Nova from Japan and Solaris from Hungary, but this California-based festival ended in 2000 after eight years of success. However, its example gives others hope and a business model to follow.

The 2000s saw the DIY ethic of the 1990s given a more professional and organised slant. In the main, these Festivals were, and are, run by fans for fans. They tend to be most successful when, as well as providing great music, they become social events in their own right, a way for people to escape their own lives for a few days.

In June 1999, Chad Hutchinson and Rob LaDuca began Nearfest, a two-day Progressive Rock festival on the eastern side of the USA. Unlike Greg Walker's California-based Progfest, Nearfest combined traditional symphonic bands with more avant-garde art-rock fare. The festival's home is the charming campus of LeHigh University near Bethlehem in Pennsylvania, a comfortable and attractive place that perfectly fits the slightly rarefied nature of the performances. The festival itself hit the ground running by combining up-and-coming American bands like Spock's Beard with some cleverly chosen overseas acts like Solaris from Hungary and Änglagård from Sweden and, most crucially, some brilliantly timed revivalists like Happy the Man and Nektar. By the time of the first Nearfest I attended, in June 2001, the event was already a fast sell-out. Rob and Chad admit that they overreached themselves in 2002 and 2003 by moving the festival to the beautifully restored Patriots Theatre in Trenton, New Jersey, and by 2004 Nearfest was back at Bethlehem, and none the worse for the experience. Indeed, by the mid-2000s it had established itself as arguably the most prestigious Progressive Rock event in the world, and an unexpected cancellation in 2011 notwithstanding, it should remain so for a while yet.

Another prestigious festival was Baja Prog, in the northern Mexican resort of Mexicali. A simple one-day event in 1997 had grown, by 2003, into an ambitious four-day extravaganza taking place over two stages, the first in the Teatro del Estado and the second in the official festival hotel of the Araiza Inn. The inn gave an opportunity for smaller bands – especially those from Central and South America – to play in the afternoon before the evening session. There was a superb international line-up in 2003 that included veterans Ange from France and Focus from Holland (albeit with only a single original member each). Also present were Magenta from the UK, playing their first significant live concert after the success of their debut album *Revolutions*, Ars Nova from Japan, and Mexican festival hosts Cast. Baja Prog went on hiatus after its twelfth edition in 2008, a victim of the worsening economic climate, and is much missed.

In Europe, several festivals have come and gone. When they do fail, it tends to be because the attendance has fallen short of the hopes (and the financial model) of the organisers. Where they succeed, as with the Prog-résiste festival at the terrific Spirit of 66 venue in Verviers, Belgium, it is by knowing the audience and pandering to it. The Night of the Prog festival began in 2006 in the astonishingly picturesque setting of the outdoor Loreley Amphitheatre on the banks of the Rhine in Germany. Although it traditionally has a capacity of 15,000, it now works perfectly well as a venue with less than a third of that number, making it viable for Progressive Rock. The Night of the Prog often draws big names.

The most successful festival in the UK has been Summer's End in the south-west, which began in 2005, founded by singer Huw Lloyd Jones. Ironically, the festival grew out of the ambition of another promoter, Sean Hunt, who had organised a festival in Chippenham, Wiltshire, in 2004. When personal circumstances prevented a repeat in 2005, Huw, who had been due to play with his band of the time, Also Eden, took up the challenge and organised a one-day festival in Gloucester. I came on board in 2006 and Summer's End became two days at the Robin Club in Bilston. From 2008 onwards we have had the perfect venue, both spiritually and practically, in Lydney in the Forest of Dean – a beautiful part of the world and a well-known holiday location. This has allowed

The crowd at High Voltage 2011 await The Enid on the Prog stage. (*Neal Palfreyman*)

a real feeling of community to build up around the festival. Festivals work when they build their own character, not just based around the music but also the venue and the social scene that arises around it. At Summer's End, we feel that the festival came of age when we moved to Lydney, where fans could not only enjoy the music but also take in the scenery. This is also true of Nearfest – the pleasing campus atmosphere, good weather and relative affluence of the town of Bethlehem make attending the event a pleasure. But if outdoor music is your thing, then where better to enjoy it than at the Night of the Prog on the banks of the Rhine?

Running a festival is not easy. Summer's End has never been financially secure, which means that every last ticket sale is vital and needs to be worked for. It also means that the internet has been important in building a community around the festival; building a mailing list has been the most vital thing of all. We rarely advertise, yet we know that the vast majority of those who might attend our festival are fully aware of when it will happen.

Many things contribute to the success of a festival. At Summer's End we encourage the artists to mix with the audience as much as possible. Some do, some don't, but this helps create atmosphere. We also attempt to make the festival as relaxed an experience as we can. Lydney Town Hall has no formal seating, so while the audience can sit, to watch the bands properly they need to stand. This does lead to a livelier atmosphere than at seated US festivals. I have fallen asleep in my seat at Nearfest – due either to boredom or jet lag – but that is hard to do when you are on your feet.

Festivals rely on the enthusiasm of those that organise them, and in the main we do what we do for the love of the music and not for financial gain. If Summer's End breaks even financially we are happy, and I know this applies to other festivals as well. Whether they are run with huge professional efficiency like Nearfest or Night of the Prog, or with a rather less formal approach like Summer's End, it is the music that matters most. Inevitably, festivals come and go or change hands depending on the stamina or financial acumen of the organisers, yet without these festivals the Progressive Rock movement would not have the momentum it now has.

Elsewhere, Progressive Rock either exists in large halls – with heritage tours by Yes and Jethro Tull – or in small enclaves where communities have built up around certain venues or organisations. In the UK, the Peel in Kingston upon Thames has built a small community around a regular series of Saturday night concerts. These concerts are vital in giving new bands a venue and an audience. The Classic Rock Society, while it does not cater for Progressive Rock alone, has done this in the north since 1991, and in recent years the society has spread its wings into other parts of the country. Few bands can tour, in the traditional sense, without losing money; however, live performance remains an important factor in the continuing success of the genre. The High Voltage Festival in London, which began in 2010, has brought high-profile Progressive Rock acts to a large audience, for example. While it has done little to promote the grassroots of the genre, it has done much to enhance the public perception of Progressive Rock in recent years. But whatever the venue, and whatever the event, live performance remains as important to Progressive Rock as it ever was.

6

THE 1980S: A SHORT-LIVED REVIVAL

There is a myth perpetuated on Progressive Rock internet forums that musically the 1980s have nothing to redeem them at all. They were, it is said, typified by vacuous 'synth pop' bands and appalling hair metal. This is, of course, a ludicrous notion. Whatever you think of punk, it helped freshen up the popular music world, and by the time the 1980s dawned, the aggression of the early punk bands had been marginalised and some real craft was creeping back into music. The other important innovation that helped perpetuate creativity was the development of relatively inexpensive polyphonic synthesizers, which allowed bands to innovate without going to massive expense.

Our story now takes three separate paths. We will examine the fortunes of the 1970s bands in the 1980s later in this chapter, and also the influential and rather surprising Neo-Prog movement of the early 1980s, but we begin in the area where many people, including myself, believe that the real innovation in popular music took place. In the art-pop movement.

ART-POP IN THE 1980S – THE NEW PROGRESSIVES?

I remember watching TV appearances by both Howard Jones and Thomas Dolby in the early 1980s. Both were one-man music machines, using banks of synthesizers, including sequencers and drum machines, to perform their songs without the need for any other musicians. The more commercially successful of these was Jones, whose debut album *Human's Lib* was a major hit in the UK and spawned several hit singles including the twee 'Your Song' and the rather more interesting Progressive Pop of 'What Is Love' and 'Pearl in the Shell'. Jones had been in a Progressive Rock band prior to his break as a pop artist, and it really showed in his music.

Dolby was less earnest than Jones, playfully exploiting his nerdish 'young boffin' image, particularly on his startlingly inventive novelty hit 'She Blinded Me with Science', which featured elderly British TV scientist Magnus Pyke.

However, his debut album *The Golden Age of Wireless* is as perfect and inventive a synth-pop album as you could possibly wish to hear. By the time of his follow-up, *The Flat Earth* in 1984, Dolby was fronting a full band and was drawing on other influences in his music. This approach was to become a consistent one as the 1980s continued. Whereas the 1970s musicians drew largely on rock music, 1960s pop and the European classical tradition for their inspiration, in the 1980s the influences became much wider. 1970s Progressive Rock was certainly important, but in Dolby's two other 1980s albums, *The Flat Earth* and *Aliens Ate My Buick*, he drew on inspiration as wide as big band jazz, the avant-garde, soul, rock and electronic music.

PETER GABRIEL AND KATE BUSH

Even though he had moved away from the typical Progressive Rock sound palate for his first two solo albums in 1977 and 1978, Peter Gabriel continued to invent and innovate. His third album, released in 1980 and often referred to as *Melt*, took this approach one step further. The most startling innovation on this album was his requirement that the drummers, including former Genesis cohort Phil Collins, avoid cymbals when playing their parts. The resulting drum patterns give the music a spare, almost tribal feel. The album combined heavy synths and some raw guitar parts – including an appearance by Paul Weller of New Wave champions The Jam on guitar. This was as inventive as anything released in the early 1980s. The percussive approach was taken a step further on the rather more experimental fourth album (*Security*) released in 1982, which replaced the relative melodicism of the third album with something considerably less accessible and more brooding. When he emerged after four years in 1986 for the huge worldwide commercial hit 'So', this had been replaced by a new soul-inspired pop approach, yet his credibility as an innovator has never been questioned and Gabriel remains the most universally respected name from the Progressive Rock era.

Meanwhile, Kate Bush, who had become a friend of Gabriel's and whose vocals were to grace his hit singles 'Games without Frontiers' and 'Don't Give Up', was also developing her music beyond her quirky singer-songwriter image. After *The Kick Inside* and the hastily released follow-up *Lionheart*, her 1980 third album *Never for Ever* saw her moving into more experimental territory. While releasing a cascade of hit singles – at least in the UK and Europe – she made innovative use of the new Fairlight keyboard, a hugely expensive and soon-to-be superseded early sampling device. Her obsession with the instrument continued on 1982's *The Dreaming*, which abandoned pop tunes in favour of dense and relatively inaccessible soundscapes created in the studio. Greeted with praise and bafflement in equal measure, the album failed to strike a chord with the album-buying public, yet remains full of Progressive Rock-inspired invention.

Bush got the balance between melody and innovation spot on when she returned in 1985 with *The Hounds of Love*, a masterpiece of an album that stretched its audience a little but not too far, as the further batch of hit singles proved. Side two of the album was one complete composition, the atmospheric 'The Ninth Wave'. It was the first time an artist had had such commercial success with a long-form piece since Yes's *Awaken* in 1977. Bush continued to take her time in producing albums, so that when the next two were released – *The Sensual World* in 1989 and *The Red Shoes* in 1993 – she had repeatedly appeared in 'where are they now?' newspaper columns. By the time *Aerial* appeared in 2005 she was an official recluse. Bush has been reluctantly accepted as a Progressive Rock artist by a community that tends to like its female artists a little more passive and a little less innovative then she has always been. Whatever her status, she has been a real innovator throughout her thirty-year career.

JAPAN AND XTC – 1970S POSEURS BECOME 1980S INNOVATORS

Actually formed in 1974 as a glam rock band, Japan developed away from guitar-based pop in the late 1970s and came to favour a stylish, Bowie-influenced art-pop. The combination of Mick Karn's bubbling bass, Steve Jansen's unusual percussion, David Sylvian's baritone and Richard Barbieri's synth soundscapes – later to be used so intelligently by Porcupine Tree – is unlike any other music made at the time. By their final two albums, *Gentlemen Take Polaroids* and the remarkable *Tin Drum* in 1980 and 1981 respectively, an inaccurate but fortuitous connection with the early 1980s New Romantic movement had catapulted them to stardom. There is a wonderful clip from *The Old Grey Whistle Test* in 1981 that shows the band performing their song 'Ghosts', surely one of the most chilling and unusual hit singles ever written. This clip and the live double album *Oil on Canvas*, which acts as a career retrospective, show that the band had absorbed the spirit of the Prog bands from the 1970s and made it their own.

XTC, on the other hand, had first appeared with their angular punk-pop in the late 1970s, but by the early 1980s the band's songwriting and arrangement skills had taken on a more refined character. Over a trio of albums in the early 1980s, the band established the innovative and very English-pastoral approach to arrangement and songwriting that was to serve them well over a long (if not always prolific) career, demonstrating that a Prog approach could still find an audience in the 1980s.

The remarkable *English Settlement*, a double album, began this process in 1982. Alongside some familiar and tuneful hit singles, there were plenty of moments of invention. Vital to the album was the use of acoustic guitar, which was played by both singer Andy Partridge and lead guitarist Dave Gregory. Of course, the album has many moods, and there are New Wave and ska references aplenty, but the pockets of invention are startling. 'Jason and the Argonauts' was as close to Progressive Rock as the early 1980s got, and this approach continued with the startlingly intricate 'Yacht Dance', with its two acoustic guitar lines weaving around each other.

This new pastoral approach continued with the even more Prog *Mummer* in 1983. The album was nowhere near as successful as its predecessor, probably because the fashionable angular pop on that album's hit singles had been replaced by something more wistful – as shown on the charming 'Love on a Farmboy's Wages' and 'Ladybird'. There were also moments that were more complex, like the powerful 'Human Alchemy'. 1984's *Big Express* featured extensive use of keyboards, especially the Mellotron, and included the band's most Progressive Rock track yet, the glorious 'This World Over'.

XTC never abandoned its first priority, which was to write great songs. However, these three albums, as well as later gems like *Oranges & Lemons*, with its huge Beatles influence, and 1992's US hit *Nonsuch*, showed that the band could blend great melodies with a Prog approach to arrangement. This culminated in the two *Apple Venus* albums in 1999 and 2000 respectively. *Apple Venus Volume 1*, with its huge orchestral arrangements and magnificent songs, remains the most-played album of theirs in my collection.

TALK TALK AND TEARS FOR FEARS – PROG BY ANY OTHER NAME

Inevitably, if the synth-pop bands were to survive, they could not stay the same forever, and several of these adapted in one direction or another. The excellent China Crisis hired Walter Becker of Steely Dan as producer and found jazz, whereas bands like Talk Talk moved in a more experimental direction.

Originally a quartet, Talk Talk's strong Roxy Music influence led to their association, like Japan, with the New Romantic scene in the early 1980s. They were successful in several territories without breaking out as stars in either the UK or the USA. The band gradually developed in sophistication with the help of an 'unofficial' band member, keyboard player and composer Tim Friese-Green, who often shared writing duties with vocalist Mark Hollis. For their breakthrough album *The Colour of Spring* in 1986, the band was involving over a dozen guest musicians, including guitarist David Rhodes and veteran percussionist Morris Pert. While still a pop record, spawning the huge hit 'Life's What You Make It', the album is hugely sophisticated, drawing on jazz and soul as well as rock. Two key tracks bookend the album: the gorgeously textured opener 'Happiness Is Easy' and the eight-minute and truly Prog 'Time It's Time'. By 1989's *Spirit of Eden* and the lesser-known *Laughing Stock* in 1992, the band had completely abandoned pop music and were intent on minimalist experimentation, with specific vocals, instruments and indeed notes used as sparingly as possible. The results were interesting, very much in the spirit of King Crimson improvisations, but it is not surprising that the audience for this music was sparse at best.

I will end this section with Tears for Fears, the New Wave group for whom Progressive Rock fans seem to have most affection. Formed by Roland Orzabal and Curt Smith in Bath, Somerset, the band originally had a teenybopper image thanks to Smith's good looks and vulnerable, untutored singing style. The intense and extremely talented Orzabal provided a weightier contrast. Unusually for a band of that era, the Progressive Rock influences were evident from the start of their career. This is less obvious in their hit singles, but certain songs from their debut *The Hurting*, something of an early 1980s classic, suggest a Prog sense of structure and dynamics, particularly in 'Start of the Breakdown' and the title track. The band's next recording, a single called 'The Way You Are' that included some complex rhythmic arrangements, was perhaps their most Prog early song. At that point, however, the band realised that a change in direction might be necessary. The follow-up album in 1985, the massive-selling *Songs from The Big Chair*, mixed pop with other influences. This beautifully structured record featured another sequence of pieces with a strong link to Progressive Rock. 'Head Over Heels/Broken (live)' showed that as a live act the band were very impressive. I saw Tears for Fears several times during this era, and they were always excellent value.

Tears for Fears
The Seeds of Love
Released 1989

By the time of the corporate 1980s, the output of successful bands had slowed so much that *The Seeds of Love*, released in 1989, was only the band's third album of the 1980s. This was typical. As it turned out, of all the albums released by the art-pop bands of the 1980s, *The Seeds of Love* contains the material most similar to the Progressive Rock of the 1970s. While the four tracks on side two of the original vinyl album contain the most obviously experimental pieces of music, even the songs on side one – which on the surface may seem to have more to do with jazz and soul than Progressive Rock – have the hallmarks of the 1970s.

Several tracks were developed out of semi-jammed arrangements played by a group of crack session musicians, including the ubiquitous (in the 1980s at least) bassist Pino Palladino, virtuoso drummer Manu Katché and guitarist Robbie McIntosh. Two other crucial factors helped shape the album: the songwriting prowess of talented pianist Nicky Holland and the discovery of singer Oleta Adams, whose presence gives some of the early part of the album its soulful vibe. Indeed, the two openers, 'Woman in Chains' and the jazzy 'Badman's Song', which both feature Roland Orzabal dueting with Adams, appear to have very little to do with Progressive Rock at all, yet the latter track has a very Prog structure. The inventive Beatles pastiche 'Sowing the Seeds of Love' references the more experimental period of the band, and the smooth, Smith-sung pop of 'Advice for the Young at Heart' closes side one with a smooth, melodic flourish.

The Seeds of Love by Tears for Fears. Prog by any other name. (*Mercury*)

Side two could not be any more different. 'Standing on the Corner of the Third World' begins in smooth, bluesy style before taking off into a complex, atmospheric ballad, while 'Swords and Knives' is pretty much straight Progressive Rock, a multi-parted, keyboard-dominated masterpiece. 'The Year of the Knife' does the same thing, but in rockier style, before 'Famous Last Words' builds tension then releases it gloriously.

A live video, *Live from Santa Barbara*, is also worth a look for a taste of the band's big-budget live show. Interestingly, the core of the band is similar to that which had toured in the early 1980s, with William Gregory on sax, Neil Taylor on guitar and Smith reverting to bass. They acquit themselves beautifully with the complex material as well as the hits. What a great Progressive Rock band they would have made!

After Smith's departure (he would rejoin some years later for a well-received reunion), Orzabal continued to record using the band name, with some initial success. Those recordings, while they are more song-orientated, retain the atmosphere, dynamics and drama of Progressive Rock, and are generally admired among Prog fans.

THE STRANGE CASE OF SKY, THE BAND THAT SHOULD NEVER HAVE BEEN

Despite all the upheavals in the pop music industry in the late 1970s and early 1980s, life for the man on the Clapham omnibus remained largely the same. The recession in the UK of the early 1980s, which prompted white reggae band UB40 to sing of the 'One in Ten' (referring to the proportion of the working population that was unemployed at the time), bit hard and touched many lives. However, many middle-of-the-road artists like Cliff Richard continued to thrive. Another of these artists riding a wave of popularity was amiable but dedicated Australian classical guitarist John Williams, whose performance of the piece 'Cavatina' had been an enormous commercial success. Williams's music began to cross genres and on his album *Travelling* he used an electric guitar for the first time.

Buoyed by this success, he formed a band, Sky, based around session musicians Kevin Peek (guitar), Herbie Flowers (bass) and Tristan Fry (drums and percussion). The masterstroke, at least initially, was the employment of former Curved Air keyboardist Francis Monkman, who lent the band a little Progressive Rock credibility. Sky's first album, which mixed interpretations of classical pieces with original material, was a huge success, and in 1980 they released their finest album, the somewhat tediously titled *Sky 2*. This album mixed a variety of classical pieces played pretty straight, with a 'rocked up' version of Bach's 'Toccata'. Many of the pieces, such as the opener 'Hotta', were fairly straightforward in structure, as influenced by disco and the melodic synthesizer music of Jean Michel Jarre as they were by Progressive Rock. However, certain tracks – particularly the side-long Monkman suite 'Fifo', Peek's multi-textured 'Sahara' and the plodding 'Scipio' – might have been created seven or eight years earlier for a different audience.

What was going on here? Progressive Rock was hugely unfashionable, as were Sky, but the musicians involved, plus the middle-of-the-road nature of much of the music, made this band hugely popular, and if they slipped in a bit of Prog, who was to notice? The band drew their popularity from a sector of society that never read the music press, and who enjoyed the melodic nature of the music rather than demand it challenge them. Yet the success of Sky also proved that there was potentially a market out there for Progressive Rock.

The band continued for the rest of the decade, although it stumbled somewhat due to line-up changes, particularly the loss of the hugely popular Williams in 1984. Rick Wakeman was even a member for short time, and I remember seeing him appear with the band on (of all programmes) *The Val Doonican Show* in the mid-1980s.

It is easy to accuse Sky of playing safe. They could have made much more challenging music than they did – and Monkman tried – but they elected instead to plough the pop-classical furrow. It is hard to blame them. Looking back, it is amazing they existed at all, and they have left us some decent music.

THE LAST TWITCHINGS OF THE OLD GUARD

The early 1980s were tough for the old guard. Genesis, after the success of *... And then there Were Three...*, released their last album to contain music to please

Progressive Rock fans in early 1980. Bookended by some Prog material, the middle part of *Duke* was either pure pop, like 'Misunderstanding' and 'Turn It On Again', or just lacklustre, like Tony Banks's 'Cul-de-Sac'. The album spawned a sequence of big hit singles, and prompted the band to move in a more 'adult pop' direction in parallel with other projects, not least of which was Phil Collins's hugely successful solo career.

Almost accidentally, Yes were to have another bite of the cherry later in the 1980s, with the success of the Trevor Horn-produced *90125* album. Based around the massive US success of the single 'Owner of a Lonely Heart', and with Jon Anderson back in the fold, the band changed into a pop-rock act at a time when corporate rock was big business. Unfortunately, the band failed to capitalise on this success of the album and tour, taking three years to produce the follow-up *Big Generator*. Although both albums have hints of Progressive Rock, these hints were no more prominent than in a band like Toto – who often introduced an epic, complex slant into their music – and so they need not detain us too long.

King Crimson
Discipline
Released 1981

Much more of a surprise than the last gasp of Yes was the seemingly sudden re-emergence of King Crimson. Towards the end of the 1970s, Robert Fripp had been increasingly active. This included an excellent solo album, *Exposure*, and work with Daryl Hall, Peter Gabriel and his own band, The League of Gentlemen. Working largely in the USA, he had managed to re-invent himself as a pioneer of the New Wave rather than a Progressive Rock dinosaur. In 1980, he set about forming a new band.

This time, Fripp had a different style of music in mind, something informed by the post-punk pop of Talking Heads (from which band he stole innovative guitarist and vocalist Adrian Belew), the intricate minimalism of Steve Reich and the rhythmic complexity of the old King Crimson. With a rhythm section comprising Tony Levin (on bass and the strange Chapman Stick) and Bill Bruford (drums), the band began rehearsing in Britain before taking a short set on tour in small British venues. I caught this tour at Keele University and was very impressed, although despite playing Crimson classics 'Red' and 'Larks' Tongues in Aspic', they had less than an hour's worth of material. They were called Discipline at that point, although it was no surprise when they changed their name to King Crimson.

The resultant album, with its striking, minimalist cover, is a masterwork. It mixes Talking Heads-style vocals and song structures with a Prog style that few people had heard before. Belew sounds like he is having a whale of a time, his vocals clearly heavily influenced by David Byrne of his former band, but his melodic sense superbly utilised. His inventive guitar playing dips in and out of Fripp's more intricate patterns. Bruford and Levin sound like they were born to play this music,

Adrian Belew, a constant member of King Crimson since *Discipline* in 1981. (*Roy Layer*)

with Levin's intricate and inventive Chapman Stick work particularly impressive. But Fripp was the boss, and his remarkable guitar patterns are what make *Discipline* so memorable.

This was not by any means the King Crimson of old. It was both intricate and melodic, as exemplified by opener 'Elephant Talk'. No wonder there were debates in the band as to the commercial potential of the project. The songwriting itself is of the highest quality. In 'Frame by Frame' it is Belew that maintains the repetition – indeed, one of the fascinations of the album is that the guitarists sound so different. The languidly delicious 'Matte Kudasai' is followed by the rather more avant-garde 'Indiscipline', which features Belew's spoken word passages over something bordering on heavy rock. 'This is dangerous place,' intones Belew in 'Thela Hun Ginjeet' – although, bizarrely, he's talking about West London rather than the mean streets of New York. 'The Sheltering Sky' is a showcase for Fripp's soloing and Bruford's rhythmic textures. The astonishing title track 'Discipline', like so many King Crimson pieces, rewards the listener's concentration.

This version of the band was to record two more albums, *Beat* and *Three of a Perfect Pair*, but neither had the impact of this first masterpiece.

Moving Pictures, the album with which Rush came of age. (*Mercury*)

Rush
Moving Pictures
Released 1981

With punk raging around them, a young Canadian three-piece called Rush were gradually building a following, and outside their homeland it was the UK that seemed to notice them first. Starting out as heavy rock band in the Led Zeppelin style, the band evolved to add complexity to match their virtuosic techniques, plus the odd sword-and-sorcery lyric, taking them gradually closer to Progressive Rock. 1976's naïve *2112* included the side-long title track, while the following year's *A Farewell to Kings*, recorded at the famous Rockfield Studios in Monmouth, Wales, was the first Rush album to include extensive use of synthesizers. By 1980 the band were using synths extensively and had had a huge hit in the UK with 'The Spirit of Radio'. They were mixing sophisticated hard rock with songs of greater complexity.

Moving Pictures, released in 1981, represents the high-water mark of the band's creative surge. It also reveals a new sophistication. Aside from the leftfield science fiction of 'Red Barchetta', Neal Peart's lyrics (he is the rarest of things, a drummer and lyricist) took on greater real-world introspection. The music was precise yet sophisticated, concise yet inventive.

'Tom Sawyer', recognised as a modern classic, begins the album with a swirl of synths and meaty riffing, while 'Red Barchetta' moves along at a real clip. By the time the band toured the album – which I caught at the cavernous and much-lamented

Stafford Bingley Hall (later to burn down) – the band were using huge screens to illustrate the music. 'Red Barchetta' was a highlight I remember specifically to this day. 'YYZ' is the ultimate Rush instrumental, hugely influential on bands as varied as Enchant from California and Porcupine Tree from southern England. After 'Limelight', side two is a little more experimental, with the epic 'The Camera Eye' giving way to the sinister 'Witch Hunt' and the final, reggae-inflected 'Vital Signs'.

Despite the extensive use of keyboards, this album is dominated by the instrumental prowess of guitarist Alex Lifeson. His guitars crunch not with aggression, but with invention. It is this that makes this great album a Progressive Rock masterpiece, rather than just an example of sophisticated hard rock. After *Moving Pictures*, the band continued to make great music, some of it even more like Prog, but 1981 was the point when everything – modernity, invention and character – came into focus.

AN UNLIKELY REVIVAL

It is interesting and slightly ironic that the movement that helped kill the Progressive Rock movement, punk, should indirectly contribute to its revival.

The rise in punk and New Wave bands also gave an opportunity for another form of music to revive its fortunes: Heavy Metal. In the same way that the big-league Progressive Rock bands distanced themselves from their audiences in the mid to late 1970s, so too did the big heavy rock bands like Deep Purple and Led Zeppelin. Although many of the groups that took part in the New Wave of British Heavy Metal (NWOBHM) from 1979 onwards had formed earlier in the 1970s, it was not until 1979 that these artists began to coalesce into a movement. This movement began to take shape around a series of legendary compilation albums, most notably *Metal for Muthas* volumes one and two. Some groups were signed to small DIY labels, while others found themselves signed to more prestigious outfits as the movement began to progress. The rock weekly *Sounds* became the chief rabble-rouser for the cause, as well as DJ Tommy Vance's *Friday Rock Show* on BBC Radio 1. The movement soon took over the annual Reading Festival, which had been a champion of rock (including Progressive Rock) in the 1970s but towards the end of the decade had been swamped by New Wave bands. I attended the festival from 1980 to 1983, and they were very different affairs to the corporate events of the new millennium, more like the football matches of the same era than festivals of music. Despite the drunkenness and the vague feeling of threat, I loved each one.

The NWOBHM was initially categorised by fast, aggressive playing, gruff lead vocals and a DIY ethic towards recording that led to some horribly recorded albums. The Marquee club in London became the spiritual home of the movement. However, within a couple of years the bands had mellowed. The successful groups had gradually recruited more impressive musicians, and some bands like Grand Prix and White Spirit, who both signed with major labels, tentatively introduced some Prog elements into their music. Chief among these were Magnum from Birmingham, whose relatively melodic and subtle style of heavy rock became increasingly popular as the 1980s wore on, via albums like *Chase the Dragon* and *On a Storyteller's Night*. Many bands began to introduce mythical or fantasy elements into their lyrics, and the NWOBHM even had its own Roger Dean via the fantasy artwork of Rodney Matthews. This new boom in heavy bands produced an environment of DIY credibility as well as a thriving club scene up and down the UK, and all of a sudden some Progressive Rock bands began to emerge on the back of it.

Like many of the groups that emerged around 1982, Marillion had been around since the late 1970s, developing their own style, hiring and firing musicians, and working hard to make names for themselves in a marketplace that was barely interested. Then, all of a sudden, they were getting some interest. Who actually made up Marillion's early audience? There is little doubt that the principle audience group came from waves of fans that had been gripped by the first wave of the NWOBHM. Many of these, like me, had been far too young to hear *Foxtrot* first time round (or *Deep Purple in Rock*, for that matter) but were drawn by the parallels between the epic nature of Marillion's music and those of metal bands like Diamond Head (whose second album *Canterbury*, released in 1982, drew considerable inspiration from Progressive Rock) and a resurgent Uriah Heep. I remember very well that authenticity and credibility were huge factors in deciding which bands metal fans liked or did not like in the early 1980s. We believed in real guitars, real singing, real keyboards and real drums. Hit singles were OK as long as you didn't try too hard to be 'commercial'. Interestingly, those who bemoaned the use of drum machines and taped instruments on stage thought nothing of their favourite bands singing some of the most hideously misogynist lyrics in the history of music. Nonetheless, Marillion, with their earnest lead singer Fish and his lyrics full of bedsit angst, had credibility in spades. If you add to the band's metal following a smattering of fans, also like me, who were too young to have found Prog during its first flowering, then there was a real audience to be had. Marillion found us first.

The band built up a following during 1981 and the first half of 1982. When Fish announced from the stage at the Reading Festival that the band had signed to EMI, we all felt a huge sense of both disbelief and elation. Progressive Rock was back! The elation continued as the band released a thirty-minute EP featuring three songs from the live set: the exuberant 'Market Square Heroes' the more typical 'Three Boats Down from the Candy' and the epic 'Grendel'. I have always disliked 'Grendel' – to my ears it is weak and derivative – yet this was still a decent enough version and a young band is allowed its moments of naïveté, after all. But the band now needed an album, and that was to be the real challenge.

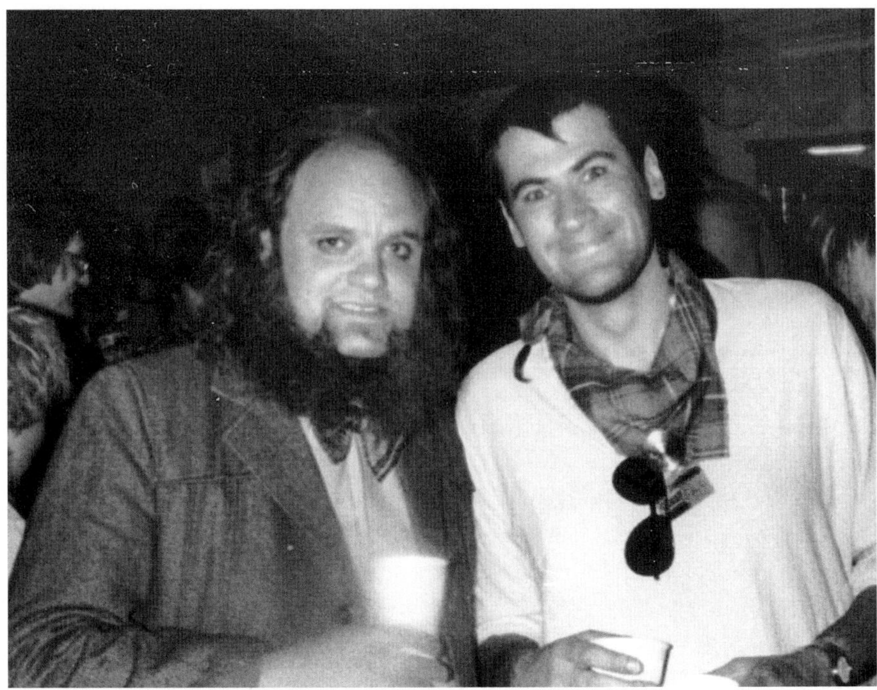

Robert John Godfrey of The Enid and Fish of Marillion in the early 1980s. (*David Robinson*)

Marillion
Script for a Jester's Tear
Released 1983

I remember to this very day the shattering disappointment I felt when I first heard this album in March 1983. The build-up had been feverish. This was to be Progressive Rock's return, but the album sounded so flat, over-produced and lifeless. The studio renditions of familiar tracks seemed so sterile compared to the live versions I had heard previously. Of course, I got over my disappointment pretty quickly and became used to these versions, but I never really warmed to the album completely. Listening to the record on my own, the excitement of joint participation was lost. Following Marillion had been a visceral and exciting experience when they were a live act, but on record the band's limitations became apparent

Nonetheless, it remains an important album, and a fine one given the benefit of hindsight. Marillion were the first band to be signed to a major label, and as the first flowering of a new movement it stands up pretty well. Overall, the material is sincere and impressive. The main instrumentalists – Mark Kelly on keyboards and Steve Rothery on guitar – make fine debuts. Rothery's guitar, in particular, soars impressively, especially on the climactic 'Forgotten Sons', and some of the arrangements show a great deal of imagination. Much of the flatness stems from

Mick Pointer's sluggish drumming, which is swamped by too much reverb and gives the music an unappealing drag at times. Pointer was to be fired a few months later, although it is worth pointing out that his recent career as Arena drummer has demonstrated considerable improvement.

Even on record, however, it is the presence of Fish that dominates. Often accused of verbosity in his lyrics, he nonetheless tackles some impressive and contemporary subjects, from class war in 'Garden Party' (a pithy and relevant subject, particularly in the early 1980s) to a chilling indictment of the treatment of war veterans in 'Forgotten Sons'. He also uses spoken word passages to remarkably telling effect. Often compared to Peter Gabriel, his delivery and lyrical choices owe as much to Peter Hammill as Gabriel, and even David Cousins of The Strawbs is referenced at times.

Unlike most of the Neo-Prog bands, Marillion were allowed a certain amount of artistic freedom as long as the hit singles kept on coming. That difficult second album *Fugazi*, released in 1984, took some gestation as the band had used up most of their material on their first EP and album.

TWELFTH NIGHT – A STORY OF HOW NOT TO DO IT

Meanwhile, life was not quite so easy for some of the other Progressive Rock bands of the early 1980s. The first band out of the blocks towards the end of 1982 was Twelfth Night from Reading. I well remember their appearance at the

Geoff Mann and Clive Mitten of Twelfth Night at the Reading Festival 1983. (*David Robinson*)

Reading Festival in 1982. The band were dressed in white jumpsuits and played an all-instrumental set until singer Geoff Mann made his first appearance with the band for a reworked version of the epic 'Sequences'. I remember walking into town the following morning and buying their self-released *Live at the Target* album. However, of all the Progressive Rock bands from this era, the career of Twelfth Night is perhaps the most frustrating, full of near misses and missed opportunities.

Twelfth Night
Fact and Fiction
Released December 1982

Of all the albums recorded during the early part of the Neo-Progressive era, *Fact and Fiction* is the one most influenced by the pop music around them at the time. It helps, obviously, that Geoff Mann often sounds like Phil Oakey of the Human League, but the title track in particular sounds like a specific and gratuitous attempt to make the charts. Elsewhere, both the material and the execution are somewhat varied, but the longer pieces 'Creepshow' and 'We Are Sane' crackle with madcap danger, and are certainly worth the price of admission, while 'Love Song' straddles the interesting line between the New Romantic movement and Progressive Rock. Overall, it is an important album and very much a product of its time in a way that IQ and Pallas (for instance) were not.

Probably the most frustrating thing about the band is that their recorded work does not quite do them justice, and two of their most important and best-remembered pieces of music – the vocal version of 'Sequences' and 'The Collector' – do not appear on studio albums at all. In fact, while *Fact and Fiction* remains a hugely flawed but important work in the Neo-Prog canon, it is probably *Live and Let Live*, an album recorded during one of Geoff Mann's farewell appearances at the Marquee in 1983, that best represents the band.

In October 1984 Twelfth Night released *Art and Illusion*, featuring new singer Andy Sears. This was a mini-album – a business decision taken by the band's management Hit and Run and later regretted by the band – and was released on the worthy independent label Music for Nations. The band were changing style at that point, moving in a fashionable 1980s direction with hints of bands like Duran Duran, but with a rockier edge. Finally they signed to Virgin, but their self-titled album on that label was a bold failure. It feels pretty inventive for its time and it holds up well alongside Pallas's *The Wedge* as an example of a band attempting to be creative within a strict art-pop template. The superb final track on the Virgin album, 'Take a Look', is a fine summation of a frustrating career that was to peter out later within a year or so, not to be revived until the new millennium.

Euan Lowson of Pallas during 'Crown of Thorns' in the early 1980s. (*David Robinson*)

PALLAS – ARRIVING ALIVE

If Twelfth Night were first out of the blocks in England and Marillion were the proud trailblazers, then Pallas from Scotland were probably the next most successful of the Neo-Progressives. The band had already released an album in 1981, making them technically the first band of the Neo-Progressive movement to put out a piece of vinyl. Pallas's approach was typified by the harder edge of their music and the theatricality of Euan Lowson, perhaps the most extreme of the 1980s Gabriel-inspired singers. His performance of 'The Ripper', which can be found on *Arrive Alive*, built to a chilling climax with Lowson simulating a rape on stage. Check it out on YouTube. It's not pleasant, but it is genuinely terrifying.

Pallas
The Sentinel
Released 1984

The band finally signed to Harvest Records and recruited Eddie Offord to produce their major label debut. However, Harvest got cold feet about releasing the entire *Atlantis Suite* as the album – as the band had intended – and insisted on some of the more commercial material that had appeared on the debut, including the melodic rock song 'Arrive Alive (Eyes in the Night)', which I will admit is my favourite song of theirs from the era. As a result, the album itself, despite a stunning gatefold sleeve by Patrick Woodroffe, feels like a compromise.

On the original vinyl version of the album, the band kicks off with the catchy 'Arrive Alive (Eyes in the Night)' and follows this up with the hard rock of 'Cut and Run'. It is only then that we get the first Atlantis piece, the epic 'Rise and Fall', which has suggestions (unusually for this period) of Yes. Side two opens with the powerful 'Shock Treatment', which is followed by two more epic Atlantis tracks, 'Ark of Infinity' and 'Atlantis'. Many reissued versions restore the tracks originally planned for the rest of the album, alongside epics like 'Crown of Thorns'.

As a casual listener to Pallas rather than a diehard fan, it is interesting to note that much of the material on *The Sentinel* feels pretty fresh today. The Pallas of *XXV*, their 2010 album, might have written the same material – a testament to the quality of their material in the early days.

Pallas were pushed in a more commercial direction after *The Sentinel*, although the *Knightmoves* EP does include the classic 'Sanctuary', and while album *The Wedge*, recorded with diminutive new singer Alan Reed, does contain some excellent Progressive Pop material, it has generally received bad press among Progressive Rock fans. *The Wedge* was to be their last album for ten years.

IQ, PENDRAGON, SOLSTICE AND THE NEO-PROGRESSIVE MOVEMENT

In the same way that most of the 1970s bands, particularly Genesis, often rejected the Progressive Rock tag, IQ have always rejected the Neo-Progressive tag, in particular outspoken keyboard player Martin Orford, one of the most talented musicians to emerge from the movement. These labels tend to exist for those looking in rather than those gazing out, so it is no wonder that they occasionally cause offence. However, to me it fits nicely and I do not consider it an insult in the slightest. These were, after all, bands drawing their influences from the 1970s rather than inventing the genre from scratch.

Orford and guitarist Mike Holmes, two of the most distinctive figures of the 1980s, formed IQ out of the ashes of The Lens and the band recorded a cassette only released in 1982, followed in 1983 by their first album proper, *Tales from the Lush Attic* on Samurai, which included the much-lauded epic 'The Last Human Gateway'.

IQ
The Wake
Released June 1985

Like the music of Pallas, an interesting feature of *The Wake* is how little the basic building blocks of IQ's music have changed in the intervening twenty-five years.

Peter Nicholls of IQ onstage in the early 1980s. (*David Robinson*)

True, *The Wake* is not the finest recorded album ever; the lead vocals often get lost in the mix and the drums sound like old boxes. In addition, some of the music is rather naïve, but the material and playing are as good as anything they have recorded since. The bass playing of Tim Essau (back with the band as of 2011) particularly stands out, but the album belongs to the delightful keyboard work of Martin Orford. Whereas his contemporaries were producing thin or synthetic keyboard sounds, Orford's palate was huge, powerful and grandiose, as shown on his intro for 'The Magic Roundabout'. It is not difficult to imagine him in a 1970s band. The material, too, was usually excellent, with the occasional surprising lightness of touch among the bombast. Unusually for the band, the song 'Corners' features a robotic rhythm based on a drum machine pattern.

After the relative lack of success of *The Wake*, the band began to move in a poppier direction with new singer Paul Menel, who replaced Peter Nicholls in 1986. The two albums that resulted from his tenure with the band (which were both released on the Vertigo label) have a mixed reputation. Like Twelfth Night, the band had acquired a major deal a little too late. For some, the poppier material and 1980s production irritate, while to others those albums were gateway albums for the band and the genre.

Pendragon were a slightly different proposition. Having supported many of the up-and-coming bands from the early 1980s, they put out two albums in the 1980s. The well-received debut *The Jewel* mixed song-orientated material with Marillion-esque keyboards and Nick Barrett's fluid guitar playing, plus a remarkably mobile rhythm section. The band's attempts to sign to a major deal got some interest from EMI but a deal failed to materialise, so the band formed their own label, Toff Records, in 1987 for the slightly more commercial *KowTow*. The time for Pendragon was still to come.

Although part of a relatively small movement, bands like Quasar, Abel Ganz and Haze had a particular sound about them. They generally had male vocalists and were a little rough around the edges, although their influences tended to come from Peter Gabriel-era Genesis, with bands like Yes, Camel and Pink Floyd thrown in to varying degrees. Add to that some metal, a touch of punk and a large dose of the 1980s pop, and these were the main influences that informed Progressive Rock in the early and mid-1980s.

SOLSTICE GET FOLKY

Not so Solstice. While the band – led by guitarist Andy Glass and violinist/keyboard player Mark Elton – were happy to be part of the same movement as these other bands, they had a very different agenda. Hailing from Milton Keynes, the band were hippies when hippies were deeply unfashionable. Taking a strong New Age world view, the band began to build a live following in early 1983 with the help of a rigorous touring schedule and an early appearance on the cover of *Sounds*. Sonically, the band owed its allegiances to folk music, Yes and Camel, but crucially the sound that the band wanted required female vocals, and so the early incarnation of the band had a long succession of singers.

Unlike Pendragon and IQ, Solstice were given a recording contract by EMI in the early days, and went out on a three-band package tour in 1984 with Pallas and Trilogy. The album, as often happened during this era, could have been better. The material was good, and included the classic 'Brave New World' and the dramatic 'Cheyenne', both in the band's live set today. However, the primitive recording and production style failed to capture the spirit of the band's live performances, and the momentum was lost. The band called it a day in 1985 with much of their best material unreleased. As with Pendragon, their time was to come.

MARILLION STRIKE GOLD WITH 'KAYLEIGH'

Marillion
Misplaced Childhood
Released June 1985

It often happens that a band releases their finest work when moving between styles. The version of Marillion that recorded *Misplaced Childhood* was moving out of the

Script for a Jester's Tear phase into something both more adult and more accessible. After the difficult but reasonably successful *Fugazi,* Marillion began work on that most hideous of things, the concept album. Less brooding than the lyrical content of *Fugazi,* but still emotionally complex, the band linked their songs together while keeping the melodic content exceptionally high. I saw the band play side one of the album early in 1985 at Hammersmith Odeon, several months before release, and it is indeed the first side that stands out as the major part of the work, treading as it does a careful line between sonic invention and pop melodicism.

It opens in typically brooding style before breaking into the massive hit single 'Kayleigh'. Whereas the singles from the earlier two albums had been bought by rock fans, 'Kayleigh' penetrated the UK public consciousness like no other song in Progressive Rock with the exception of 'Dust in the Wind', which had done pretty much the same thing for Kansas in the USA in 1977. It lifted Fish from rock star to a public figure overnight. 'Lavender' and the triumphant 'Heart of Lothian' were also hits, although 'Bitter Suite', sandwiched between them, is perhaps the finest piece on the album, with some delicious keyboards from Mark Kelly. Side two is less impressive musically, although it has its moments, particularly the opening 'Waterhole (Expresso Bongo)' and the closing 'White Feather', but elsewhere it feels a little wordy and less distinctive musically in comparison to side one, which remains a high-water mark in Progressive Rock.

Misplaced Childhood was also to be the high-water mark for Marillion themselves. Deservedly, the album was a huge global success, leaving the band with much to live up to. Relationships between Fish and the band began to falter as a result of this, and *Clutching at Straws*, with the benefit of hindsight, shows why. An album about addiction and alienation, it contains some openly autobiographical lyrics based around a character called 'Torch'. Much too downbeat to be the success that its predecessor had been, it still did well enough in the UK, and included some hit singles in 'Incommunicado' and 'Sugar Mice' as well as some fan favourites in 'White Russian' and 'Slàinte Mhath'. The tour was not a happy time, and neither were attempts to record a new album in 1988, so Fish left the band. Most felt that Marillion was over. Some, like me, felt that this was an opportunity to change a name that might have seemed bearable in 1982, but in 1989 seemed a little, well, silly. Nobody read Tolkien any more, surely? After some auditions that included contributions from Stu Nicholson of Galahad and Nigel Voyle of Welsh band Cyan (later to morph into Magenta), the band finally carried on with singer Steve Hogarth and suffered a drop in record sales, despite the excellence of their 1989 album *Season's End*. Marillion's major label days were numbered.

THE VOICE AND THE VENUE

The Neo-Prog movement burned brightly but briefly. That such a vibrant (if small) movement should have, in Marillion, only one major success is an absurdity, but the truth is that the record companies missed the boat by signing other bands too late and then failing to give them the support they needed to put out the albums that they wanted to make. But the interference-free days of the early 1970s were over. I expected another golden period for Progressive Rock. I was to be disappointed.

What successes the movement had were boosted by two important contributors. While many bands had places to play locally, in London the movement coalesced around the Marquee club in Wardour Street in the same way as it had at the end of the 1960s. As I was away at university in Newcastle-under-Lyme in 1982 and 1983, so my trips to the Marquee were limited, but I remember the atmosphere, the heat and the distinctive black decor. As a venue it supported punk, metal and Neo-Prog; the size of the crowd and the quality of the support were vital barometers of how a band was progressing. Playing the Marquee was special, as was having a session on the *Friday Rock Show*. This was a late-night programme on BBC Radio 1 featuring tracks from metal and Prog bands that ran from 1978 until 1993. The opening show was a broadcast of Yes live at Wembley. To be featured on the show – in particular, to be able to record a session for the show at the BBC's legendary studios at Maida Vale – was a high point in any young band's career. A huge supporter of the Neo-Progressive movement was its presenter, the honey-voiced Tommy Vance, whose enthusiasm and knowledge were vital in the development of the movement, even if it was short-lived. Vance died in 2005 at the age of sixty-five, and we miss him. All six Neo-Progressive bands that I have discussed still exist in some form today. They all had talent, and they all deserved better. Eventually, they found it.

BACK TO THE MAINSTREAM

Aside from the invention to be found in art-pop and the last twitching of the Neo-Prog movement, the late 1980s were the bleakest years for Progressive Rock fans. I remained on the lookout for the odd moment of Prog in mainstream music, and occasionally found it, often hidden within the stadium rock that became so lucrative towards the end of the 1980s. As already mentioned, American band Toto remained a good source, for instance 'Change of Heart' from *Isolation*, with its extended middle section, or 'Home of the Brave' from *The Seventh One*, another extended track with multiple sections were a pleasant and rewarding surprise. Pink Floyd emerged without Roger Waters to release a pretty decent comeback album in *A Momentary Lapse of Reason*.

I also remember watching the TV chat show *Wogan* in 1986 for my first introduction to a band called It Bites. At first glance, the band looked like any other mid-1980s pop group, all big hair and glossy production, but – hang on – wasn't that a quirky time signature? The band's debut single 'Calling All the Heroes' was a big hit in the UK, and the cover of their debut album *The Big Lad in the Windmill* recalled the 1970s, even if the content only hinted at a Prog sensibility.

It Bites
Once Around the World
Released April 1988

The band's second album charted in the UK and showed that the band had moved on a little from the pop sensibilities of *The Big Lad in the Windmill*. While side one of the record (I bought it on vinyl initially) ploughs a pop and rock furrow, side two, almost unexpectedly, becomes a full-on Progressive Rock album. 'Old Man and the Angel', initially available only as a 12-inch single for the full version unless you bought the CD, is deliciously complex in its long instrumental section, while 'Plastic Dreamer' weaves lovely vocal patterns around its main melody. However, the biggest surprise (unless you had seen the band live, as it was a mainstay of their live set in 1986) was the fourteen-minute title track, a Genesis-inspired mixture of hard rock, Progressive Rock, guitar pyrotechnics and Dixieland jazz. The stars of the album were Francis Dunnery for the versatility of his guitar work and particularly keyboard player John Beck, who was able to mix classic 1980s block chords with Prog invention.

The band were to move in a hard rock direction before disintegrating at the end of the decade, but for Progressive Rock fans at the end of the 1980s, this album was an oasis in a huge desert. Perhaps something was stirring, however. In 1989, Jon Anderson, Steve Howe, Rick Wakeman and Bill Bruford made an album with several epic tracks and a cover by Roger Dean. It was not quite Yes, but it *was* Prog. Perhaps there was some hope after all.

7

ART AND ILLUSION: COVER ART AND DESIGN

Given that much of the appeal of Progressive Rock is derived from atmosphere and dynamics, it is no surprise that album cover design has always been an important factor in the development of the genre. When the 12-inch long-player was first developed, the usual form was to put a picture of the artist on the album cover. It was The Beatles that first began to challenge this. It is true that there is no Beatles album that does not have some sort of depiction of the band on its cover except *The White Album*, but both Klaus Voormann's cartoonish cover for *Revolver* and the famous Peter Blake collage that adorned *Sgt. Pepper's Lonely Hearts Club Band* suggested a different way, and Progressive Rock artists took full advantage of it.

By the 1970s specially commissioned paintings tended to dominate, often by specific artists that became synonymous with certain groups. An exemplary early artist was Barry Godber, who painted the astonishing cover of King Crimson's *In the Court of the Crimson King*. Had he not died so early in life, he might have designed covers for countless Progressive Rock albums.

ROGER DEAN

The king of these auteurs was a polite, well-educated English gentleman called Roger Dean. Dean is best known for his work with Yes, but he also designed albums for Greenslade, Gentle Giant and Uriah Heep among many. Compare, for instance, his work with Gentle Giant and his work with Yes, and it is clear that his muse lies with Yes. 'Give us an octopus, Roger,' someone has clearly said to him in the discussions for 1972's best-known Gentle Giant album, and that is precisely what he has given them. It is a Roger Dean octopus, for sure, but there's little imagination there. Compare that to *Close to the Edge* by Yes, from the same year. This was the same album that first introduced the serpentine Yes logo. The front cover of the album is a triumph of minimalism, a green cover shading from dark to bright, with the title and the name of the band at the top. However,

Right: A very dapper Roger Dean introduces AOR supergroup Asia at the High Voltage Festival in 2010. (*Neil Palfreyman*)

Below: The stunning gatefold painting of *Close to the Edge*, one of Roger Dean's finest. (*Rhino*)

open up the gatefold sleeve and real treasures are revealed – Dean's extraordinary skyscape, a lake seemingly perched on the top of the world with waterfalls cascading into clouds. Impressive though this image is on the remastered 1993 Rhino version on CD, the impact of the 12-inch vinyl gatefold on a sixteen-year-old kid with an overactive imagination is unrepeatable.

Dean's covers for Yes albums have been hugely popular. The band has occasionally drifted away from him to use other designers, but it is interesting to note that whenever they decide to go back to basics – which has happened more than once over the years, from 1980's *Drama* album to 1998's *The Ladder* and of course 2011's *Fly from Here* – they return to a Dean design, as if they need to say, 'Look, we want you to know that we are still the band you know and love, so here's a Roger Dean cover to reassure you.'

As a result, Dean remains the most important figure in Progressive Rock art and design.

PAUL WHITEHEAD

Synonymous with Tony Stratton Smith's Charisma label rather than any specific band except perhaps Genesis, Paul Whitehead's surreal and very English compositions graced some very important albums of the early 1970s. A very distinctive artist, although perhaps not quite as instantly recognisable as Roger Dean, he designed the first three Genesis albums for Charisma, *Trespass*, *Nursery*

Paul Whitehead's famous cover for *Foxtrot* by Genesis. (*Chrysalis*)

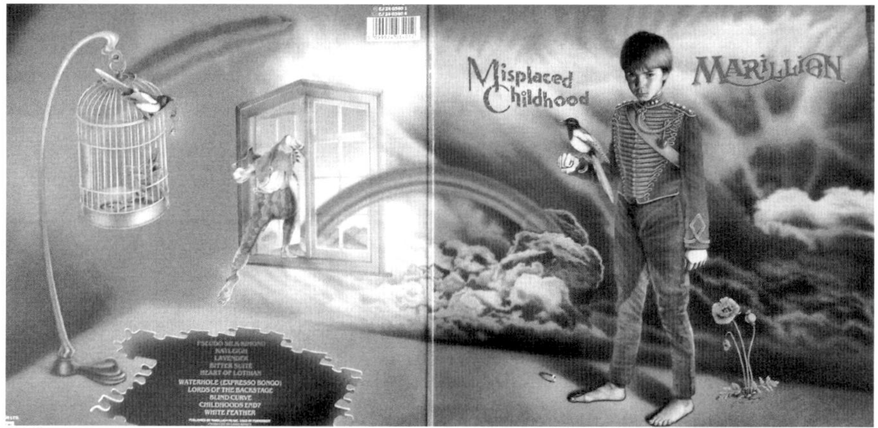

The stunning Paul Wilkinson cover for Marillion's *Misplaced Childhood*. (*EMI*)

Cryme and *Foxtrot*, as well as several albums from the Van der Graaf Generator stable, including *Pawn Hearts* and the Peter Hammill classic *Fool's Mate*. Other albums included several with Italian band Le Orme and various albums with the newer breed of Progressive Rock artists. Like Dean, he has maintained his links with the contemporary Progressive Rock community, exhibiting at Nearfest and designing the logo for the festival in 2000.

MARK WILKINSON

Moving forward ten years, Mark Wilkinson has become closely linked to the Fish-era albums and singles of Marillion. His work is clean, colourful and beautifully accurate, but the surreal and allegorical nature of his covers is another thing entirely. Two images became important linking factors in his albums and singles with Marillion: the two-faced jester first introduced on the band's first 12-inch single 'Market Square Heroes', and the drummer boy used for the band's best-known album *Misplaced Childhood* and on the massive hit single 'Kayleigh'.

HIPGNOSIS

Best known for its work with Pink Floyd, the Hipgnosis agency – first constituted to work on the second Pink Floyd album, *A Saucerful of Secrets* – became famous in the 1970s for a different type of cover art. The agency, led by Storm Thorgerson and Aubrey Powell, specialised in photographic set pieces rather than artwork, most famously the astonishing cover of Pink Floyd's *Animals*, where an inflatable pig is suspended over Battersea Power Station. Today, this sort of cover night have been produced using Adobe Photoshop, yet often the Hipgnosis team set up visually striking and complex shots live, often going to great expense to do so.

The agency became more fashionable as the 1970s wore on and designed covers for many of the key Progressive Rock acts of the 1970s, including Genesis (the striking cover for *The Lamb Lies Down on Broadway* being one, though they also designed the more florid *Wind & Wuthering*), Yes (including the much-derided *Going for the One* and *Tormato* covers) and Peter Gabriel (the first three self-titled albums). Despite Hipgnosis's reputation for innovation, not every album was of the highest quality, and their company policy of only asking artists to pay what they thought the cover was worth occasionally backfired on them. Renaissance's *Ashes Are Burning* has simply a poor band photograph with a logo dumped on the top, although later covers like *A Song for All Seasons* were much better.

OTHER DESIGN TRENDS

Were there any other unifying factors that set Progressive Rock cover design apart? Broadly speaking, no, although the trend towards illustrating the lyrics rather than the artist was particularly prevalent in Progressive Rock. This was not always a subtle device. That Caravan chose to illustrate *Girls that Grow Plump in the Night* with the image of a slumbering woman was both obvious and in keeping with the very English humour of the band. The stunning and very influential cover of Emerson, Lake & Palmer's *Brain Salad Surgery* from 1973, painted by Swiss surrealist painter H. R. Giger, had to be toned down for sexual content, while their 1971 classic *Tarkus* was illustrated with a huge amount of artistic licence by British painter William Neal, who depicted the title character as half-armadillo, half-tank.

Artists were not always completely absent from their covers. A character not unlike Ian Anderson often appeared on the cover of Jethro Tull albums (see *Aqualung* and *Too Old to Rock 'n' Roll: Too Young to Die!*) despite Anderson's frequent denials that these figures actually depicted him. *Trilogy* by ELP showed the three band members in profile, looking not unlike Roman emperors, and King Crimson's *Red* is both Beatle-esque and starkly modern, pre-empting the grittier work to come towards the end of the 1970s.

In the 1980s, the DIY nature of the music was mirrored by the album artwork. Budding artists like Peter Nicholls of IQ designed their own covers, both for artistic reasons and to keep costs down. When artists like Marillion or Pallas were able to sign major label contracts, more money could be spent – as the stunning gatefold sleeve designed by painter Patrick Woodroffe that came with *The Sentinel* was able to show. Steve Hackett's late 1970s and early 1980s solo albums have a wonderful continuity to them – usually portraits of Steve painted by his then-wife Kim Poor in that distinctive airbrushed style of hers.

1. Yes in 1974, on the *Tales from Topographic Oceans* tour in the USA. Note Roger and Martin Dean's stage design. (*Rich Greene*)

2. Bill Bruford, that most travelled of Progressive Rock drummers, played in Yes, King Crimson, Genesis, UK and his own band, Bruford. (*James Cumpsty, www.billbruford.com*)

3, 4, 5. Three famous guitarists. Clockwise from top left: Steve Howe of Yes, Anthony Phillips, the first Genesis guitarist, and Steve Hackett, the second Genesis guitarist. (*Chris Walkden*)

6, 7. Progressive Rock's two great keyboard players. Right, Keith Emerson onstage at Nearfest in 2006 with his huge modular Moog synthesiser (*Kevin Scherer*). Below, Rick Wakeman onstage at a Classic Rock Society concert in 2002. His keyboard rig contains modern digital machine the Korg Triton and a vintage Minimoog. (*Chris Walkden*).

Above: 8. Carl Palmer of ELP and Asia onstage at the High Voltage Festival in London, 2010. (*Neil Palfreyman*)

Left: 9. Richard Sinclair of Caravan and Hatfield and the North at Nearfest. (*Kevin Sherer*)

10. 11, 12. Two flautists and a singer. Clockwise from top left: Ian Anderson of Jethro Tull at the High Voltage Festival, July 2011 (*Neil Palfreyman*), Thijs Van Leer of Focus (*Stephen Lambe*), and Peter Hammill of Van der Graaf Generator (*Kevin Scherer*).

Left: 13. Frank Bornemann of German Prog pioneers Eloy at the Night of the Prog Festival, Loreley, 2011. (*Neil Palfreyman*)

Below left: 14. Franco Mussida of Italian band PFM at Nearfest. (*Kevin Scherer*)

Below right: 15. Christian Décamps of French band Ange, also at Nearfest. (*Kevin Scherer*)

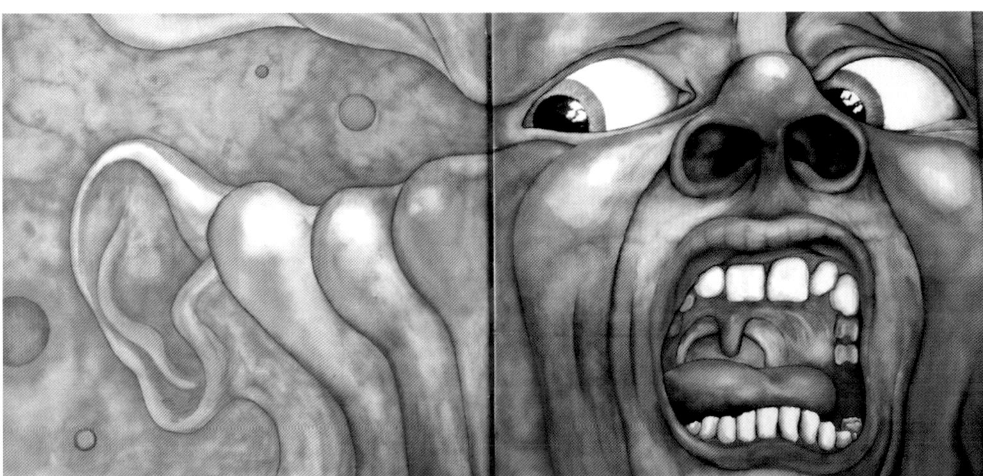

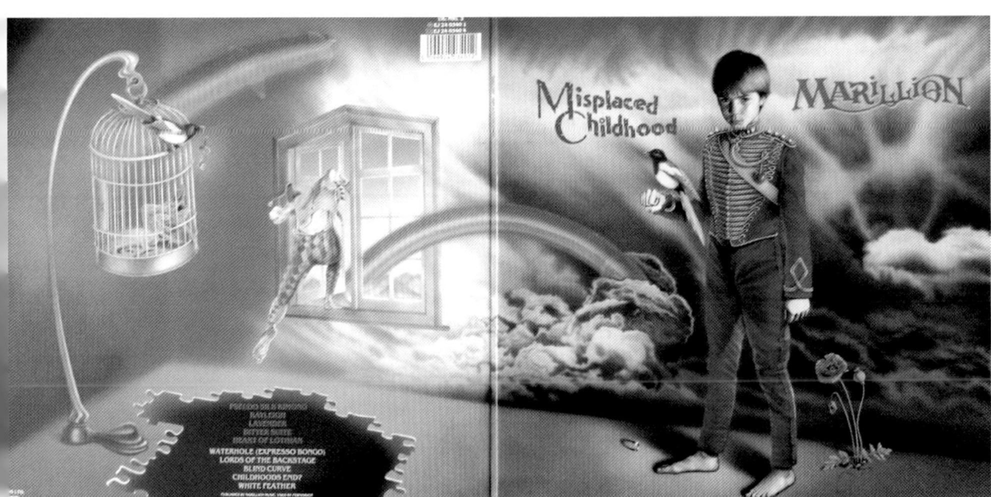

16, 17, 18. Classic gatefold sleeves. From top to bottom: the inner gatefold of *Close to the Edge* by Yes, designed by Roger Dean (*Atlantic*), *In the Court of the Crimson King* by King Crimson, designed by Barry Godber (*EG*), and *Misplaced Childhood* by Marillion, designed by Mark Wilkinson (*EMI*).

19, 20. Two very different bass players:. Left, Tony Levin, star of the 1980s incarnation of King Crimson and a long-term member of Peter Gabriel's band (*Kevin Scherer*). Below, Geddy Lee and the huge Rush stage set in 2010 (*Peter Hutchins*).

Above: 21, 22. Fish onstage with Marillion in the early 1980s (*David Robinson*) and in concert in 2006 (*Chris Walkden*).

Below: 23. Peter Nicholls of IQ (in typically heavy make-up) and Geoff Mann of Twelfth Night together in concert in the early 1980s. (*David Robinson*)

Above left: 24. Alan Reed of Pallas at the Marquee in the mid-1980s. (*David Robinson*)

Above right: 25. Pallas onstage in Wath in Yorkshire in March 2011. (*Chris Walkden*)

26. Sandy Leigh, the singer in an early Solstice line-up in 1983. (*David Robinson*)

27, 28. Two faces of Nick Barrett of Pendragon. Above, onstage with Pete Gee in the mid-1980s, and below, in a typical pose in 2011. (*Chris Walkden*)

29, 30, 31. Heroes of the 1990s revival. Clockwise from top left: Thomas Johnson of Änglagård (*Chris Walkden*), Brett Kull of Echolyn (*Kevin Scherer*), and Sylvia Erichsen and Jacob Holm-Lupo of White Willow (*Stephen Lambe*).

32. 33, 34. The leading lights of the New Progressive movement. Clockwise from top left: Steven Wilson of Porcupine Tree (*Neil Palfreyman*), Roine Stolt of The Flower Kings at the Summer's End Festival in 2010 (*Chris Walkden*) and brothers Neal and Alan Morse at an emotional Spock's Beard reunion during the High Voltage Festival in July 2011 (*Neil Palfreyman*).

35. The amazing effects during the Genesis reunion tour in 2007. Note the shots of Peter Gabriel in 'Supper's Ready' flower outfit on the screen. (*Neil Palfreyman*)

36. A big crowd watch Dream Theater at the Night of the Prog Festival, Loreley, July 2011. (*Neil Palfreyman*)

37, 38, 39. Three of the new female stars making waves in Progressive Rock. Clockwise from top left:Christina Booth of Magenta (*Chris Walkden*), Amy Darby of Thieves' Kitchen (*Chris Walkden*) and Emma Brown of Solstice (*Stephen Lambe*).

40, 41, 42. Three of the busiest men in modern Progressive Rock at the start of the new millennium. Anticlockwise from top: bassist John Jowitt of Arena, Ark and formerly IQ, guitarist and singer John Mitchell of It Bites, Arena, Kino and Frost*, and singer and multi-instrumentalist Daniel Gildenlow of Pain of Salvation and Transatlantic. (*Chris Walkden*)

This continued into the CD era, when design, understandably, became less vital to the overall perception of an album. In this brave new download-only world of the new millennium, the need for visual art that is not on film or video has all but ended. What is the point, for instance, of spending a fortune on album cover design when the casing is only a few inches across? Having said that, the Retro-Progressive movement of the new millennium *has* inspired some interesting artwork. Killusion of Germany, for instance, while more normally associated with the dark world of extreme metal, produced some brilliantly stylised covers for bands like Norway's White Willow, and one particularly gruesome cover for Welsh band Magenta's 2008 album *Metamorphosis*.

ED UNITSKY

If Roger Dean dominated the 1970s and Mark Wilkinson the 1980s, then the most important figure since the turn of the millennium has been Ed Unitsky from Belarus. It is no coincidence that the world of the internet has allowed talented people, whether they are musicians or visual artists, to make careers for themselves. In the great tradition of Progressive Rock artists, Ed produces spellbinding fantasy landscapes, often in direct collaboration with the artists themselves. Although occasionally reminiscent of what has gone before, more usually his work has a strong character of its own, with extreme detailing so unusual for CD reproduction that it almost feels wasted. Nonetheless, his

:the music that died alone

Ed Unitsky's cover for The Tangent's debut, *The Music that Died Alone*. His stunning artwork cries out for a gatefold sleeve. (*Inside Out*)

The distinctive 'Mad Hatter' Charisma label. (*Virgin*)

work is so reminiscent of the 1970s that contemporary Progressive Rock artists, particularly those that favour a retro style, have flocked to him, and it does not seem to matter that the eventual size of his reproduced work means that it is impossible for it to be as immersive as it would have been in the vinyl era.

VINYL LABELS

Imagine the ritualistic thrill of playing a 12-inch album. You examine the front and back and read the track titles, wondering what they will sound like. You open up the gatefold and take in the panorama that opens up for you. Then you take the inner record cover out of its sleeve and remove the vinyl disc itself. Hopefully it is a heavy grade of vinyl, although the medium became lighter and poorer in quality as the 1970s and 1980s drew on. The final thing you see before you put the album on the spindle of your turntable is the record company label. To me, these are as evocative as anything else in the record-listening process. As a Yes obsessive, the green, white and orange Atlantic label was always very familiar, but of course most Progressive Rock fans will have been equally excited by the 'Mad Hatter' Charisma label, which was far more evocative and English than the original pink label. For me, the A&M label meant Progressive Rock rather than the easy listening artists most associated with the label and even the resoundingly boring orange Epic label held a wonderful mystique. It was all part of the experience.

8

THE 1990S: SIGNS OF LIFE

As the 1980s gave way to the 1990s, the world was largely devoid of Progressive Rock. However, the history of popular music always runs in cycles, and something was stirring. The fact that this 'something' was called grunge and based in Seattle is not as irrelevant as it may seem. The beginning of the 1980s had seen a new creativity among songwriters as the rawness of punk had gained sophistication. However, by the end of the decade many of these bands had either become huge international brands, like Tears for Fears, or had moved into rather more experimental waters, like Talk Talk. The 1980s were also synonymous with the 'hair metal' of Bon Jovi and Guns N' Roses, who sold out huge venues and made massive amounts of money for promoters, labels and drug dealers. Meanwhile, former indie bands like U2 from Ireland were also tapping into the zeitgeist and had joined the posse of bands flocking towards the arenas and stadiums.

The whole concept of stadium rock had begun in the 1970s, of course, with events like the ELP-headlined California Jam. The biggest Progressive Rock bands had played their part in the development of a stadium circuit in the USA. The picture of Steve Walsh of Kansas screaming into a microphone on a summer's day in front of a huge stadium of people somewhere in the USA *circa* 1978 lingers in my memory. I would love to have been there. By the end of the 1980s there were no Prog bands playing this circuit. Not even Yes. Once again, the rock world had lost touch with its audience, and it was time for a change.

Grunge had first begun to emerge in the mid-1980s and it exploded onto the rock scene with the huge commercial success of Nirvana, Soundgarden, Alice in Chains and Pearl Jam in the early 1990s. Mixing metal with a touch of punk and the alternative rock that had also been emerging towards the end of the 1980s, this new movement brought with it a new DIY ethic that seemed to affect *all* music in the same way that punk had nearly fifteen years earlier. This coincided with the rise of house music in Europe and the development of rave culture, which itself grew out of the alternative festivals circuit so cruelly repressed in Margaret Thatcher's Britain of the mid-1980s.

What did this mean for Progressive Rock? By 1989 my interest had waned so much that I did not even bother to see Anderson Bruford Wakeman Howe when they played London towards the end of 1989, although I did buy the album. I still followed Marillion, although I was not sure what to make of new singer Steve Hogarth. The Neo-Progressive movement limped on at the end of the 1980s. IQ's late 1980s attempts at commercialism failed and they were dropped by their label Squawk, part of Vertigo. Some new bands, like Ark from the West Midlands, did emerge, although their timing was not the best and they were active at the Neo-Progressive movement's lowest ebb.

However, there were stirrings. In the late 1980s, Utah-based enthusiast Greg Walker started the Syn-Phonic mail-order business, followed by Malcolm Parker's GFT business in the UK in 1992. Parker's Cyclops label began in 1994, aiming initially to give a home to new British bands making music in the Prog style but also taking on overseas acts where he saw potential. Initially, Cyclops was just a vehicle to release music that had already been recorded, but as the business grew, Parker was able to advance money to bands to record in the way that a conventional label would. The role of these two individuals is hard to understate. Walker in the USA and Parker in the UK, alongside perhaps Ken Golden of Laser's Edge in the US and David Robinson of F2 in the UK, pioneered the promotion of Progressive Rock worldwide. They took the germ of an idea – that perhaps a market still existed for Progressive Rock – and made it a reality. Elsewhere, opportunities were also developing. By the middle of the 1990s, the Musea label in France and Progress Records in Sweden (run by Hansi Cross of Swedish band Cross) were doing the same thing. The pattern for all these organisations was consistent. Not only did they run mail-order organisations, collecting together as many artists from as many different sources as they could negotiate, they also acted as low-budget labels and distributors, with their own roster of artists. For all these organisations working on a shoestring, the development of the CD was important, since they were easier to package and store. Vinyl, romantic though it was, is always difficult to post. It also has to be remembered that even in the early 1990s, the most obvious and cost-effective way for an artist to duplicate and distribute their music was via cassette. These new labels gave them access to the then-expensive process of CD duplication.

The best-known organisation to emerge during this period was the German label Inside Out. Formed by Thomas Weber in 1996, the label began by providing distribution for US artists like Shadow Gallery before developing its own roster of American and European artists. Although heavily handicapped by the failure of parent distributor SPV in 2009, Inside Out remains the best route to market for any aspiring Progressive Rock band, and the majority of the biggest acts to emerge in the 1990s had their biggest sales when signed to the label.

After a few years in the wilderness, I returned to the Progressive Rock fold in around 1994. At the time, Malcolm Parker of GFT would advertise his wares in the back of the more serious UK music magazines. It is likely that I first saw

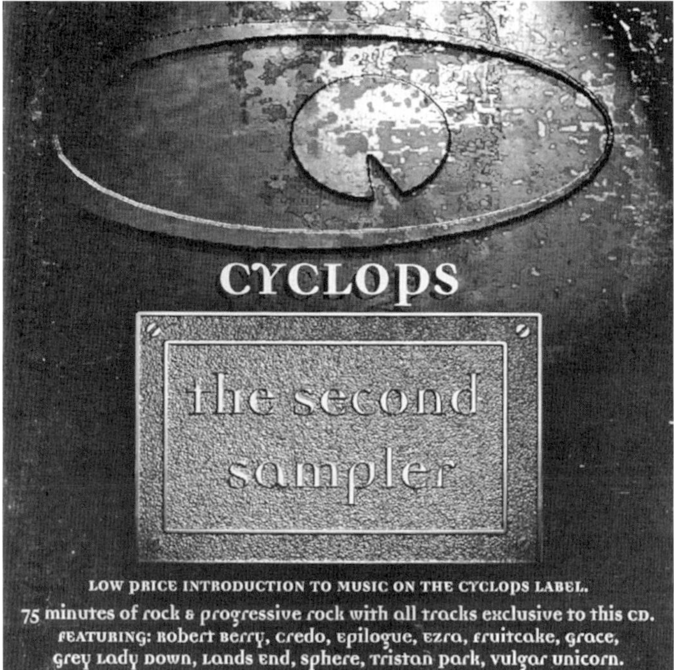

The Second Cyclops Sampler. As 1990s as Cool Britannia and *Ab Fab*. (*Cyclops*)

an advertisement in the back of *Q* magazine, though the creation of *Mojo* in 1993, with its deliberately retro classic rock slant, also provided a vital medium for such businesses. I bought the first of six samplers released between 1994 and 2006 by the label. These samplers were essential in re-introducing me to a genre I had loved, and the music was a real eye-opener, even though the actual quality was hugely variable.

Music choices were made by leafing through GFT's huge and endearingly amateurish photocopied catalogue. Pre-internet, there was no way to hear the music without buying the album. Chances needed to be taken and as a result mistakes were sometimes made, yet purchasers learned to trust Malcolm's workmanlike descriptions. If Malcolm told you that X sounded like Y, you believed him, and this minimised the failures. Nonetheless, everyone who bought CDs from him has items in their collections that they hate. It was all part of the fun. It always intrigued me, however, that Malcolm would use the conventions and clichés of Progressive Rock as selling points. It is understandable that he should do this, yet to market an album as having 'three tracks over ten minutes long' or a 'twenty-minute multi-part suite' struck me as one-dimensional. Should a piece of music not be whatever length it needs to be? If you start out with a twenty-minute piece in mind, well, you are likely to get *Tales from Topographic Oceans*, for better or for worse.

The Second Cyclops Sampler
Released 1995

Of the six Cyclops samplers, I have chosen the second one, released in 1995. According to the inner sleeve, there were twenty-nine albums in the Cyclops catalogue at that point, but this is the one I feel best represents the character of the label at the time; it certainly contains the music I played the most often. It is a fascinating snapshot of where the UK Progressive Rock industry was in the mid-1990s. Interestingly, Parker was always at pains to present new songs or alternative versions so that the samplers could be bought in their own right and the purchaser did not feel ripped off. With the benefit of hindsight, he perhaps went too far with this, so some of the samplers represent a ragbag of music rather than the best of what the label had to offer, but on this sampler Cyclops is well represented.

The album kicks off with 'Dirty World' from American Robert Berry. Berry is an interesting figure. Like Billy Sherwood, he has skirted the fringes of the mainstream Progressive Rock world for many years. As well as playing in 3 with Carl Palmer and Keith Emerson, he also joined the Hackett and Howe AOR vehicle GTR just as they were imploding, and his excellent *Pilgrimage to a Point* album remains a personal favourite. 'Dirty World', however, is a good pop song, but does not represent his Prog leanings. Credo's 'The Letter' is still a live favourite with the resurgent new version of the band, and contains strong hints of Fish-era Marillion. 'Please' by the little-known Staffordshire band Epilogue is a typical song of the era, a Pallas-inspired slice of pop-rock with a strong synth riff. Welsh band Ezra, another band still with us today, provide the Floyd-influenced 'Somewhere', not their finest moment. Norwegians Fruitcake give us the deliciously lush yet brief 'Where I've Been'.

Another band from Staffordshire, Grace, were the local Prog heroes when I was at university there in the early 1980s, and their track 'The Miracle' represented a real resurgence for them as one of the Cyclops label's best bands. The same can be said for Grey Lady Down, who were the best-selling band on the label throughout the 1990s. From the ebullience of the biography in the booklet of this sampler, it would seem that they were about to hit the mainstream, citing gig slots with Pendragon and The Enid as well as performances with 1990s stalwarts Jadis. Certainly, their music had all the right ingredients to appeal to the Neo-Prog fans that had survived the 1980s, but despite a big following they never escaped beyond the confines of the Prog community, and the band came to a end in the early 2000s, only to re-emerge in 2011. The live version of 'The Flyer', featured here, is typical of the band's output.

US band Lands End were another favourite, with a leisurely, almost ambient, keyboard-based approach that I really enjoyed. I particularly loved their obsession with analogue synths. Sphere's 'Three Simple Words' is interesting in that it represents an early attempt at a sound that was eventually to develop into fully-fledged fusion. It treads a line between Neo-Prog and something more complex and does it rather successfully. An all-instrumental version of the band would eventually change its name to Sphere3 and release an album a few years later. However, I rather like this version of the band, with its Genesis and Camel influences. Next it is back to the US for another band with promise, Tristan Park, and their rather catchy 'The Space Between'. The album finishes with 'Lost for Ever/Supersmoke', a surprisingly adventurous track from Vulgar Unicorn, a band that featured Bruce Soord, later to front the post-rock Cyclops band The Pineapple Thief.

Revisiting this album has been a poignant and rewarding experience. First of all, it holds up exceptionally well from an artistic point of view. Several of the bands featured still exist, though only Credo and Grey Lady Down, both active again after long breaks, play live with any regularity. Both Cyclops and GFT have been through tough times in recent years. Malcolm Parker was slow to embrace the internet as a medium and while both mail-order business and label still exist, the rise of Amazon and the ability of bands to exist independently of labels mean that both have shrunk to shadows of their former selves. But as all the Progressive Rock fans in the UK who returned to the genre in the 1990s will testify, we owe him a debt of thanks. The USA owes the same debt to Greg Walker.

NEO-PROG IN THE 1990S

By the end of the 1980s, the very British Neo-Progressive movement had gone underground, but maintained a reasonable grassroots following. Grey Lady Down on the Cyclops label and Gary Chandler's Jadis (which included Martin Orford and John Jowitt of IQ for a while) were the leading lights of that movement, but the most successful of these bands were Arena. The band formed in 1995 when former Marillion drummer Mick Pointer teamed up with Clive Nolan of Pendragon. The band has had something of a revolving-door membership since then, but has the distinction of being the first group to introduce John Mitchell to the world. As a guitarist and singer, the talented Mitchell was to loom large over the UK Progressive Rock scene, and eventually became the replacement for Francis Dunnery in a resurgent It Bites. Arena's music is grandiose and dramatic, with a deliberately epic sweep, and is best typified by *The Visitor*, released in 1998, although all their albums, with compositions mainly by Nolan, are worthy of attention by those who like a little melodrama in their Prog.

Solstice
Circles
Released 1997

While IQ found their feet after the return of Peter Nicholls, for Solstice this renewed interest and the re-release of their first album suggested to Andy Glass that he should reform a version of the band to release their unrecorded 1980s songs. The resulting album, *New Life*, contained superb material but was not quite

The cover for the reissue of *Circles* by Solstice, with trademark mandala. (*F2*)

as well recorded as it might have been. While the *New Life* line-up did not continue for long, a further line-up with young vocalist Emma Brown now fronting the band recorded an album of brand-new material, *Circles*.

To me, this is Solstice at their best. Andy Glass's delicious guitar work is at its most emotional on dreamy opener 'Salu', while the title track is a plea for the rights of everyone to welcome the solstice at Stonehenge. Another hypnotic piece, 'Soul to Soul', is followed by the up-tempo 'Thank You'. The deliciously delicate 'Medicine' is followed by 'Sacred Run', perhaps one of the band's best up-tempo pieces, and the beautifully melodic closing instrumental 'Coming Home'.

Circles showed that Andy Glass's ability to write a glorious, uplifting melody had not diminished over the years, and while the full sonic potential of the band was not to be realised until 2010's gorgeous comeback album *Spirit*, *Circles* had possibly their most emotional, positive and uplifting material – traits in both the band and the genre that I greatly admire.

This was actually a heady time in the UK. The developing scene embraced both new and old bands modestly, but with warmth. One of the main catalysts of this surge in interest was the Classic Rock Society, which was founded in 1991 in the Rotherham area. Beginning with some local gigs and a short, stapled fanzine, by the end of the decade it had become an organisation of genuine international stature, drawing decent crowds to its concerts and festivals at the Oakwood Centre in Rotherham.

THE USA BECOMES THE NEW HOME OF PROGRESSIVE ROCK

Gradually, with mail-order dealers actively seeking out new artists to promote, a genuine Progressive Rock scene began to emerge. The amazing difference between this and either of the two waves that had gone before it was the incredible array of countries that seemed to be producing new bands. The most obvious example of this was the USA. Compared to the UK, Germany and Italy, for instance, the US had never had its fair share of Prog bands in the 1970s. As the 1990s wore on, huge numbers of bands of the highest quality began to emerge, led by Echolyn from the East Coast, Iluvatar from Baltimore and Discipline from Detroit. All these bands had a strong British influence, but mixed it up with far less self-consciousness and rather more imagination than their 1990s British counterparts. Discipline, for instance, led by the charismatic Matthew Parmenter, combined the stylings of Genesis and Van der Graaf Generator to by turns chilling and inspirational effect. The influences on these bands were interesting. Most of them channelled the 1980s Neo-Prog of Marillion and a variety of the first wave of bands. This made for a more varied and interesting mix of sounds compared to the bands coming out of the UK.

GLASS HAMMER AND ECHOLYN

No two bands demonstrate this interesting variation in influences better than Glass Hammer and Echolyn. Hailing originally from Chattanooga in Tennessee, Glass Hammer was the brainchild of multi-instrumentalists Steve Babb and Fred Schendel, and in some ways the project they formed became a Progressive Rock apologist's nightmare, particularly as their debut album *Journey of the Dunadan* was based on Tolkien. Over the years the band have built up a strong following with music often heavily reminiscent of Yes, and are wise not to take themselves too seriously. Usually building their music around strong concepts and good melodies, the band have gathered around them a strong and talented team of guest musicians, and are recommended to anyone whose tastes are shamelessly retro.

On the other hand, Echolyn, from Pennsylvania, moved in a jazzier, more Gentle Giant-influenced direction. Their second album *Suffocating the Bloom* meshes traditional Progressive Rock with fusion-orientated material, and shows admirable musical ambition and great playing skills. However, almost out of the blue, in 1994 something amazing happened. Echolyn were signed to major label Sony.

Echolyn
As the World
Released March 1995

As the World is a vitally important album in the third coming of Progressive Rock. Not only is it a remarkably dense and exciting record in its own right, produced by

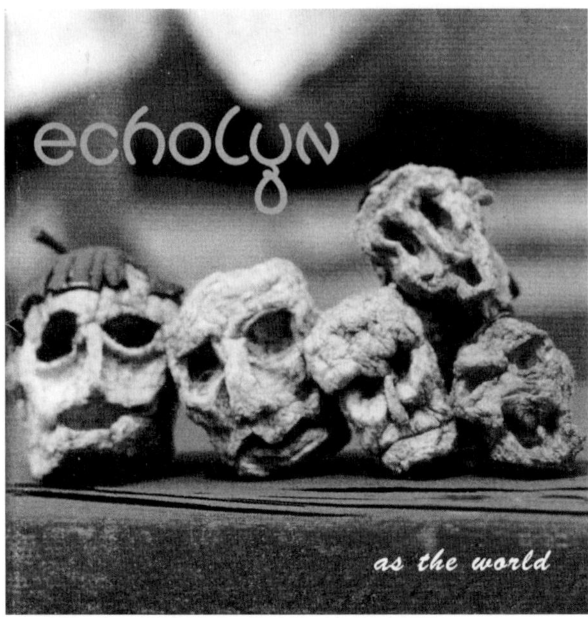

The strikingly original cover of Echolyn's only album for Sony, *As the World*. (*Sony/Cyclops*)

a group of young American musicians at the top of their game, but it was the last album by a 'traditional' Progressive Rock band to be produced on a major label. It would never happen today, but in the 1990s there was still an opportunity for one enthusiastic label executive to sign a favourite band, and this is what happened to Echolyn. After the recording, Sony lost interest in the band, forcing them to tour the album without label support. Released by Sony only in the USA, the album was licensed to small Prog labels elsewhere in the world, including Malcolm Parker's Cyclops label in the UK.

I am not a supporter of very long albums as a rule, but *As the World* is a dense and very satisfying piece of work. I had the same reaction to it as I had with the music of Gentle Giant, in that once I found a way into the music, the whole album opened up before me, and I loved every moment. The melodies are difficult to pick out at first, but once the feel of the album – with its powerful playing and superb harmonies – is established, the tunes reveal themselves gradually. Most of all, this is an album that rewards repeated listening.

Vocals are a vitally important part of *As the World*, and while the harmonies are deeply impressive, the sweet voice of guitarist Brett Kull and the slightly harsher, grunge-influenced tones of Ray Weston contrast impressively. Instrumentally, Kull's hard-rocking guitar combines with Chris Busby's keyboards beautifully. Busby is a unique musician, his often dissonant playing combining traditional Prog textures with influences from fusion and contemporary classical composers. His piano playing, in particular, is a joy on *As the World*. Tom Hiatt on bass and Paul Ramsay on drums, both skilled and mobile players, are vital to the overall success of the band's left-of-centre approach.

It is ironic that the band should deliver their most dense and inaccessible album to a major label. Had Sony received 2000's *Cowboy Poems Free*, with its relative accessibility, it is just possible that Echolyn might have made a career for themselves with the label. As it is, *As the World* is unique, a completely non-commercial album released with big record sales in mind. However, if you fancy a challenge and do not mind having to work your brain when listening, it could be that this amazing record will reward you for years.

THE EMERGENCE OF SPOCK'S BEARD

Despite Echolyn's major label outing, the most successful US band to emerge during the 1990s was the hugely popular Spock's Beard from California. Formed by brothers Neal and Alan Morse, bass player Dave Meros and session drummer Nick D'Virgilio, they came together in a similar way to groups like Yes and Focus in the 1970s. These were not fledgling musicians learning their craft, but experienced professionals looking to play the music that they loved for fun. As a result, their hugely melodic sound combined plenty of different influences from pop to AOR, jazz, folk and even show tunes. This led, just occasionally, to accusations of insincerity. Spock's Beard were, at least after a while, as commercial as Progressive Rock could possibly be. Alongside the multi-part suites and Gentle Giant-inspired multi-part harmonies, the band have always thrown in songs like 'June', which is almost a pastiche of Crosby, Stills & Nash.

The opening moments of *The Light* feel like the beginning of a musical, and the album offers a remarkable four-track *tour de force*. This first album impressed without selling in huge quantities, and each successive album did a little better, mixing up AOR with full-on symphonic Progressive Rock, so that by the *Day for Night* album in 1999 the band were selling well, aided by the excellent distribution offered by the Inside Out label. They even had some chart success in continental Europe. Alongside Sweden's The Flower Kings, the band was as successful as a contemporary Progressive Rock band can get.

Spock's Beard
V
Released 2000

V was the fifth album by Spock's Beard with Neal Morse in the band, and has many of the group's most notable characteristics. In particular, if you only ever hear one track by the band in your life, make it the sixteen-minute album opener 'At the End of the Day'. Hugely melodic and a bit over the top, it is a euphoric experience and contains almost all the elements that made the Neal Morse-fronted version of the band so engaging. 'Revelation', on the other hand, is a brooding, minor-key piece that breaks into full-on metal at times, whereas 'Thoughts (Part II)' is one of

The expressive Ryo Okumoto of Spock's Beard at the 2011 High Voltage Festival. (*Neil Palfreyman*)

the band's Gentle Giant tributes, a showcase for some manic instrumental band interplay and startling vocal harmonies. The band follow this with the charmingly light 'All on a Sunday', later simplified for a single release, and the ethereal 'Goodbye to Yesterday'.

The twenty-seven-minute 'The Great Nothing' closes the album with great style. Spock's Beard had attempted long form music before – with 'The Healing Colours of Sound' on *Day for Night* – however, whereas that piece had felt like a series of songs strung together, 'The Great Nothing' feels more like one coherent piece of music, a precursor perhaps of Morse's solo material or his long tracks with Transatlantic. It is a hugely confident masterpiece.

THE SCANDINAVIANS ARE COMING

Somewhat surprisingly, the most creative territory apart from the USA during the 1990s was Scandinavia. Whereas the reverence for Progressive Rock in the USA was almost casual – 'It's just another music genre, after all; what's all the fuss about?' – for the people of Norway and Sweden it was more of a religious ritual. Analogue keyboards were held up as sacred relics and beards were grown long.

Several bands are worthy of particular note in the 1990s. Anekdoten from Sweden had their roots as that most unlikely of things, a King Crimson tribute band. Their early music is somewhat attritional and very powerful, with strong bass rhythms and huge, powerful, dark sweeps of Mellotron. However, the band that had the biggest cult following of the 1990s, perhaps due to their miserly two-album history and successive appearances at Progfest in the USA, were Änglagård. Rather than the power of Anekdoten, Änglagård's music was far more symphonic, although with a delicious lightness of touch that was unique to the band, with its interweaving Mellotron and synth textures and folky flute. Hailing from the Oslo area of Norway, the evocatively named White Willow took a route more influenced by folk. The band was, and remains, the brainchild of guitarist and composer Jacob Holm-Lupo, whose initial intention was to combine the Progressive Rock of King Crimson and Genesis with a lighter, folkier touch derived from Norwegian traditional music.

Änglagård
Hybris
Released 1992

Anekdoten
Nucleus
Released 1995

White Willow
Ignis Fatuus
Released 1995

These three albums, released within three years of each other, demonstrate the huge quality, breadth and depth coming out of Scandinavia at the time. Despite the obvious differences in tone and approach of these three bands, there are some unifying factors. There was certainly no virtuosity for virtuosity's sake on display, and while Änglagård's music is the most intricate from a compositional point of view, each band relies on thematic development and delicate repetition of those themes to build tension and complexity.

Hybris contains four long pieces of music over the course of a relatively short album. Many cite its sequel *Epilog* as a better record since it dispenses with the lead vocals sung in Swedish, but to me the vocals add charm and atmosphere even if they are not themselves the most impressive part of the album. It is not hard to appreciate why the Progressive Rock community, particularly in the USA, embraced them so fully, as the band's music has a real spirit of authenticity about it. In particular, Thomas Johnson's use of the Mellotron is wonderful, by turns chilling and moving. The use of the flute, also a significant feature of White Willow's music, is also delicate and beautifully affecting. Most importantly, this album recalls a simpler time – almost as if punk, and the 1980s British Prog revival that came after it, had never occurred.

Whereas the music of Änglagård mixed influences with some dexterity, for the mid-1990s incarnation of Anekdoten it was mid-1970s King Crimson that was a

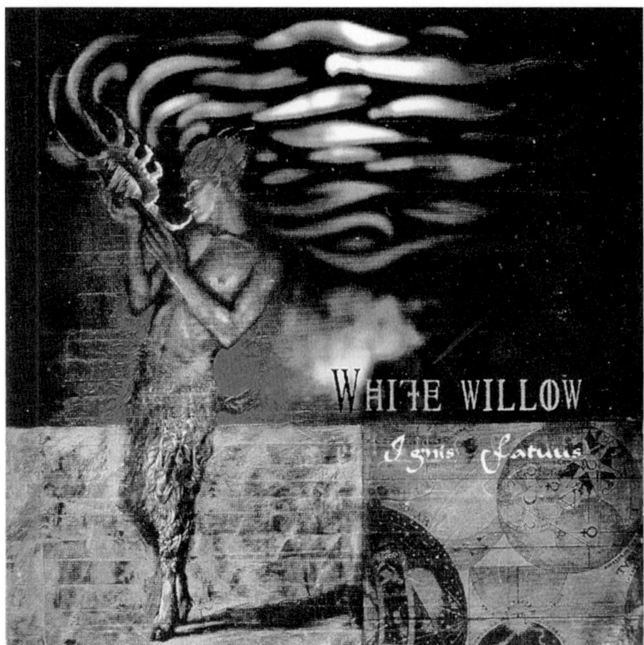

Ignis Fatuus, the wonderful 1995 debut of Norway's White Willow. (*Laser's Edge*)

starting point. Imagine the intensity of the track 'One More Red Nightmare' varied for an entire album and you have Anekdoten's uncompromising approach to their music. Their second album *Nucleus* is summarised by the attritional nature of its title track. This is powerful stuff, with complex sweeps of almost metallic guitar combining with Mellotron and vocals, bringing to mind the alienation of Radiohead a couple of years later. This brooding intensity continues on 'Harvest', while the infamous 'Book of Hours' builds chillingly in power with the Mellotron and guitar sections interspersed with periods of brooding tension. Only on final track 'In Freedom' does the mood lift, with the Mellotron used for beauty rather than as an instrument of terror. The music of Anekdoten, particularly on these early 1990s albums, is powerful, inaccessible, uncompromising and difficult to listen to; however, it does reward those that give it time, and *Nucleus* in particular is an album of stark and disturbing beauty.

Of the three bands mentioned here, it is the music of White Willow that I find most rewarding. With White Willow the lead vocals and vocal melodies are the most vital, and while on their debut *Ignis Fatuus* not all the vocals are delivered by female singers, this was to become a major feature of the band's sound. Here, the music is deliciously varied and romantic, with a strong, almost Gothic romanticism that hints at warm summer evenings in the Norwegian countryside and, just occasionally, dark winter solitude. Opener 'Snowfall' in a manifesto for the band, a sweet vocal melody over brooding flute, Mellotron and synths. 'Lord of Night', on the other hand, introduces Tirill Mohn's violin and Jacob Holm-Lupo's lead guitar for the first time. This is how the album continues, combining dark instrumental passages with some delicately pastoral acoustic moments. Occasionally the music even takes on a Renaissance character, with harpsichord featured on several pieces. The brief 'Till He Arrives' remains a personal favourite, and it is delicate and gloriously melodic. The album closes with a couple of longer, more intense pieces that hint at a rockier future for White Willow.

Änglagård were to split up after *Epilog*, which means that their legend remains intact, based as it is on two fine albums and a handful of well-regarded live appearances. They have reformed occasionally and at the time of writing a third album was due in 2012. Anekdoten have changed a little, with more emphasis on post-rock in their music. White Willow, though far from prolific, continue to make albums and play live occasionally. While their music has lost the pastoral quality of *Ignis Fatuus*, all their releases are worthy of attention, with *Storm Season* from 2004 particularly recommended.

THE FLOWER KINGS

If ever there was a Progressive Rock band that split the existing audience, it must be The Flower Kings from Sweden. To many they are the second coming of the great bands of the first Progressive Rock era (such as Yes and Genesis), while other Prog fans, and I will admit that I tend towards this camp, have not engaged with them at all. Certainly the band are superb musicians, and have produced some music of great quality over the years. Not only that, but since convening to provide a touring band for veteran guitarist Roine Stolt, previously of 1970s band Kaipa, they have been hugely prolific, producing ten studio albums between 1995 and their last album at time of writing, *The Sum of No Evil* in 2007. Generally it is the earlier albums, particularly *Retropolis* in 1996 and the double album *Stardust We Are* the following year, that seem to be the most loved, but my personal favourite Flower Kings album is *Space Revolver*.

The Flower Kings
Space Revolver
Released 2000

One of the reasons I have failed to engage completely with the work of The Flower Kings is that I often find the construction of their pieces a bit 'Prog by numbers'. The music is beautifully constructed and played and expertly written and, unlike some of the band's detractors, I even like Roine Stolt's voice. However, I find their music a little devoid of soul. Nevertheless, I find *Space Revolver* rather charming and I have 'engaged' with this album like no other by The Flower Kings.

Structurally, the record revolves around the two-part epic 'I Am the Sun'. Its opening theme, initially played on the organ then repeated on other instruments, is both grandiose and moving, setting the listener up for the rest of the album.

What follows are a couple of decent epics, 'Monster Within' and 'Slave to Money', and also some shorter pieces, which add a lot of charm to the album, particularly 'Dream on Dreamer' and the much-derided 'Chicken Farmer Song'.

Fortunes for The Flower Kings were mixed in the 2000s, with some albums, like the double *Paradox Hotel*, being well-received while others such as *The Rainmaker* suggested a decline. By 2011 Roine was concentrating on other projects, specifically a rather more mellow Progressive Rock band called Agents of Mercy, but was anticipating a return to Flower Kings activity in the near future.

THE RISE OF PROGRESSIVE METAL

Progressive Rock has always had links with more the aggressive, guitar-orientated world of Heavy Metal. After all, both genres grew out of the progressive music boom of the late 1960s. However, in the early 1990s metal bands began to look beyond the clichés of their own music and towards Progressive Rock as an inspiration. Songs sometimes became longer and more complex, and musicianship became more versatile and virtuosic, especially in the rhythm section of bass and drums. Initially, these bands were American and were typified by the superstars of the genre, who won big followings among younger metal fans. Queensryche, Fates Warning and particularly Dream Theater were to become the kings of this new hybrid.

While these bands sold albums by the bucketload, their hybrid of Heavy Metal posturing and Progressive Rock textures did not always sit well with

Opposite and right: Jonas Reingold and Roine Stolt of The Flower Kings at the Summer's End Festival in 2010. (*Chris Walkden*)

traditional Progressive Rock fans, and only Dream Theater, with their tendency to revere the bands of the 1970s and their reliance on rather more adult lyrical content, have been completely accepted by the Progressive Rock community. As always, the *laissez-faire* attitude on continental Europe and particularly in the Scandinavian countries has led to some interesting music combinations. Pain of Salvation, led by singer and multi-instrumentalist Daniel Gildenlow, has moulded the Progressive Metal genre to fit his own particular worldview. His conceptual material is particularly strong, tacking subjects as diverse as religion and philosophy on *"BE"* and world politics on *Scarsick*. Meanwhile, Opeth have gradually moved from extreme death metal into far more lush, almost symphonic ground. The UK has few bands to have penetrated the international scene besides the excellent Threshold, currently fronted by the talented and somewhat mercurial Damian Wilson. In Holland, Arjen Lucassen has been hugely successful with his *Ayreon* project, which combines lush Progressive and Celtic textures with dramatic metal and extensive use of analogue instruments. In truth, his epic science fiction stories are somewhat silly in themselves, but he does write great material and his albums are worth getting for the sheer volume of Prog and metal stars involved in them. His most impressive album remains *The Human Equation* from 2004, featuring James Labrie from Dream Theater in the lead role, and it is no coincidence that other singers involved have included artists of the calibre of Bob Catley of Magnum, Neal Morse of Spock's Beard and Daniel Gildenlow of Pain of Salvation.

Mike Portnoy of Dream Theater and Transatlantic onstage in 2010. (*Roy Layer*)

Dream Theater
Metropolis Pt 2: Scenes from a Memory
Released 1999

Recorded at a time when concept albums were not particularly fashionable, Dream Theater's masterpiece arrived in 1999. In terms of the balance between metal and Progressive Rock, it gets things just about right, and while the metal elements are certainly strong, particularly in the 'shredding' guitar work of John Petrucci and the macho vocals of James LaBrie, the keyboard work of Jordan Rudess is prominent and varied, making this an album that both metal and Prog fans should be able to enjoy.

The story is also engaging and unusually sensitive for a metal album, particularly as the main character Nicholas has been a woman, Victoria, in a past life. The rather melodramatic themes of murder and betrayal are less unusual. Musically, the album also works nicely, with passages of introspection balancing the bombast convincingly. If you have not dipped into Progressive Metal before and would like a starting point, this is probably the album to go with.

FEMALE-FRONTED SYMPHONIC METAL

While the number of woman fronting Progressive Rock bands has grown in the last twenty years, in Heavy Metal it has skyrocketed. This is particularly prevalent in the other subgenre of metal to demonstrate a significant Prog influence, which is symphonic metal. Often fronted by women who sometimes sing in an operatic style, these bands also employ extended song forms and huge orchestral sweeps, with keyboards again prominent. The most important bands of this genre have tended to be from Europe, and include groups that have had considerable international success. Examples are Within Temptation and the now defunct After Forever from Holland, Nightwish from Finland, Lacuna Coil from Italy and Leaves' Eyes from Germany. With their passionate, emotive lyrics and increased level of sensuality, many of these bands have found a formula that is strangely commercial. Arjen Lucassen even tried his hand at one, forming the excellent Stream of Passion fronted by diminutive Mexican singer Marcela Bovio a few years ago.

THE 1970S BANDS IN MIDDLE AGE

What happened to the 1970s bands in the 1990s? Genesis continued to play their pop/rock show in huge venues, with only the occasional nod towards their Prog past. Meanwhile, Yes had a frantically busy decade, with increasingly desperate attempts to recapture their Prog past. 1990's *Union* album was a near-disastrous attempt to combine the unreleased Anderson Bruford Wakeman Howe album with part-finished work from the version of Yes based on the West Coast of the USA, which included Chris Squire and Alan White. The eight-man arena tour that followed was largely well-received. The band then reverted, bizarrely, to the *90125* line-up for 1994's decent but poorly received hard-rock album *Talk*. By 1996, Howe and Wakeman were back for another slightly ill-conceived venture, the part-studio, part-live *Keys to Ascension* albums, which included two reasonable stabs at a new 'Close to the Edge' with the twenty-minute-plus epics 'That, That Is' and 'Mind Drive'. That Wakeman had re-discovered the Minimoog helped, but it could not disguise the overall lack of energy in the playing. In 1998, the band resumed regular touring, promoting the much-derided *Open Your Eyes* album and the better-received *The Ladder*, which included concerts at the Royal Albert Hall in London and the band's first purpose-made DVD in 1999.

One band to undergo a surprising burst of activity were Camel, who released three decent albums in the 1990s, all of them conceptual in nature. Andrew Latimer had moved to the USA and took the name of the band with him. The first release was *Dust and Dreams* in 1991, which told the story of John Steinbeck's novel *The Grapes of Wrath* using both poignant instrumental themes and some well-judged songs. *Harbour of Dreams*, based around the idea of Irish immigration to the USA, followed in 1996, with the atmospheric and slightly disappointing *Rajaz* arriving in 1999. The band also played some well-received but modest tours during the decade.

Once again, it was up to Robert Fripp to set the creative bar highest, and in the early 1990s he began to see King Crimson not as a four-piece but as a six-piece, adding Chapman Stick player Trey Gunn and drummer Pat Mastelotto to the *Discipline* line-up, which included Bill Bruford, whose ties to E. G. Records, with whom Fripp was in dispute, ensured that he could not sign on immediately. The resulting EP, *Vrooom*, and the album that the EP helped finance, *Thrak*, combined the music of *Red* with the lyrical and vocal content of the 1980s version of the band. Powerful, almost discordant at times, this was proof that the Prog bands from the 1970s could still innovate. Whereas Yes were obsessed with the integrity of its line-up, with new musicians seen as interlopers, King Crimson thrived on new blood and new ideas, meaning that the band never stayed still creatively.

POST-ROCK, POST-PROG

The mid-1990s saw a huge explosion in interest in rock and pop music in the UK with the advent of what came to be known as Britpop. Dominated by the upbeat music of Oasis, Blur and Suede, as well as the female-fronted bands Elastica and Sleeper, this was music that tapped directly into the zeitgeist. As well as being multi-racial, this was music in which women could participate equally with men. While Oasis referenced The Beatles and Blur The Kinks, other bands took a more reflective and inward-looking approach, and one of those was Radiohead.

Radiohead
OK Computer
Released 1997

OK Computer is a Progressive Rock album almost by accident, and is amazingly important in that it created a genre of its very own. By showing that bands could be successful and make music that took chances, Radiohead provided inspiration for groups as varied as Elbow from Manchester and The Pineapple Thief from Dorset.

I will be honest here. While I understand why it was successful, I do not like the album much. It is a bleak and unsettling piece of music and while I agree that it does have some beautiful moments – the orchestral sweep of opener 'Airbag', for instance, or the charming, chiming 'No Surprises' – for most of the album I struggle to engage with the music. However, I appreciate what the band were trying to achieve and I admire them for that.

OK Computer is largely responsible for showing 'indie rock' bands that it was fine to look beyond the traditional verse-chorus structure, and that other textures were also acceptable. When Elbow released their beautiful song 'Newborn' in 2001, even though many critics shouted 'Prog Rock', the band could cite Genesis as an influence and not be crucified for doing so. When they played 'One Day Like This' with a string section at the Glastonbury Festival some years later, it was generally agreed that it was one of the magisterial moments of the event that year. Thirty years earlier, it would have been seen as pretentious.

9

THE VOICE AND THE WORDS

George Martin once commented that while John Lennon's priority in songwriting was the lyrics, Paul McCartney's was the music. If you ask a typical Progressive Rock fan whether they consider lyrics to be particularly important to the enjoyment of the music as a whole, it is probable that they will answer 'no'. Yet when the critics talk about rock and pop music, it is always the great poets that are most lauded. Bob Dylan is spoken of in hushed tones, not just for the poetry of his writing but also for the way he was influenced by other writers. There were threats of suicide among fans when 1980s indie band The Smiths split up, so obsessed were some by the way that Morrissey's lyrics had spoken to them about their own lives. Even at the more mundane end of the lyric-writing spectrum, a song will strike a chord with millions – for instance 'Angels' by Take That heart-throb Robbie Williams. In these cases, performance and arrangement are almost secondary. It is the lyrics, sung along to at concerts and played at funerals, that are remembered. We have all, at one time or another, been touched by a heartfelt lyric that seemed to speak to us personally. So where are the poets of Progressive Rock?

THE VOICE

First of all we need to examine the role that vocals have in Progressive Rock. In pop music, the lead vocal carries the song, and so a strong vocalist, whether it be Smokey Robinson, Elton John or Beyoncé, is essential. In Progressive Rock, the vocalist often – but by no means always – takes a back seat. Not only does Progressive Rock contain lengthy instrumental passages, but like jazz it also includes a significant number of bands that make no use of vocals whatsoever. Classic examples would include Dutch band Focus, of course, while more modern exponents include FROM.UZ of Uzbekistan, and Quantum Fantay from Belgium, whose stock-in-trade is joyful Progressive Rock.

Bands from both the classic and modern eras, given the relative paucity of lead vocals in their music, have often 'made do' with instrumentalists taking vocal duties. Camel, for instance, did not have a dedicated lead vocalist until singer-for-hire Chris Rainbow joined the band in the early 1980s. While the presence of Greg Lake as singer (and the lyrics of Peter Sinfield) on the first two King Crimson albums gave the vocals greater weight than in some bands, by the time of the *Larks' Tongues in Aspic* line-up in 1972 King Crimson were more focused on instrumental improvisation, and despite the excellent singing and songwriting of bassist John Wetton, vocals took more of a back seat within the band. When King Crimson reformed for the *Discipline* album in 1980, Robert Fripp, having absorbed the sounds of the New Wave scene in New York, brought on board innovative singer Adrian Belew to add his David Byrne-inspired vocal stylings to a mixture of material that was as song-orientated as it was innovative.

Not that all bands ignored vocals. Just listen to the delicious vocal section in Gentle Giant's 'On Reflection' from the *Free Hand* album, for instance. This is a rare example of a 'round' in Progressive Rock, beautifully executed and often played live in a different arrangement. The band were one of the few groups in the 1970s to make full use of multiple vocalists, principally by contrasting the brasher rock-and-roll styling of Derek Shulman (who had been lead vocalist in the earlier white soul group Simon Dupree and the Big Sound) with the velvet-smooth singing of Kerry Minnear. While Shulman tended to handle Minnear's vocals in a live setting, on record the keyboard player provided a subtle and often beautifully judged contrast. His performance on the medieval-tinged ballad 'Think of Me with Kindness' from *Octopus*, for instance, remains one of the most touching examples of simple songwriting in Progressive Rock.

Meanwhile, the Prog mainstream was dominated by two vocalists of rare distinctiveness and power: Peter Gabriel of Genesis and Jon Anderson of Yes.

Altos are very rare in rock music, and not to everyone's taste, so despite the fact that he was already a well-known figure in the London club scene, it cannot have been an obvious decision to build a band around Jon Anderson. Having said that, one of the stated aims of the band when it began rehearsing in 1968 was to demonstrate the influence of vocal groups like The 5th Dimension, the American ensemble whose best-known songs in the UK included 'Up, Up and Away' and the uplifting 'Aquarius/Let the Sunshine In' from the musical *Hair*. In addition to Anderson's disarming yet powerful voice (it is amazing what a career in the clubs will do for your singing), he had a willing foil in bassist Chris Squire. Squire had a voice almost (but not quite) good enough to front his own band, as he demonstrated on his excellent 1975 solo album *Fish out of Water*. Squire's range and chorister's pitching contrasted beautifully with Anderson's, and their harmonising as a duo became a Yes trademark over the years. However, The 5th Dimension influence really kicked in when three or more vocalists harmonised. Two magisterial examples included the middle piano and vocal section from 'South Side of the Sky' from 1971's *Fragile* and the 'I Get Up I Get Down' section from *Close to the Edge* the following year. Third vocalist Steve Howe was a much weaker singer than the other two, but his vocals 'work' because of their similar timbre to Squire's.

Peter Gabriel, however, influenced a whole generation of vocalists in the 1980s and beyond with a very stylised and throaty rasp. While we have already discussed the spectacle of his showmanship, what makes him a great vocalist is his passion, drama and sheer soul. While backing vocals were less important to Gabriel-era Genesis than they were to Yes in the same period, Phil Collins's voice blended beautifully with Gabriel's, both in the studio and in concert. Listen, for instance, to the beautiful 'nah, nah, nah' vocal section in the middle of 'The Cinema Show' on *Selling England by the Pound* to hear what the band were capable of as a unit, although more often Gabriel is used as a powerful and unpredictable solo presence, as in 'The Battle of Epping Forest' from the same album.

Given the speed that Progressive Rock moved away from the blues, it is hardly surprising that hard rock and blues vocalists were harder to find once the genre had become established in the early 1970s. In America the story was different however, and Kansas vocalist Steve Walsh, with his clean yet powerful tone, found himself beautifully suited both to the band's English-inspired Progressive Rock and their American-style AOR excursions. Once again, we find a second vocalist playing a significant role in a band, this time violinist Robby Steinhardt, whose voice was close enough to Walsh's to blend when harmonising, but distinctive enough to lend a different tone to the music during his occasional lead vocals.

However, if Progressive Rock has a second language, it must be Italian. While many bands, including PFM and Le Orme, initially sang their lyrics in Italian, Emerson, Lake & Palmer employed Peter Sinfield to provide lyrics for PFM once they had signed to the British band's label Manticore. But the most expressive and perhaps most appropriate vocalist in Italian Progressive Rock was operatic tenor Francesco di Giacomo of Banco del Mutuo Soccorso. While they, too, signed to Manticore and released a debut in English in 1975, their music works far better sung in Italian, where the full operatic flavour and romanticism is allowed to shine through, never better typified than on the passionate '750,000 anni fa ... L'amore?' from *Darwin!*.

It would be unfair to call every singer in the early 1980s British revival a Peter Gabriel clone, but, just as the music generally took more influences from Genesis than from the other bands of the 1970s, Gabriel seems to have been the most noticeable influence on its vocalists. Part of this is simply to do with the way certain people from certain social backgrounds sing. Gabriel came from a white, middle-class English upbringing and so did many of the people he inspired. However, it was also the surreal theatricality he brought to his Genesis performances that impressed many of his imitators. The 1980s revivalists gave a more literal slant to this theatricality. As well as applying striking face make-up, Marillion's Fish donned flak jacket and helmet for the band's emotional anti-war set closer 'Forgotten Sons', while Peter Nicholls of IQ used different costumes to assist with the full concert performance of the band's 1997 double album *Subterranea*. Early performances by Scottish band Pallas were often characterized by extreme, horror-inspired theatrics.

Fish, as the most charismatic character from the 1980s revival, was often accused of imitating Peter Gabriel, yet in retrospect it is his reverence for Peter Hammill that comes across in his vocal delivery and lyrics. Besides, within a couple of albums he had successfully imposed his own personality on the band's considerable fanbase, and the Gabriel comparisons largely disappeared.

One other way to make sure that a group had a strong vocalist was to hire a woman. In the early 1970s there were few, Progressive Rock being largely a masculine pursuit and the music industry being a somewhat misogynist one. Sonja Kristina of Curved Air is a notable exception, of course, and not only did she bring to the band a powerful sexuality, she was no passenger when it came to creativity. Annie Haslam, who followed Jane Relf as singer in Renaissance, was a more passive presence in the band. She played no part in the writing process and presented an unassuming stage presence, concentrating largely on her superb vocal performances.

Whenever a band hires a female singer, they are required to sidestep the typical taunt that 'she's only in the band for her looks'. It is quite possible that some singers have won their places entirely on the basis of sex appeal, but in an environment like Progressive Rock where the music comes first, the voice tends to take precedence. Of the 1980s bands, only Solstice chose to use a female vocalist, and a small army sang in the band at various points until Emma Brown joined in the mid-1990s; she has stayed ever since. For band leader Andy Glass, the presence of a female singer is partly due to a vague urge to reproduce Jon Anderson's alto tones and partly to do with the more spiritual side of the band. He feels it suits the band's music. Having said that, female singers in pure Progressive Rock bands, as opposed to crossover groups that mix Progressive Rock with metal, folk or world music, are rare. Christina Booth of Magenta is probably the most prominent of these, but others include Leslie Hunt of US band District 97. As Progressive Rock follows a largely masculine demographic, female singers often push the bands they are in towards other areas of music. So groups like Iona, Karnataka and Mostly Autumn (whose singer Heather Findlay is a particularly powerful presence) tend to combine Progressive Rock influences with pop, heavy rock and Celtic to varying degrees, producing an interesting hybrid that leaves some hardcore Progressive Rock fans feeling a little uncomfortable.

THE WORDS

From day one, Progressive Rock set itself apart from other forms of popular music. If it was to do this artistically, then the lyrics had to play their part. Yet audiences tend to want lyrics that they can engage with and the most common way of doing this it to write about romance. However, your average Progressive Rock lyricist would prefer to write about something else. So what to choose as

Heather Findlay at the Cambridge Rock Festival, August 2011. (*Stephen Lambe*)

subject matter? Whereas The Beatles, for instance, had drugs as an inspiration, Progressive Rock has no significant history of major drug use. Most bands used soft drugs, and Rick Wakeman, in particular, liked a drink. Progressive Rock has practically no drug casualties, living or dead. Most of the significant members of Yes, Genesis, King Crimson, ELP and Gentle Giant are still alive, and many are active in music. LSD, for instance, appears not to have been a major influence on any of the major Prog lyricists, most of whose work would seem to be influenced by other stimuli, such as literature, film or historical subjects. The most distinctive lyric writer in Progressive Rock has always been Jon Anderson of Yes. Often unfairly ridiculed, Anderson used the sound of the words he was singing to build atmosphere and paint subliminal pictures in conjunction not only with the music but also other stimuli – the stage sets and album covers, for example. This is a typical Anderson lyric from the 1970s:

> A seasoned witch could call you from the depths of your disgrace,
> And rearrange your liver to the solid mental grace,
> And achieve it all with music that came quickly from afar,
> Then taste the fruit of man recorded losing all against the hour.
> And assessing points to nowhere, leading ev'ry single one.
> A dewdrop can exalt us like the music of the sun,
> And take away the plain in which we move,
> And choose the course you're running.

Regardless of what these lyrics – which are from the title track of *Close to the Edge* – illustrate, in context they are urgent and powerful. Strong and effective emphasis is placed at the end of each fourth line, in this case 'hour' and 'running', particularly as the expected rhyming couplet does not appear. Some lines are impenetrable, while others stand on their own as lone truths (line six, for instance).

From the same album, this time from the track 'Siberian Khatru', comes the following sequence of words:

Outboard, river,
Bluetail, tailfly,
Luther, in time,
Suntower, asking,
Cover, lover,
June cast, moon fast,
As one changes,
Heart gold, leaver,
Soul mark, mover,
Christian, changer,
Called out, saviour,
Moon gate, climber,
Turn round, glider.

Here there is no attempt at meaning, yet the sound of the words as sung has great power. The repetition of 'er' words is vital, as are the rather obvious rhymes of 'cover' with 'lover' and 'June cast' with 'moon fast' and the repetition of 'tail' in line two. Each word is chosen to scan perfectly, with strong rhythm, while the actual melody repeats every other line, becoming more insistent as the music builds. Most importantly, the words themselves paint an otherworldly picture without saying anything at all. Some obvious examples include 'suntower', 'soul mark' and 'moon gate', which, when read in conjunction with the music and cover art, conjure up heady, abstract images.

THE CONCEPT ALBUM BECOMES THE ROOT OF ALL EVIL

It is absurd to make the assumption that an artist cannot be allowed to write an entire album of music that has one subject or tells one particular story. Yet in the wake of many of the efforts of Progressive Rock artists, the 'concept album' – as it became called – is synonymous with pretention and overindulgence. While in most cases these albums had concepts that were based around the lyrical content, there was a tendency also to repeat themes or maintain a consistent musical tone.

If the critics of Progressive Rock are anything to go by (and they aren't), all concept albums are about pixies and elves. It is true that Tolkien was a strong influence on many bands of the early 1970s, but then Tolkien was very much in fashion in those days, and such imagery can also be found in folk and in hard rock, especially on 'Misty Mountain Hop' and several other songs on *Led Zeppelin IV*. No Progressive Rock band loves Tolkien quite as much as Robert Plant, but tracks by Rush and Camel have pieces specifically derived from parts of *The Lord of the Rings*. That Marillion gave themselves the name that they did, with its cringe-inducing naiveté, was probably not the best idea in the world, but as the band have been with us for thirty years it is high time we got over it.

Meanwhile, fantasy and science fiction have always been prominent in Progressive Rock lyrics. Often the story is allegorical, intended to tell us about ourselves. For instance, Pallas's *The Sentinel*, although about Atlantis, also parallels the Cold War, while Magma's tales of Kobaia have a strong ecological theme, albeit in a guttural version of German that is not meant to be translatable, word for word. IQ's magnificent double album *Subterranea* tells a futuristic story of an individual fighting against an oppressive regime that has imprisoned him and is using him as a part of a social experiment. Jon Anderson's remarkable *Olias of Sunhillow* is the surreal story of a planet's inhabitants escaping to find another home, and Le Orme's *Felona e Sorona*, inspired by *Romeo and Juliet*, is part love story, part tale of warring planets. Eloy's *Power and the Passion* tells the story of a man transported back to the fourteenth century.

As lyric writers get older, however, fantasy themes tend to be replaced by rather more sophisticated, personal or adult subject matter. Rush drummer Neal Peart, for instance, switched to more thoughtful subject matter from the early 1980s onwards. Fantasy subjects disappear from the work of Jon Anderson and Peter Hammill after their early work, and in both cases their lyrics become more personal or analytical, albeit in very different styles.

Although Progressive Rock bands have not always tackled their subjects with much sophistication, politics have often provided interesting subjects. As well as Pallas's allegorical *The Sentinel*, the Cold War provided inspiration for Camel in *Stationary Traveller* and Steve Hackett in *Defector* in the early 1980s. Political corruption inspired *The Power and the Glory* by Gentle Giant and Pink Floyd's biting *Animals*. As the years have gone on, politics has become less important to lyric writers than society in general, and the late 1990s and 2000s have been notable for a series of albums with the alienating nature of modern society at their core. Porcupine Tree's 2007 album *Fear of a Blank Planet* was a chilling exposé of an alienated youth, while *OK Computer* by Radiohead examined the alienating power of machines.

Progressive Rock has rarely played a part in Christian or worship music as a genre, yet it still has a strong undercurrent of lyrics inspired by religious faith, particularly among US artists. This can be overt – as with Neil Morse's *Testimony* and *Testimony 2* and the born-again work of Ajalon and Cryptic Vision – or

Peter Hammill, the Bob Dylan of Progressive Rock. (*Roy Layer*)

more subtle, as on Echolyn's single-track album *Mei*. On the other hand, many bands, such as Jethro Tull, have taken a stance against organised religion. More often, Progressive Rock lyrics either look outwards at society or inwards at the human condition. Peter Gabriel's lyrics on *Selling England by the Pound*, for instance, took on a more analytical character after the surrealist nature of his storytelling on earlier albums.

Given that the current crop of lyric writers tend to be men in their late thirties or early forties, it is hardly surprising that the subject matter of their songs tends towards the sort of subjects that interest men of that age. Nostalgia and mortality loom large, as does the continuing legacy of two world wars. The Holocaust also provides poignant material. At a festival in 2010, I remember seeing both Pallas and Twelfth Night use similar photographic stills from the gates of the Aushwitz concentration camp ('Arbeit macht frei'). It is the First World War, the futility of which still causes horror a century later, that provides the most resonant material. This is true only, of course, of British lyricists, for whom the horrors of that war have remained in sharp focus, partly thanks to the continued popularity of Siegfried Sassoon and Wilfred Owen, and also in the *Regeneration* novels of Pat Barker. Not only does the subject matter resonate strongly, the mechanics of trench warfare make for the sort of dramatic storytelling beloved of the Neo-Progressive movement. Examples include Paul Menel's wonderful lyrics on IQ's 'Common Ground', British band Credo's hugely poignant 'From the Cradle… To the Grave', Magenta's epic 'The Ballad of Samuel Lane' and, most famously, Twelfth Night's powerful 'Sequences', which featured Geoff Mann singing the lyrics dressed in a First World War officer's uniform.

If the genre has a Bob Dylan, then it is probably appropriate that it should be Peter Hammill of Van der Graaf Generator. Hammill's themes are often inward-looking, examining the human condition, madness and alienation. Dense, ripe and poetic, even if his lyrics do not penetrate they are certainly able to intimidate. Like the work of his contemporary Jon Anderson, the sound Hammill's lyrics make is as important as the words, on the first listen at least. While Fish was clearly influenced by Hammill, so is Andy Tillison of The Tangent, perhaps the most impressive lyricist of the most recent generation. Tillison has the palate to tackle very personal subjects, as in 'The Full Gamut' from *Not as Good as the Book,* or world politics in 'Four Egos, One War' from the same album. He is particularly poignant in 'In Earnest' and the reflective 'Perdu dans Paris', while 'GPS Culture' satirises our reliance on modern technology.

This chapter can only scratch the surface of the importance of lyrics in Progressive Rock. Suffice to say, most successful bands have thrived on the added depth and resonance that decent lyrics bring.

10

INTO THE NEW MILLENNIUM: THE INTERNET AND A THRIVING NICHE

The revival of the 1990s was fuelled by word of mouth and mail-order services, and the rise of the internet in the late 1990s changed everything, for good and ill. New technology demonstrated that not only were there bands still making music all over the world, but that this music was now accessible to anyone. However, by the turn of the millennium the internet had not only become the prime source of information about Progressive Rock music, it had become the main way of sourcing examples of the music itself. Not only could you look at a band's website and download short clips of the music, you could also email them, and sometimes they would even reply. Music had become a two-way dialogue.

There were plenty of different strands to this chapter of the Progressive Rock story, for while some of the bands that had become popular in the 1990s in the UK – like Grey Lady Down and Jadis – found their careers faltering, for others it was a new beginning. Meanwhile, slowly but surely, the term 'Progressive Rock' began to lose its bad name and became just another genre to be referred to as an influence. Thus, the rise of bands like The Mars Volta and Tool incorporated Progressive Rock structures into other types of music, creating exciting hybrids of styles. The Mars Volta's first album, *De-Loused in the Comatorium*, is a remarkably creative work, drawing from punk, metal and Prog in equal measure. Swedish Death Metal band Opeth continued to change styles, with singer Mikael Åkerfeldt often switching between the traditional Death Metal growl and a clean singing style much more to the taste of Progressive Rock fans.

PORCUPINE TREE – THE NEW SUPERSTARS

The metallic influence on Progressive Rock that had begun with Dream Theater continued and began to spread, typified by the work of the new superstars of Progressive Rock, Britain's Porcupine Tree. Steven Wilson formed the band in the 1980s as a pastiche of a typical Progressive Rock band, an in-joke between himself and some friends. Before long, the joke had taken on a life of its own, and by the mid-1990s Porcupine Tree were a genuine touring band combining trance and ambient music with a Pink Floyd sensibility. Formerly on the psychedelic label Delirium, the band moved to indie label Snapper for their well-received albums *Stupid Dream* and *Lightbulb Sun* around the turn of the millennium. However, the band was to reach a far wider audience with their next album, which was to take them in a more crowd-pleasing direction.

Porcupine Tree
In Absentia
Released 2002

After the post-rock pleasures of the band's 2000 album *Lightbulb Sun*, which combined Progressive Rock with indie songwriting, Porcupine Tree cranked up their guitars and edged further into Progressive Metal territory for 2002's *In Absentia*, their first (and only) album for major label offshoot Lava Records. This is not the band's most Prog album – keyboard player Richard Barbieri's contributions, for instance, seem less important than usual – but it *is* important in that the band were the first Progressive Rock act to be signed to a major label since Echolyn in 1994. While the album represents a shift towards louder guitars, it does so without compromising on quality or intelligence.

Opener 'Blackest Eyes', a huge fan favourite, combines guitar crunch with sensitivity, while 'Trains' is a relatively simple semi-acoustic piece and 'Lips of Ashes' is very Prog, combining atmospherics with Steven Wilson's layered vocals. 'The Sound of Muzak', an impassioned attack on the destruction of music as an art form, is both pithy and catchy while the amazing 'Gravity Eyelids' begins in familiar ambient fashion before upping the tempo with a burst of metal. 'Wedding Nails' is an up-tempo instrumental, while the manic 'The Creator Has a Mastertape' is a frenzied study of paranoia. 'Heartattack in a Layby' builds tension before breaking into a glorious, if sinister, choral section. 'Strip the Soul' provides some concluding menace before the album washes away on a sea of keyboards in 'Collapse the Light into Earth'.

The band had made the leap from cult Progressive Rock band into the mainstream. While *In Absentia* was not the major success the label might have hoped for, it sold significantly better than the Snapper albums, and after its release, with the band finding a home on metal label Roadrunner Records, each successive album has done better and better. *Deadwing* continued in the same style, increasing the obvious Progressive Rock influence considerably, especially on the lengthy title track. 2007's bleak *Fear of a Blank Planet*, as well as including a contribution from Robert Fripp, featured a solo from Alex Lifeson from Rush on the extraordinary seventeen-minute epic 'Anesthetize'. By this point, the band's albums were appearing in the UK charts, and their stage shows were becoming increasingly elaborate, with huge screens adding to the atmosphere

Porcupine Tree play their largest concert ever at a sold-out Royal Albert Hall in 2010. (*Neil Palfreyman*)

of their performances. The band took their ambition one step further for *The Incident* in 2009, with the album containing one lengthy song cycle, which they played live in its entirety.

THE EASTERN EUROPEANS ARE COMING!

The new millennium saw the emergence of bands from all over the world, but certain countries showed that their reverence for Progressive Rock had never been tarnished by the critical contempt that bands in the UK and the USA had suffered. In certain territories, artists were able to create a hybrid of Progressive Rock and classical music. Generally instrumental in nature, and incorporating classical instrumentation into a rock framework, Univers Zero from Belgium remain the most adventurous and hardcore of these groups, playing music with a strong twentieth-century classical influence. However, more accessible hybrids were forged by bands like Isildurs Bane from Sweden, and in particular After Crying from Hungary.

After Crying
Struggle for Life
Released 2000

The only live album in this list of key recordings, *Struggle for Life* probably sums up the music of After Crying best, despite it being their eleventh recorded work of one type or another. Although the band is most often labelled 'symphonic', their music here is incredibly varied, from the brooding atmospherics of opener 'Viaduct' to the final charge of their thirty-minute 'Conclusion', which includes short solos for most of the band and a shameless tribute to Emerson, Lake & Palmer. Elsewhere, John Wetton makes an appearance for a cover of King Crimson's 'Starless' and at times the music moves off into classical recital territory with (for instance) 'Sonata for Violoncello and Piano'.This piece features bassist Pejtsik Péter doubling on cello – on which instrument he is also a virtuoso.

In fact, this is the main character of the music of After Crying. The lines are completely blurred between classical and rock music, and both are given equal weight without any sort of self-consciousness. The King Crimson cover version, as well as tributes to ELP and Frank Zappa, shows that the band are not afraid to reference their heroes, and this is actually quite refreshing.

However, one particular country saw a greater level of creativity than any other in the late 1990s and early 2000s. Poland. The sixth most populous country in Europe, it had been a political flashpoint in the 1980s due to the success of its non-communist trade union Solidarity, usually cited as one of the main causes of the fall of the Iron Curtain in 1989. Poland was accepted into mainstream European politics much earlier than many of its Eastern European rivals, becoming an Associate member of the European Union in 1994 and a full member ten years later.

This meant that Polish artists gained more artistic freedom and the economic power to escape the confines of their country. Although not every Progressive Rock artist was signed to its principal label, Metal Mind, the power of this independent label is second only to Inside Out in the Progressive Rock world, and has been particularly successful not just in promoting its own extensive roster of artists, but also giving the more popular overseas artists a way to record DVDs. Pendragon, in particular, have taken particular advantage of this and even smaller bands like British groups Credo, Tinyfish and DeeExpus have been able to record DVDs in Poland. Clive Nolan's Progressive Rock opera *She*, featuring Christina Booth of Magenta and Alan Reed of Pallas, was also premiered in Poland.

Polish bands themselves have made a huge impact on the Progressive Rock scene. Riverside have become one of the biggest bands of their type in the world, playing to large audiences, albeit in modest-sized venues, all over the planet. Satellite, a band that grew out of 1990s band Collage, were the brainchild of

Mariusz Duda of Riverside onstage in Holmfirth in 2011. (*Chris Walkden*)

drummer Wojtek Szadkowski, who has become one of the most prolific and creative forces in European Progressive Rock, his other projects including Strawberry Fields, Peter Pan and Travellers. Also from Poland are the excellent Quidam, whose music is split into two phases: the albums released in the 1990s, featuring female vocalist Emila Derkowska, and the more contemporary and emotive material produced with Bartek Kossowicz on vocals. While it breaks no new ground, 2007 album *Alone Together* is heartily recommended. It seems that whenever one looks, another excellent band has emerged from Poland. As the other Eastern European countries like Romania and Bulgaria catch up, who knows what treasures will be unearthed?

A CONTINUED REVIVAL IN THE CLASSIC PROGRESSIVE ROCK STYLE

In the early 2000s, The Flower Kings continued to churn out album after album of Retro-Progressive Rock to a modest but adoring public. However, they were not alone and other bands began making music in a style that looked specifically and directly back to the 1970s for its inspiration. One of these bands was Magenta from south Wales. Multi-instrumentalist Rob Reed had laboured for over ten years in his well-received band Cyan before he recruited singer Christina Booth. Booth had also sung with Reed in local pop acts Cold and Trippa, and he decided to using her wonderful singing voice on his next project, a high-concept double album about faith that pastiched the sounds of Yes, Genesis and Pink

Floyd. *Revolutions* was released in 2001. The band have gradually established their own identity since then, mixing hardcore Progressive Rock with shorter pieces. A single, 'Speechless', even made it into the lower reaches of the UK charts in 2007.

Significantly, Magenta are one of few popular bands in modern Progressive Rock to have been successful without the backing of a mainstream independent label. Most of the successful bands of the 2000s, such as Spock's Beard, The Flower Kings, The Tangent, Jem Godfrey's Frost* project and Australian band Unitopia have been signed to the Inside Out label, which has the reputation and the distribution to maximise a band's sales. Magenta initially signed to F2, run by David Robinson – who also owns the progrock.co.uk mail-order company in the UK – but from the mid-2000s the band self-released everything on Reed's own Tigermoth label.

Magenta
Seven
Released April 2004

After the unabashed successes of *Revolutions,* Rob Reed decided not to repeat the *Tales from Topographic Oceans*-inspired format for the band's next album. Instead, Magenta wrote a seven-track record made up of shorter (although still epic) pieces. This was to be a masterstroke, and *Seven* remains one of the best-loved Progressive

Magenta's best-known album *Seven*. (*Tigermoth Records*)

Rock albums of the 2000s. Christina Booth was back again, as was Chris Fry on guitar and Tim Robinson on drums, with most other instruments, including bass and keyboards, played by Reed himself. The album saw the band starting to form an identity of its own, and some of the obvious influences from the 1970s began to merge together into something more individual.

Here, the lose concept is of the seven deadly sins, although the subject matter remains relatively oblique. 'Gluttony', a long-term live favourite, references Yes but only in passing, while 'Envy' has a melody that suggests Renaissance at their most melodic, with a Genesis-inspired middle section. 'Lust' is another Retro-Prog orgy, while 'Greed', perhaps the weakest track on the original version, was extensively reworked for the 2009 fifth-anniversary reissue. 'Anger' is a gentle piece full of sadness, although it was reworked as a dramatic live track later in the decade, while 'Pride' mixes pop with Celtic-tinged Prog. The album closes in dramatic fashion with 'Sloth', whose quiet beginning gives way to a huge, David Gilmour-style solo from guest guitarist Martin Shellard.

TRANSATLANTIC

'Supergroups' have existed in rock since Crosby, Stills, Nash & Young first sat on a stage, and Progressive Rock has had one or two. In 2000, Neal Morse of Spock's Beard, Roine Stolt of The Flower Kings, Pete Trewavas of Marillion and Mike Portnoy of Dream Theater formed a band called Transatlantic. The group began ambitiously, headlining Nearfest in 2000, and their aim was always to be as openly Prog as possible. Their opening statement, *SMPT:e*, was awash with delicious melodies and extended jamming.

Transatlantic
Bridge Across Forever
Released 2001

While many fans cite 'All of the Above' from the band's debut as their finest individual piece of music, for me their second album, released in 2001, is their best as a whole. Typically for the band – for whom excess was not something to be shied away from – it contains just four pieces of music over its sixty minutes and opens in fine style with 'Duel with the Devil'. This is typical Transatlantic, very retro and completely unrestrained, with every band member playing as many notes as possible as strenuously as possible. 'Suite Charlotte Pike', despite some nice melodies and Roine's first vocal of the album, is somewhat dispensible. The title track, sung by Morse, is charming. The album finishes in typically unrestrained fashion with 'Stranger in Your Soul', a thirty-minute *tour de force* with big solos, delicious harmonies, and the opportunity for all four members to sing lead.

Neil Morse and Roine Stolt of Transatlantic onstage at the High Voltage Festival in 2010. (*Neil Palfreyman*)

With Morse pursuing a solo career in Christian music, albeit a very Prog incarnation of it, the band did not reconvene again until 2009, when they released *The Whirlwind*. Like Porcupine Tree's *The Incident* from the same year, it is a single song cycle clocking in at over seventy minutes. It is not to everyone's taste. For some, Transatlantic's extreme and shameless take on Progressive Rock is more than a touch excessive. To others, including me, the band have played some of the best live shows of the new millennium. Not only is their reverence to the genre a joy, but the way they have captured the imagination of audiences worldwide is refreshing. Their music is joyous and unrestrained but completely over-the-top in an era when to be like that is, at last, possible. It is still a wonder that such music could attract such an audience as I saw when the band played in front of 2,000 people in a packed Shepherd's Bush Empire in London in May 2010 – a concert later released as part of a sumptuous DVD package.

THE TANGENT

One final band to have significant success with a 1970s approach to their music has been The Tangent. The brainchild of Parallel or 90 Degrees keyboard player Andy Tillison, the band were originally a supergroup featuring the ubiquitous Roine Stolt and colleague Jonas Reingold from The Flower Kings, plus David Jackson of Van der Graaf Generator. However, they have made a succession of wonderful albums since 2003's *The Music that Died Alone*. The band combine classic Prog keyboard pyrotechnics with a touch of the jazzier Canterbury sound, combined with Tillison's reflective, highly intelligent and often politicised lyrics.

By 2010, The Tangent had become a more conventional band made up of British musicians. Their 2010 'live in the studio' DVD *Going Off on Two* is highly recommended.

The Tangent
A Place in the Queue
Released 2006

Back in 2006 album three saw The Tangent beginning to throw off the shackles of the supergroup tag. Roine Stolt had departed, to be replaced by fellow Swede Krister Jonsson, and Theo Travis was now on sax and flute. With Andy Tillison taking over all lead vocal duties, *A Place in the Queue* was a far more cohesive album than its predecessor, *The World that We Drive Through*. The album opens and closes with two twenty-minute epics, and begins with perhaps the band's finest piece, the poignant and inspiring 'In Earnest'. 'Lost in London' has a strong Canterbury feel, and after 'DIY Surgery', a delicious and brief jazz workout, they launch into 'GPS Culture', another of their finest pieces with its gorgeous Moog fanfares. There is a touch of Van der Graaf Generator in 'Follow Your Leaders', before the fun disco interlude 'The Sun in My Eyes' and the dramatic twenty-five-minute title track.

Aside from the obvious talent and intelligence of Andy Tillison, what makes The Tangent stand out among the current crop of contemporary Retro-Prog bands is that they are one of few bands to demonstrate no discernible Genesis influence. For them Yes, Van der Graaf Generator, Caravan and Hatfield and the North are much more obvious inspirations. With *A Place in the Queue,* the pieces all came together on an album of real quality.

THE 1980S BANDS FIND THEIR NICHE

Is it any coincidence that all the bands that had been most popular in the 1980s were once again active in the 2000s? I think not. Marillion had spent the 1990s adjusting to life after the departure of singer Fish. The band were able to keep the standard of music high enough after his departure, but while they were appreciated by the 1990s underground, the band found that the mainstream was not so interested in them and spent most of the decade adjusting to life on its fringes. However, the band found that the internet suited them and that there was still a smaller but equally passionate fanbase out there. For 2001's *Anorachnophobia*, the band asked their fans to pre-order the album via their website in return for a special edition to be received ahead of release. Almost 15,000 fans took the band up on the offer and a new type of sales model was forged that would subsequently be much-copied by other artists. Marillion

Peter Nicholls of IQ in 2011. (*Neil Palfreyman*)

have seen their fanbase gradually increase since, and their tours now bring in similar crowds to their early 1980s heyday, even if their albums do not sell in the same quantities. The band were also the first to earn a living by releasing lots of product via Racket Records – live albums and DVDs abound – and the connection between the band and its fans has always been warm and innovative. The Marillion weekends, in effect band-organised fan conventions, in the UK, Holland and most recently Canada, have never been repeated by any other group within or outside the mainstream. Musically, the band has settled into a niche of ambitious, emotional rock music. Although tracks from the Fish era are still occasionally played, and once in a while they blow off their Prog chops in the studio – as in 'Ocean Cloud' from the special edition of *Marbles* from 2004 – unlike many of their contemporaries, they have moved on musically and do not feel constrained by the old hits.

IQ
Dark Matter
Released 2004

IQ never really went away. However, they have never been prolific, releasing a succession of very fine, beautifully crafted albums every five years or so. There have been several line-up changes, most significantly the departure of Martin Orford in 2007, but the nucleus of the band has remained vocalist Peter Nicholls and guitarist

Mike Holmes. The band have maintained their very dedicated following and remain one of the most significant world forces in Progressive Rock.

The quality bar has always remained high, and 1997's *Subterranea* is regularly cited as a classic of narrative Progressive Rock, but for me their finest album musically is this, the last to feature Martin Orford on keyboards and the powerful rhythm section of Andy Edwards on drums and John Jowitt on bass. As is usually the case with IQ, it is the sense of dark drama and melody that most impresses. While *The Wake*, for instance, was one the best albums of the Neo-Prog era, *Dark Matter* rises head and shoulders above it musically. The melodies are sophisticated, the production crisp and dynamic, and the playing exemplary. The album is bookended by two wonderful extended pieces, 'Sacred Sound' and the multi-part twenty-four-minute *tour de force* 'Harvest of Souls'. While the Genesis influences remain, this is an album on which IQ really sound like, well, IQ.

Pendragon
Pure
Released 2008

Another band to maintain a career in its own bubble and with this own label (Toff) has been Pendragon. 1991's *The World* saw the band return to epic songwriting, and each subsequent album has had its share of very fine material. The band are one of very few in the contemporary Progressive Rock scene to still be able to undertake

Clive Nolan, keyboardist of both Pendragon and Arena. (*Chris Walkden*)

full, 'old-style' tours, as they have a strong following in mainland Europe, especially in Poland. Like IQ, the band has been able to build on a solid following from the 1980s, and in the latter half of the 2000s the band really raised their game with an album that received the best reviews of their career – the magnificent *Pure*. Not only was the album dark, powerful and in many ways groundbreaking in its modernity, the recruitment of the remarkable Scott Higham on drums helped galvanise the band during some astonishing live performances.

Songs like 'Indigo' and 'Eraserhead' border on the metallic and show that Pendragon had taken plenty of inspiration from contemporary sources like Porcupine Tree. Add to that treated vocals and relatively basic keyboards and you get something that might have failed in less imaginative hands. However, these influences are combined with such superb material and melodies that the album is a complete triumph. Indeed, it might just be the band's defining statement, thirty years into a turbulent career. 'It's Only Me', the moving album closer, is probably the best song Pendragon ever recorded. It's that good.

PALLAS, TWELFTH NIGHT AND SOLSTICE

Pallas reconvened in 1999 for the well-received, if relatively hard-rocking, *Beat the Drum*, followed by the grandiose and much more Prog *The Cross & the Crucible* in 2001 and the confident *The Dreams of Men* in 2005. By 2009, the band, based in Aberdeen, had drifted apart from singer Alan Reed, who was based in London. The subsequent split, with a level of acrimony almost unheard of in the relatively sedate world of Progressive Rock, led to the new album *XXV*, which returned to the story of *The Sentinel* with new singer Paul Mackie.

After twenty years apart, Twelfth Night returned for some rapturously received live concerts in 2007, followed by a further series of shows in 2010, this time using members of Neo-Prog contemporaries Galahad to fill out the band's sound. The band continue to re-release their back catalogue on David Robinson's F2 label, and while this new activity does not represent a full-time reunion, fans have been partially satiated at least. Similarly reconvening in 2007 and also releasing their back catalogue via the ubiquitous F2 label, Solstice have been rather more active. Finally fulfilling the potential they demonstrated back in 1984, and with a stable line-up, the band released the beautiful *Spirit* album in 2010.

HERITAGE BANDS

What is a heritage band? A heritage band is any group that tours for a living, playing its back catalogue rather than releasing new product. 2000 was an important year for Yes in that it was the last time the band could be seen touring

Andy Glass of Solstice at the 2007 Summer's End Festival. (*Chris Walkden*)

in support of a new album, 1999's *The Ladder*. Since then, the band have played little or no new material in their live set, instead relying on concerts built around the 1970s back catalogue. When singer Jon Anderson fell ill in 2008, the band – some felt somewhat callously – replaced him with a singer from a tribute band and went on tour anyway. Ian Anderson and guitarist Martin Barre still play the circuit as Jethro Tull, but with interchangeable musicians filling the other positions in the band.

The question of what happens when certain members of a band do not wish to tour or are incapable of doing so has raised some interesting philosophical issues. Is this Yes or is it a tribute band? Or both? Focus currently tour with original members Thijs van Leer and Pierre van der Linden, but without guitarist Jan Akkerman, who plays Focus material in his own live set. Is this band really Focus? Does it matter?

Touring well into late middle age, even the artists themselves would admit they are not quite what they were. In 2007 Genesis reconvened for a huge stadium tour, playing a mixture of their 1980s and 1990s hits with a fair few 1970s classics thrown in. The rumours had been rife that they might have toured *The Lamb Lies Down on Broadway* as a five-piece with Steve Hackett and Peter Gabriel involved, but in the end the band went with the 1990s line-up fronted

Christian Vander of Magma in a rare moment away from the drum kit. (*Kevin Scherer*)

by Phil Collins. In short, they chased the money, and who can blame them? In July 2010, Emerson, Lake & Palmer reconvened for one final concert, a ninety-minute set headlining the inaugural High Voltage Festival in London. The band played well, but it was clear that extensive touring would probably be beyond them.

Many other bands reformed, revived or saw their audiences grow and their profile increase. Magma, PFM, Le Orme and Banco all made high-profile appearances at Nearfest. Camel played a farewell tour in 2003, and any further activity was put on hold following the serious illness of Andrew Latimer. Gentle Giant always resisted the temptation to reform, but did return in partial (and perhaps tribute) form as the band Three Friends, which featured former members Malcolm Montmore, Gary Green and (briefly) Kerry Minnear. All three Shulman brothers were conspicuous by their absence.

An exception to the heritage band process was, as always, the enigmatic Robert Fripp. Fripp reconvenes line-ups of King Crimson when he sees fit, but has admirably steered clear of the desire to rely on past line-ups and former glories. He does call on past collaborators to be involved in Crimson line-ups, but for every Tony Levin there is a Trey Gunn, a hugely skilled younger musician who can help keep the music fresh. Fripp reconvenes King Crimson when he feels that the band has something to say or music that he feels has the King Crimson spirit. Having said that, even he has stuck largely to the formula he has employed for Crimson since the 1980s, and *The Power to Believe* in 2003 continued his long-term collaboration with Adrian Belew.

Kansas
Somewhere to Elsewhere
Released 2000

Bands that were popular in the 1970s release few new albums today, even if many of them were active in the 2000s as live entities. However, Kansas caused something of a shock in 2000 by releasing a reunion album that compares favourably with their output from the 1970s. Significantly, the chief creative force was a guest, Kerry Livgren, who had not been involved in the band since the early 1980s, and the album returned, briefly, to the line-up from the 1970s, with the diplomatic addition of long-term bass player Billy Greer.

Like their classic albums, *Somewhere to Elsewhere* mixes up Prog material – as on the terrific opener 'Icarus II' and the delicious, piano- and violin-led 'Distant Vision' – with shorter melodic material like 'When the World Was Young' and the Southern rock of 'Disappearing Skin Tight Blues'. However, it is the symphonic material that stands up best. The album coaxes a terrific performance out of vocalist Steve Walsh. While his singing shows some of the ravages of age, here it works beautifully, giving the music a poignant quality.

Released on the Magna Carta label, this album was to be a surprising oasis of creativity for a band that has otherwise dragged itself, slightly wearily and without Livgren, around the US heritage circuit. Of this album they can be proud.

REISSUE FRENZY

The CD era gave record companies the opportunity to convince fans to buy their vinyl all over again, promising increased sound quality and exclusive bonus tracks. Key albums, including the big sellers from the Progressive Rock era, were soon released on CD. Within a few years, however, it became apparent that if you offered the fan something even better, they would buy it yet again. The 'remastering' process began with the Led Zeppelin catalogue in 1992, and most of the major artists from the 1970s followed within ten years. In the modern age, mastering is a digital process that enhances the quality of a given recording. It is not related to remixing, where the original sound balance is altered to bring certain sounds up or down in the mix (which record companies rightly assumed would not be tolerated by fans). The mastering process is not always successful. There have been repeated debates in the press and within the Progressive Rock community about the tendency to master music 'loudly', meaning that musical subtleties are lost. Given the huge dynamic range of many Prog albums, most fans want a 'dynamic' remaster and not one that just hits the listener with volume.

The companies involved in this process varied greatly. Robert Fripp has controlled the release of King Crimson remasters personally, accompanying these with a phased series of archive concert recordings. The Yes catalogue was released by Rhino (a reissue label owned by Warner) with a varied series of extras, including alternative versions, studio run-throughs and demos. Gentle Giant supervised their own 'vinyl replica' reissues via Alucard, a company run by Kerry Minnear. The Genesis 'Definitive Issue Remasters' were released by Virgin.

But it was not only the big boys who received the reissue treatment. Small companies like Esoteric, run by Mark and Vicky Powell, have dug deep into the 1970s and have re-released some of the key works by relatively big players like PFM. Their print runs are short, but their catalogue is large and highly recommended for those wanting to dip into some of the more obscure bands from the Prog era. It would seem that there is enough interest out there for even the least successful albums from the Progressive Rock era to be released.

THE TOUR DVD – THE NEW LIVE ALBUM

In the 1970s and 1980s, if a band wanted to put out a live concert, then vinyl was the only way to do it. There were TV appearances and the odd concert film, of course, but the live album was the only way of getting a band's whole live set out to audiences wanting to relive the live experience. Towards the end of the 1980s, live concerts could be filmed at great expense and then released on VHS video. However, in the 1990s, DVDs started to become a viable way of getting music out to a paying public as part of the album/tour process. Bands could play a long tour as Yes and Rush did, for instance, and film one night of it, giving fans a souvenir of the show even if it wasn't precisely the same gig. This is fair enough – if artists can make this pay it is fine, and if live product gets released a little more frequently than it might have been in the 1970s or 1980s, then what is the harm? Marillion, in particular, have made a career of releasing as much product as possible to a hungry fanbase.

But this can go too far. Why not, for example, have a company record the concert you were at, and make it directly available to you after the show for a hefty fee via download or CD? No need for bootlegs anymore – you can pay for the show you were at, and have it immediately. If I sound a little cynical here, it is because I feel there is some exploitation going on. You go to a concert and you enjoy it. You pay to download it. You play it once. You realise it wasn't quite as great as you thought at the time. You never play it again. What a waste of money.

DVD has become a useful medium for audio as well. With DVD audio often mixed in 2.0 (stereo) and 5.1 (surround sound), the opportunity has arisen to create 5.1 versions of original albums as well. This format has never completely caught on, but it does give an interesting opportunity for a remix engineer to get his hands on a classic album and produce a complementary, reverential alternative

The cover to Transatlantic's sumptuous two DVD, three CD set commemorating their May 2010 tour. (*Inside Out*)

version. The king of 5.1 mixes is Steven Wilson of Porcupine Tree, a man trusted by Robert Fripp to manage the phased 5.1 reissues of King Crimson's music and who also remixed Caravan's *In the Land of Grey and Pink* for 5.1 reissue in 2011. In 2009 Wilson was nominated for a Grammy for his surround mix of Porcupine Tree's *Fear of a Blank Planet.*

THE TRIBUTE BAND PHENOMENON

The original 'tribute acts' were Elvis Presley impersonators. Fuelled by the belief, or at least wish, that 'the King' was still alive, and by the relative ease of impersonating him, acts spread their way across the world. Sometimes these were little more than lookalikes, while at the other end of the scale these performers put on huge, expensive revues in Elvis style. *Elvis: The Musical* ran in the West End of London just after Presley's death in 1977, and made a star of Shakin' Stevens, who has built a lifelong career out of a thinly veiled Elvis impersonation.

Next came The Beatles tributes. Some picked specific periods to copy, others went for highlights from the band's whole career. Australia became the home of the growing tribute industry around the early 1990s. Australia is a notoriously difficult place to tour in due to the logistics of getting there and travelling around. Combine the lack of front-line tours with a pleasingly gregarious and improvisatory national character, and the scene was set for the rise of the tribute act.

The first Prog-related tribute band to win international renown was The Australian Pink Floyd, which began in the late 1980s in Adelaide. Amazingly, this band now reproduce, with unerring accuracy, the music of Pink Floyd in huge arenas all over the world, showing that the appetite for such music is far from satiated, despite relatively regular touring from both Roger Waters and David Gilmour.

The best-known tribute for one of our other core bands has to be The Musical Box from Canada, who reproduce the music and look from specific Gabriel-era Genesis Tours. These are meticulously researched to reproduce specific set lists, costumes, instruments and even stage patter from this era – no mean feat given that from an early stage in the band's career, Gabriel used surreal storytelling to mask the band's retuning. Other Genesis tributes are less specific in their reproductions of the music, and bands like The Carpet Crawlers in the UK are as happy with Collins-era pieces as they are with the Gabriel era, mixing up the performances in a way that the original band might not have. The same is true of Yes tribute bands. Some, like Yessongs from Italy, pick whole Yes concerts to reproduce, whereas others, like the veteran British group Fragile, mix the songs up in a way that would never suit the politics of the real band.

Two things that tribute bands understandably crave are authenticity and credibility. There are several ways that this can be achieved:

1. Get a member of the original group to endorse you. This has happened frequently, but the most famous example is the appearance of The Australian Pink Floyd at David Gilmour's fiftieth birthday party.

2. Better still, get a member of the original group to play with you. Again, examples are numerous but Steve Hackett has played with The Musical Box and Yes guitarist Steve Howe played several dates and even a small tour with Fragile, and appeared to love every minute.

3. Even better still, get a member of the band to become a permanent member. This is what sometimes happens when a member of a band decides to play the music of that band without using the actual name of that band. Two strong examples would be Three Friends, the Gentle Giant tribute act that featured Garry Green (and Kerry Minnear for a while) and thus managed to win huge credibility with Progressive Rock fans. The other is Mick Pointer's Script, who specifically and eerily reproduce the earliest performances, *circa* 1982, of Marillion with Pointer, the band's original drummer, and a group of well-known musicians, including Nick Barrett from Marillion contemporaries Pendragon. The band features Liverpudlian Brian Cummings as 'Fish'. He also performs as both Phil Collins and Peter Gabriel in a Genesis tribute act.

Brian Cummins inhabits the role of Fish with Mick Pointer's Script at the Night of the Prog Festival, Loreley, 2009. (*Stephen Lambe*)

Being the singer in a tribute band can pay dividends, of course, as you never know who might be in the audience. In 2008, when Yes went looking for a replacement for Jon Anderson (who had been sidelined by health problems) they picked a Canadian called Benoit David from tribute band Close to the Edge. At time of writing, David remains in the band and sang on their 2011 album *Fly from Here*.

Tribute bands are a moral dilemma. Look at any successful club schedule, and you will see a host of such bands playing, sometimes four or five nights per week. With tickets for the world's biggest acts at a premium price in huge venues, what better than to see an approximation in a small venue with a pint, a palatable ticket price and a decent view? Millions of people say yes to this every year. Are such bands crowding the schedules so that newer bands cannot get live experience and build followings, or are they keeping the clubs in business, allowing artists that play their own material a vital venue to play, albeit with fewer nights of the week to choose from? Are people 'wasting' their live experience by picking music that comforts them when they could be listening to new music, or do tribute bands fuel the passions so that they seek out new music anyway? Time will tell.

WITHER PROGRESSIVE ROCK?

In the second decade of the new millennium, there is an almost astonishing amount of new music to choose from. This is available to download almost immediately from a variety of sources, both legal and illegal. Myspace, Facebook,

Spotify and Bandcamp (among many others) provide an amazing array of artists from all over the world. Very few of these are signed to labels, so they are fighting for the same group of people to buy their CDs, download their music and buy their T-shirts. Many of these bands are... not bad. However, few are wonderful, inspirational or original. In the 1970s and 1980s, record companies provided a filter between the consumer and the artist. This was an imperfect system, and mistakes were made on a regular basis. However, picking the wheat from the chaff is now a much more difficult job. Artists, especially those that are trying to build a following, are far more accessible via email or in person, and this tends to affect our judgement. We tend to *like* the bands that we follow. We love them much less frequently.

Meanwhile, Progressive Rock itself seems to be splitting, twisting and reinventing itself. Gothic rock band Anathema from Liverpool had always shown a strong Pink Floyd influence, but in 2010 they released *We're Here Because We're Here*, a beautiful, ethereal and emotional album full of delicate textures and moments of tension and release. Bands like Amplifier have shown that a Prog sensibility is possible even with a basic guitar, bass and drums framework. A young band from London, Pure Reason Revolution, released one of the most impressive, original and authentic Progressive Rock albums of the last few years. Bands like Elbow and Mew actually have chart success with music that has a cinematic sweep and do not feel obliged to pay too much attention to the traditional verse-chorus structure of songwriting.

Vincent Cavanagh of Anathema onstage in 2011 at the Night of the Prog Festival, Loreley. (*Neil Palfreyman*)

Pure Reason Revolution at Nearfest in 2007. (*Stephen Lambe*)

Pure Reason Revolution
The Dark Third
Released 2006

This young band from London emerged from the Radiohead-inspired post-rock herd with an album of Pink Floyd-influenced majesty. The band were initially signed to Sony, but *The Dark Third* was released on the Inside Out label outside the UK – unusual for a band so young. It features some unusually impressive slide guitar playing on its atmospheric opener 'Aeropause'. The contrast between the ethereal vocals of Chloe Alper and youthful voice of Jon Courtney are vital to the album, as are the band's trademark, Beach Boy-inspired harmonies. The pivotal track on the early part of the album is the eleven-minute *tour de force* 'The Bright Ambassadors of Morning', named after a lyric from Pink Floyd's 'Echoes'. It begins with ambient swirls of synths and haunting voices before moving into the song proper, with its haunting and repetitive refrain and a huge, aggressive, post-rock ending. Combining an epic sensibility, fine melodies and remarkable creativity, 'The Bright Ambassadors of Morning' is one of the most significant Progressive Rock songs of the new millennium.

The rest of the album is almost as impressive, although a little less epic in its sweep, combining sensitive songwriting with powerful instrumental passages. While Pure Reason Revolution do not have the virtuosity of their peers, they display no shortage of imagination. The other appealing aspect of the band is their haunting and atmospheric lyrical ambiguity, throwing in an otherworldly sense of the fantastic.

The band were to change direction after *The Dark Third*, and while their delicious harmonies remained, by the time they played Nearfest in 2007 they were moving in a more synth-driven, pop direction. But this album really caused a stir in 2006, and showed that the youngsters could still compete with the veterans.

It now seems perfectly acceptable to combine influences without any need for self-consciousness. Music has become a melting pot, and with all types of music available, from Irish jigs to Australian folk, why not incorporate that into your music? Iona, for instance, combine long Prog compositions with a philosophical take on Christian worship and strong Celtic influences. As well as keyboards, lead guitar and powerful lead vocals courtesy of Irish singer Joanne Hogg, the band have utilised a full-time uilleann pipe player for the last fifteen years, giving the band music a unique, powerful and folky feel. When pop producer and songwriter Jem Godfrey wanted to indulge his love of Progressive Rock, he formed Frost* using the best musicians he could find, including the ubiquitous John Jowitt and John Mitchell. The resulting album, *Milliontown*, combined epic Prog sensibilities (i.e. complex keyboard and guitar interplay) with a strong contemporary edge (treated vocals and lush pop melodies).

SET THE (QUALITY) CONTROLS FOR THE HEART OF THE SUN

It is difficult for any band to get noticed amid the sheer noise of worldwide internet activity. But just like forty years ago it is sheer quality that makes a difference, as two releases of the last few years show.

Thieves' Kitchen
The Water Road
Released 2008

Thieves' Kitchen had been toiling away on their jazz-influenced Progressive Rock without making huge amounts of headway since their first album, *Argot* in 2000. By 2008, personnel changes had produced the perfect line-up, with vocalist and multi-instrumentalist Amy Darby in place and, crucially, the recruitment of Änglagård keyboard player Thomas Johnson. They joined guitarist Phil Mercy, drummer Mark Robotham and bassist Andy Bonham for this exquisite album, which combines the adventure of their previous work with a deliciously serene and consistent atmosphere. Mercy provides the jazz textures, while Johnson, particularly in his use of delicate piano figures and wonderful sweeps of Mellotron, provides the atmosphere.

The opening twenty-one-minute track, 'The Long Fianchetto', is also the finest. It takes its time to develop, in true Änglagård style, not stating its main theme until five minutes in. Darby's lead vocals enter over delicious acoustic guitar, Mellotron and Fender Rhodes. The next instrumental section is again very reminiscent of Änglagård before gradually and emotionally re-establishing its main theme. Like many of the very best pieces of Progressive Rock, 'The Long Fianchetto' has emotion at its heart, and uses thematic development very skilfully to build and then release tension.

The rest of the album is also wonderful. 'Returglas' jumps and skips playfully, while 'Chameleon' is another long-form piece, this time with some delicious soprano sax from Paul Beecham. 'Om Tare' is a powerful piece of fusion, while 'Tacenda for You' showcases the low-register singing of Amy Darby and 'When the Moon is in the River of Heaven' showcases Johnson's keyboard skills, as does the brief 'Plaint'. The final piece, 'The Water Road', develops its themes with flute and oboe. Unashamedly retro, and a feast for Mellotron lovers, *The Water Road* is beautifully composed, played and realised. Due to an injury to Phil Mercy's hand – caused, ironically, by his playing position when using a double-necked guitar – the band were unable to capitalise on the rapturous critical reaction to the album, but it remains a modern-day, retro-inspired classic.

Big Big Train
The Underfall Yard
Released 2009

If Thieves' Kitchen's *The Water Road* suggested Scandinavia in its sweeps of Mellotron at left-of-centre atmospherics, this album by veteran 1990s band Big Big Train could not sound more English. The band have not played live for some years, and have developed a studio mentality based around the best musicians and performances possible, recruiting Spock's Beard drummer Nick D'Virgilio on their recent albums plus former XTC guitarist David Gregory. As a result, getting the band together in one place has been an irregular occurrence.

The Underfall Yard – both the epic title track and the album – is awash with evocative lyricism and magnificent playing. In many ways it stands as a companion piece to *The Water Road* in that it is unashamedly retro in character and contains similar instrumentation, albeit with a stronger Genesis influence. The emotionalism of the performances stands out. This is no stuffy Prog-by-numbers effort. This album pulls at the heartstrings. A real benefit to the band was also the recruitment

A Big Big Train promo shot. (*Neil Palfreyman*)

of new singer David Longton, whose voice recalls Gabriel, Collins and particularly Steve Hogarth of Marillion, often in the same phrase. In true Progressive Rock style, he is also a fine flute player.

The band followed this with the 2010 mini-album *Far Skies Deep Time*, which maintained the incredibly high standard of *The Underfall Yard*. Big Big Train have carved out a niche for themselves, not by hard touring, but the high quality of their output – a lesson for many bands.

DOWNLOADING – A NEW MORALITY?

There is a great Italian interview with Gentle Giant from about 1972 where the band are asked why they do not play for free. Simply because, they answer, they have to earn a living to eat and make further records. It almost seems absurd that the question should be asked, yet since the turn of the millennium the music industry has been rocked, and partially dismantled, by the free availability of music online. Almost anything you could possibly want to get your hands on is available with the aid of a Google search. Torrent sites make illegal downloading possible at the click of a mouse, while Spotify and YouTube make licensed music freely available to millions and can make superstars of the unknown and the untalented.

When Martin Orford of IQ decided to quit music completely at the end of 2008, he cited disillusionment with the illegal pirating of his music, which was preventing him from earning a living. He had a point of course, but what he perhaps failed to realise was that the whole landscape of music had changed. There are hundreds of Progressive Rock bands out there all over the world, and they want attention. Furthermore, many of them are actually quite good. In 1990, if you wanted to buy a Progressive Rock album your choices were relatively limited. A few bands had the market to themselves, and so sales on vinyl and, later, CD were good. Now the world is awash with great bands. IQ are not alone anymore, and they have a smaller slice of the pie.

Furthermore, everyone is active at the moment. There have been a series of startling reformations in the last few years, most notably that of Genesis for one last tour, but Renaissance and Van der Graaf Generator from the 1970s, Twelfth Night and Solstice from the 1980s, and even bands as diverse as Grey Lady Down and Änglagård from the 1990s are all back with us. Significantly, it is not the prospect of earning money that seems to be attracting these bands. Instead, it is the prospect of being heard. Citizens of Hope indeed.

EPILOGUE

DARLINGS OF THE PRESS AT LAST?

By 2011, the rehabilitation of Progressive Rock seemed almost complete. The more intelligent and balanced magazines like *The Word* and *Uncut* in the UK seemed to have a different attitude to those of *NME* (in the UK) and *Rolling Stone* (in the USA), to whom Prog remained a four-letter word. In 2009, BBC Four in the UK screened a ninety-minute documentary called *Prog Britannia*, a humorous yet affectionate examination of the genre up until the end of the 1970s. Many of the old clichés were trotted out, but compared to *Top Ten Prog Rock* on Channel 4 several years earlier, this was respectful and well-mannered. The High Voltage Festival in 2010, which featured Emerson, Lake & Palmer, prompted a good deal of press coverage, some of it ironic but most at least partially reverential.

Classic Rock magazine in the UK has followed the Progressive Rock scene in a small way since its inception in 1998, firstly with Nick Shilton's 'Hemispheres' column (which was how I first heard about Magenta in 2001) and later with the Progressive Rock reviews section, often hosted by Geoff Barton. This coverage did not sit particularly well with the rest of the content of the magazine, so the occasional Prog specials were always something to look forward to. It was with some excitement that we welcomed *Classic Rock Presents Prog* for the first time in 2009. On the whole, this has done a fine job in promoting bands old and new to a general audience, and while there is little depth to be found in its pages, it is usually an excellent read.

Elsewhere, *Rock Society*, produced by the Classic Rock Society in the UK, continues to support bands producing new music to a somewhat smaller readership, and in the USA *Progression* also covers the scene with a keen eye. The rise of the internet has also seen a growing number of internet-based radio stations and specialist podcasts, which provide a vital service in bringing new releases to an admittedly small number of listeners. Occasionally, the music penetrates a wider audience, and *Stuart Maconie's Freak Zone* on BBC 6 Music, a digital station, plays some Progressive Rock and has featured Bill Bruford as a guest.

That the new breed of bands playing 'classic' Progressive Rock have not reached a wider and younger audience is hardly a surprise. Progressive Rock is a specialist genre once again, with an ageing audience. However, the success of Porcupine Tree, Dream Theater and Elbow should give us all hope. Wherever there are people willing to put in a little work to get more than a catchy tune and a trite lyric out of music, then Progressive Rock, in some form, has some hope for survival. See you in another forty years.

Three major sources of contemporary Prog pleasure: *Classic Rock Presents Prog* (*Future Publishing*), *Rock Society Magazine* (*Classic Rock Society*) and *Progression* from the USA (*John Collinge*).

ACKNOWLEDGEMENTS

I am hugely grateful to all those who have given encouragement and assistance during the creation of this book and during my time in the Progressive Rock world. In particular: my father, my late mother, my brother Philip and my sister Rosemary; Jonathan Reeve and Campbell McCutcheon at Amberley Publishing; Mike Davies, who suffered two Nearfests with me in 2001 and 2002; Christina and Mike Booth, Chris Fry, Rob and Steve Reed and Chris Jones of Magenta; Jacob Holm-Lupo in Norway; Russ Elliot of www.musicaldiscoveries.com and Tiz Hay for encouraging me to write in the first place; my colleague-in-arms Huw Lloyd Jones, 'Saviour of Prog' and founder of the Summer's End Festival, as well as his ever-suffering family; Miles Bartaby, Steve 'Tommo' Tomlin, Andy Faulkner and Gareth Burfoot of the Classic Rock Society; Chris Walkden; David Robinson; members of the Magenta and Progressive Ears internet forums; Bill Bruford; Oana and Mr Jimmy; the bands Tinyfish, Also Eden, The Tangent and Unto Us; and finally my gorgeous wife Gill, the Prog Widow, whose patience in trying circumstances is much appreciated.

PHOTOGRAPHIC CREDITS

I would like to thank the photographers that have generously given their time and patience to source photographs for me. Except for two pictures of Bill Bruford, no stock or photo library images have been used in this book. In particular, thanks to: Chris Walkden; Neil Palfreyman; David Robinson of www.progrock.co.uk; Kevin Scherer for the treasure trove of Nearfest pictures; Roy Layer for the Ottowa Bluesfest photographs; Rich Greene; and Peter Hutchins.

FURTHER READING

Aside from the ever-useful Wikipedia, the hugely comprehensive www.progarchives.com has been a massive source of information during the writing of this book.

Over the years I have read many, many books on various aspects of Progressive Rock. Some have been published commercially, while others have been released with a small niche market in mind. Here are some of them.

BOOKS ON PROGRESSIVE ROCK

20th Century Rock and Roll: Progressive Rock (Canada: Collectors Guide Publishing).
Couture, Ronald, *Essential Mini-Guide to Progressive Rock, Past and Present* (Progarchives).
Holm-Hudson, Kevin, ed., *Progressive Rock Reconsidered* (Routledge).
Lucky, Jerry, *The Progressive Rock Files* (Canada: Collectors Guide Publishing).
Macan, Edward, *Rocking the Classics: English Progressive Rock and the Counterculture* (OUP).
Martin, Bill, *Listening to the Future* (USA: Open Court).
Powell, Mark, *Prophets and Sages* (Cherry Red Books).
Romano, Will, *Mountains Come Out of the Sky* (Backbeat Books).
Smith, Bradley, *The Billboard Guide to Progressive Rock* (USA: Billboard).
Snider, Charles, *The Strawberry Bricks Guide to Progressive Rock* (Lulu).
Stump, Paul, *The Music's All that Matters* (Quartet).

GENERAL BOOKS THAT COVER PROGRESSIVE ROCK

Coe, Jonathan, *The Rotters' Club* (Viking Press).
Jewell, Derek, *The Popular Voice* (Sphere).
Maconie, Stuart, *Cider with Roadies* (Ebury Press).
Moore, Allan F., *Rock: The Primary Text* (Ashgate).

BIOGRAPHIES OF PROGRESSIVE ROCK MUSICIANS

Banks, Peter, with Billy James, *Beyond and Before* (Golden Treasures Publishing).
Bruford, Bill, *The Autobiography* (Jawbone).
Dancha, Kim, *My Own Time: The Authorized Biography of John Wetton* (Northern Line).
Emerson, Keith, *Pictures of an Exhibitionist* (John Blake).

Hewitt, Alan, *Sketches of Hackett: The Authorised Steve Hackett Biography* (Wymer Publishing).
Wakeman, Rick, *Say Yes* (Hodder & Stoughton).

BAND BIOGRAPHIES AND STUDIES

Blake, Mark, *Pigs Might Fly: The Inside Story of Pink Floyd* (Aurum).
Collins, Jon, *Marillion/Separated Out – The Complete History 1979–2002* (Helter Skelter).
Forrester, George, Martyn Hanson and Frank Askew, *Emerson, Lake & Palmer: The Show that Never Ends* (Helter Skelter).
Hewitt, Alan, *Opening the Musical Box: A Genesis Chronicle* (Firefly).
Holm-Hudson, Kevin, *Genesis and The Lamb Lies Down on Broadway* (Ashgate).
Martin, Bill, *The Music of Yes* (USA: Open Court).
Randall, David, *In and Out of Focus: The Music of Jan Akkerman and Focus* (SAF).
Rees, David, *Minstrels in the Gallery: A History of Jethro Tull* (Firefly).
Smith, Sid, *In the Court of King Crimson* (Helter Skelter).
Stump, Paul, *Gentle Giant: Acquiring the Taste* (SAF).
Watkinson, David, *Yes: Perpetual Change* (Plexus).
Welch, Chris, *Close to the Edge: The Story of Yes* (Omnibus Press).
Wild, Andrew, *Play On: The Authorised Biography of Twelfth Night*.

GENERAL REFERENCE WORKS

The Billboard Book of Top 40 Albums.
Guinness British Hit Albums.
Guinness British Hit Singles.
The Illustrated Encyclopedia of Rock (Salamander).
Larkin, Colin, *Virgin All Time Top 1000 Albums* (Virgin).
Larkin, Colin, *The Virgin Encyclopedia of Seventies Music* (Virgin).
The New Rolling Stone Encyclopedia of Rock and Roll (Simon & Schuster).
Rock: The Rough Guide.

AND FINALLY THE FINEST BOOK EVER WRITTEN ABOUT MUSIC

Ross, Alex, *The Rest is Noise: Listening to the Twentieth Century* (Harper Perennial).

INDEX